STRANDS OF BLOOD

Life, Family, Bleeding, Redemption

JULY 21, 2025

MARCUS E. CARR, JR., MD, PHD, COL USAR (RET.)

Printed by crossingpress.org

Table of Contents

3

I. DOCTOR STORIES

An Introduction

Sherri has suggested on several occasions that I record some of the stories I tell about my experiences as a doctor. For some reason, I love telling these stories. Sometimes, when I talk about these experiences, it's almost as if I were there again. My attempt to capture on paper what I have verbalized many times follows. I make little effort at grammatical or political correctness because I want to record the stories as I tell them orally. These stories were initially intended for my family and friends, but they reflect aspects of the human condition that seem to be relevant to most people. I hope that you enjoy reading them as much as I enjoyed telling them.

Davidson College to UNC

I spent some of the best years of my life in Chapel Hill, North Carolina, but I did not start there. I attended Davidson College as an undergraduate. Davidson is an excellent school. When I was there in the late 1960s and early 1970s, most of the 250 students in each class went on to pursue graduate or professional studies. Davidson has produced (and continues to produce) more than its fair share of ministers, lawyers, medical doctors, and academicians. During my time there, Davidson had two significant drawbacks. First, there were no females. Second, there were Saturday classes. They solved the Saturday class problem while I was there, and they became co-educational (thank goodness) a few years after I left. There were other minor annoyances, such as the daily chapel, the minimal number of allowed class cuts, and freshman beanies (that is right…freshman beanies… and no talking outside of a building for freshmen until homecoming). However, it was a wonderful place. We also had a great basketball team. With only a thousand students, we were regularly in the top ten and made it to the NCAA National tournament at a time when only 16 teams went. The only team we could not beat was the Charlie Scott-led University of North Carolina.

How did I wind up at hated UNC in Blue Heaven? The answer is not simple. It was an evolution of circumstances. I was a young teenager when NASA was born. President Kennedy challenged the space program to send a man to the moon and bring him back by the end of the decade. So, I wanted to be an astronaut. I diligently studied math and science in high school and went on to attend Davidson, where I majored in physics. Unfortunately, I continued to grow, and astronauts were not large people. The Mercury astronauts had to be less than 5 feet 11 inches (180 cm) and could not weigh more than 180 pounds. The capsules were small, and every pound of extra weight stressed the Redstone rocket's ability to launch the capsule and astronaut into Earth orbit. I could still make the weight in high school,

6

but I was several inches over the height limit by the time I reached college. Okay, I would be a physicist.

Unfortunately, as soon as we reached the moon, the space program began to power down. This (and other events) significantly impacted the need for physicists. I received a letter from the American Institute of Physics stating that the unemployment rate for PhDs in Physics was 28 percent, but that they expected this trend to "bottom out" by the mid-1970s. Bottom-out…I need a new focus.

So, how could I convert a BS in physics into a viable career? I reasoned that people in the medical field always seemed to have reliable employment. If I wanted to pursue research, the NIH appeared to fund a significant amount of academic medical research. The question became, what endeavors would be an excellent cross between physics and medicine? Luckily, it became apparent that there would be multiple possibilities. Two areas seemed relatively new and exciting – Molecular Biology and Biomedical Engineering. The first would put me right on the cusp of gene research. The second allowed the application of engineering approaches to solve medical problems.

I had no true preference. I applied to Vanderbilt University's Molecular Biology program and the University of North Carolina's new Biomedical Mathematics and Engineering (BMME) program. I got into both, but UNC offered a full-ride commitment from day one. Vanderbilt offered money only after the first year was completed. To my way of thinking, this was a "no-brainer." I was off to UNC-Chapel Hill and the Southern part of heaven!

At UNC, I took the required introductory engineering courses and quickly jumped into research in Dr. Jan Hermans' laboratories. Dr. Hermans was a Dutchman and a world-renowned physical biochemist. In addition to engineering courses, I took biochemistry courses. My financial support was provided by the newly funded UNC SCOR (Specialized Center of Research) grant for hemostasis and thrombosis.

7

UNC was a hotbed of blood-clotting research and had been since the arrival of Dr. Ken Brinkhous in the Department of Pathology. Dr. Brinkhous was widely recognized as the father of hemophilia research and was undoubtedly the primary reason the University of North Carolina (UNC) received the enormous grant. Only three medical centers in the US got the award during the first round. While Dr. Brinkhous may have been the primary clotter, there were multiple other world-recognized experts at UNC (Webster, Wagner, Roberts, etc.).

Dr. Hermans was not a "clotter" per se, but a good polymer chemist. Since the end-product of the coagulation cascade is a massive polymer formed from fibrinogen, Dr. Hermans was set to use physical-chemical techniques to measure clotting and the structure of the clot. As a young member of his team, I helped develop techniques and instruments to measure the size and strength of fibrin polymers.

Dr. Hermans was rather intimidating for some folks, but we always seemed to click. Some students like a significant amount of guidance when starting a project. This was not what Dr. Hermans was best at. He was an idea man and an excellent mathematician. If he walked in and said, "I bet we could measure Y by doing X," then he wanted you to find a way to do "X" and then try to use "X" to measure "Y." It did not matter if "X" worked perfectly (or at all, for that matter) if you produced data (even if it was insufficient). Jan could take what you had attempted and figure out how to do it better (i.e., correctly). He could also analyze a minimal data set to determine whether the measurement was effective and whether the approach had merit. Thus, at the front end of a project, Dr. Hermans was a "minimalist," but on the back end, he was remarkable. Once I recognized this pattern, my work progressed rapidly, and within four years, I had completed my PhD.

Somewhere in the middle of my graduate work, it became apparent that being a biomedical engineer in the mid-1970s meant I would either work for an MD or have to be one myself. I chose the second option and began applying to medical school. I was not initially admitted because I was in the middle of my research. When it became apparent, however, that I would complete the program, I got my acceptance letter to the UNC School of Medicine. There is no question that the contacts I made during graduate school, both in the MD and Ph.D. programs, were critical to my admission. I will always be grateful to the BMME program and Dr. Hermans for launching me on the path I followed for the next 40 years.

JEREMIAH 29:11 For I know the plans I have for you," declares the Lord, "plans to prosper you and not to harm you, plans to give you hope and a future.

PROVERBS 16:9 In their hearts humans plan their course, but the Lord establishes their steps.

PROVERBS 19:21 Many are the plans in a person's heart, but it is the Lord's purpose that prevails.

ISAIAH 55:8 For my thoughts are not your thoughts, neither are your ways my ways," declares the Lord.

II. MEDICAL SCHOOL – UNC-CHAPEL HILL, NC

Third-Year Psychiatry Rotation

(Dorothea Dix Psychiatric Hospital)

Dorothea Dix was an early advocate for humane medical care for the mentally ill in the United States. Due to her efforts, North Carolina was one of the first states to establish a hospital for treating such patients. Authorized in 1849, it opened in 1856 and was initially named Dix Hill in honor of Dorothea's father. A hundred years later, the name was appropriately changed to Dorothea Dix Hospital to honor her dedication and early advocacy for what were often hidden or forgotten (or both) patient populations.

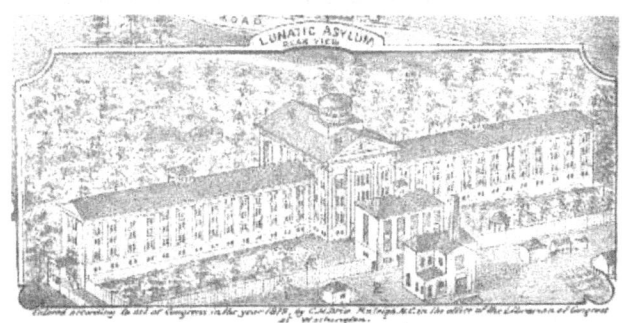

During the third year of medical school, students ("M-3s") rotate through five basic medical fields: Internal Medicine, Surgery, OB/GYN, Pediatrics, and Psychiatry. Medicine and Surgery were each 12 weeks long, and the other rotations were six weeks each. You could also consider an elective rotation or take some time to begin searching for your residency. You needed a clear idea of what you wanted to do by the end of the third year, as you would be interviewing in the fall of the fourth year. Knowing this, I had front-loaded my schedule with back-to-back Medicine and Surgery rotations. While this was great for getting ahead, it was also intense and tiring. Call schedules were either every other or every third night for both. My third rotation was Psychiatry, with virtually no call and weekends off, and I was looking forward to a bit of rest and a little time to read. I was about to learn that exhaustion can come in many forms. These are just a few of my experiences.

Professor Rounds
(Wilson's Disease, LSD and Spider Webs, Today is Tuesday)

On Friday mornings, we would have Professor Rounds at Dorothea Dix Hospital. These typically involved presenting one of our patients to one of the chief physicians. Unfortunately, I do not recall the professor's name. He was a distinguished-looking, white-haired gentleman who seemed to enjoy discussing our cases and occasionally showing us the unique aspects of the large Dorothea Dix Campus. Typically, one student would be picked to present a case, and then we would discuss it as a group. The professor would add color to the discussion by giving background information and describing similar cases he had seen.

On several Fridays, we had tours of the other buildings. I remember distinctly the day we went to a building where primarily the elderly were being treated. We entered the main door as a group and were greeted by a large bulletin board to our right. It was the bulletin board I remembered from elementary school, with flowers cut from colored construction paper and carefully attached around the edge. The central feature of the board was a calendar, and above the calendar, in large block letters, it said, "TODAY IS TUESDAY." Well, I suppose that pretty much sums it up. It was always Tuesday in that building. It is easier to stay oriented when the day never changes. I had a feeling that the routine from day to day did not change much either.

We visited a research building another Friday to see "Spiderman." No, he was not the superhero, but he was rather famous. Dr. Peter Witt was an MD and Pharmacologist who came to Dorothea Dix in 1967 as research director for the North Carolina Department of Mental Health. When we went by his lab, he had been in Raleigh for about ten years and continued his work on the impact of various stimulants, depressants, and CNS active drugs (LSD, for example) on the memory and motor skills of spiders. This was done by exposing good web spinners to the drugs and seeing what kind of webs they spun. The results were fascinating, but I had trouble understanding how this information would be used to improve our understanding of the effects on people. Nonetheless, it was cool.

Primarily, we reviewed our cases. Elsewhere, I discuss Jack's case of the half-Jesus truck driver; here, I will discuss another fascinating case, that of the star patient of Fred G, another wonderful classmate. Fred's patient also had schizophrenia, but he was younger, in his late teens, and had been in treatment for several years. Even more fascinating was his inherited underlying disease. He had Wilson's Disease. Wilson's disease is an abnormality of copper metabolism that causes the patient to gradually accumulate toxic levels of copper due to an inability to excrete the metal ion. The classic physical finding is a yellowish-brown ring in the iris of the eye, known as a Kayser-Fleischer ring, located around the pupil.

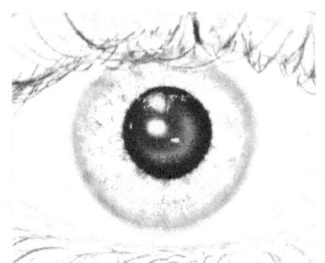

Copper is particularly toxic to the liver and, without treatment, leads to cirrhosis and liver failure. There are other toxic effects on the

13

heart and CNS, and psychiatric abnormalities are not uncommon in untreated patients. There is treatment. If the diagnosis is confirmed, the patient can be administered chelating agents that bind the metal ions, allowing them to be excreted in the urine. This type of therapy removes copper from the blood, but if administered chronically, it can also remove copper from the affected organs.

During his interview with the Professor, it became clear that the patient's older sister also suffered from Wilson's disease. The young man shared the story of his sister, who had a swollen belly. "Like she was going to have a baby, but she was not pregnant. She just got weaker and weaker and then died." It was a classic description of ascites in a patient with liver failure. The diagnosis was not made in his sister until after her death. Fortunately, due to her illness, the diagnosis was made earlier in his case, and he had begun treatment.

The treatment must have been effective, as he appeared to be a healthy young man. He acted that way as well, having been removed from younger female patients' rooms on several occasions. On at least one occasion, he introduced himself as a doctor and started to perform a physical examination.

He spent most of his time walking around the ward in a red and white running suit, accompanied by a matching red and white sweatband. Indeed, this is the outfit he wore to professor rounds. Fred had prepared me for what was to happen next. "This fellow is a real character. It will be fun to watch him spar with the attending."

The conversation became interesting when the Professor began discussing whether the patient heard voices or possessed special powers.

"Well, sometimes I hear and feel things. And, yes, I do have special abilities."

The professor continued, "Well, can you give us an example of what you consider a special power?"

At this point, the young man leaning way back (lounging) in his chair sat up and looked around at the group. A book was lying on the edge of the table. He reached out and flicked the edge of the book with his index finger and said, "Well...I just fried somebody." He then paused for a moment and gazed around the group once more. Then he reached out, flicked the book again, and said, "But don't worry. I just brought them back." I could feel Fred punch me in the back, and it was all I could do not to smile.

The last time I saw the young man, he was still walking the ward halls in his red and white sweats.

MARK 5:15 When they came to Jesus, they saw the man who had been possessed by the legion of demons, sitting there, dressed and in his right mind; and they were afraid.

JAMES 1:8 Such a person is double-minded and unstable in all they do.

Thanksgiving and a Broken Nose
(I had a skiing accident…)

Thanksgiving has always been one of my favorite holidays. I love the food, the time with family, and the football. During my third year, Thanksgiving occurred during my psychiatry rotation. Although the work schedule had not been particularly heavy, I needed a break by the time the holiday rolled around.

As usual, at that time of my life, we went North to Virginia to visit with Tony, my brother-in-law, and his family. It was always a great time, and this time was no exception. On the Friday after Thanksgiving, Tony's son Steve and my two boys, Joe and Jon, decided that the weather was perfect for outdoor basketball. We went to a local concrete court and got in line to play.

We were not the only ones with this idea, and the court was loaded with players, all just waiting their turn to play the winner of one of the ongoing games. As is typically the case, you get to keep playing if you win. The two corollaries to this arrangement are: if you want to keep playing, you need to win, and if you must play a group that has been on the court for a while, they will likely be quite competitive…

When we arrived, the courts were full, but some people were heading home when we managed to get into a game. Well, that was not bad because no one was waiting to play the winner when we finished our game (which we won). Well, you know what that means: We keep playing the same team until one of us becomes the champion of the universe.

It is always great to be a male—the mindset is so easy, predictable, and always ready to play! I have to say, even in my thirties, it was always great to be in a game.

As one might imagine, we split the first two games and the next two. Well, that means the winner of the fifth game was the Champion of the Universe. We were evenly matched. I had noted a pattern in the defense played by the player guarding me. Whenever I tried to drive toward the basket from the side, he would take away the baseline by planting himself perpendicular to it. On two occasions, I was able to back in, spin to my right around the guy, and then have a short, easy shot. If it worked twice, why not a third time?

As I made my now patented spin move, another player stepped out from behind the defender. We hit face-to-face with a loud, cracking sound. As we both fell backward, blood was soon everywhere. The other fellow had a nice laceration through the eyebrow above the left eye. I had a very deformed, obviously broken nose with an accompanying generous nosebleed. When I had a chance to gather myself, I looked at the other player and told him he would have a better cosmetic outcome if he had a few stitches to close his cut. The game was clearly over, and a couple of his teammates took him to the local hospital.

Jon was with me when I looked around for my support group, but Joe and Steve were next to the chain-link fence on their backs with their feet up against it. Neither of them had a high tolerance for the sight of blood, and there had been plenty to see. Now that most of that was over, although my nose continued to bleed, they got over their lightheadedness and took me to the emergency room.

When we arrived, the other fellow was preparing to receive his stitches, and the ER doctor took a minute to examine my nose. Diagnosis – broken nose and associated nosebleed. Well, that made sense. I was given an ice pack, tilted my head back, and waited for my nose to stop bleeding.

When he was through with the other headbanger, the doctor returned to me. The nose was still bleeding. At this point, I explained to him that I was taking an aspirin each day.

Ken Brinkhouse had been one of my mentors at the University of North Carolina. He was a renowned scientist and was generally considered one of the primary individuals responsible for defining the clotting factor deficiencies that cause the bleeding disorders of hemophilia. When I first met him, he was well into his seventies but was spry, pencil-thin, alert, and looked much younger. He was one of the first to espouse the benefits of daily aspirin, both as an anti-inflammatory and antiplatelet agent. He thought that aspirin would not only reduce the risk of stroke and heart attack (which, years later, was confirmed in clinical trials) but, with a twinkle in his eye, he told me it might even slow atherosclerosis. Well, that was enough for me. I started taking an aspirin per day in 1972, and I had been taking them for six years when the incident on the court occurred.

That was the problem. Aspirin will block the ability of little pieces of blood cells called platelets to stick to each other. The ability of platelets to aggregate at the site of injury is a critical step in stopping bleeding. Therefore, if you are taking aspirin, you are more likely to experience bleeding. If you are taking aspirin regularly, you may bleed a lot if you are injured. That is why they stop aspirin at least a week before any surgery.

I sat in the emergency room as my nose continued to bleed for the next two hours. Finally, the rate appeared to be slowing, as evidenced by reduced blood on the gauze pads, and I was allowed to go home. The only question I was asked about the fractured nose was if I knew a good ENT doctor. Luckily, I knew several, having done a rotation in ENT six weeks earlier as part of my surgery rotation. "Well, you'll need to drop by and let them realign your nose early next week."

The following day, a Sunday, I drove home with a headache, a black eye, and a crooked nose. I called my attending physician at Dorothy Dix and told them I would need to be a day late to have my nose realigned. I arrived at the ENT clinic early on Monday to see if they could accommodate me. Knowing everyone was a big help, and Sharie B, the chief resident, agreed to see me before starting his regular clinic. He looked at my nose and said, "You are going to need a little relaxer before I move that around." He continued, "Have a seat while I get you a six-pack." In this case, a six-pack was 5 milligrams of IV valium. Most people would think that 5 mg of Valium is not enough to do much. However, when given intravenously, it packs a wallop! It is also a very sclerotic agent, and the vein it was injected into basically turned into a tendon from which no one could draw blood (though many have tried) for the next 40 years.

Through my valium haze, Dr. B asked if I was ready to allow him to "manipulate" my nose. I told him he could "cut it off if need be." With probes and forceps, he moved my nose back into alignment. Unfortunately, the nasal bone attached to the skull was crushed. So, although the nasal cartilage was now aligned with the bone, there was nothing to keep it in place. Shari decided the best way to handle the situation was to pack both nostrils and cover my nose bridge with a metal flange. The metal was held in place by white tape, which crossed my nose from one cheek to the other. There was also tape that went up the center of my nose onto my forehead. That vertical piece of tape was held in place by two more perpendicular pieces across most of my forehead. I looked like 'Jason' from the horror movies. I realized later that the worst part of this treatment plan was the need to leave the pack in my nose for four weeks. The pack is usually removed within one to two weeks after a nose job. Four weeks is a very long time…

On Tuesday, I reported to Dorothy Dix to continue the last two weeks of my psychiatry rotation. The reaction from my patients was rather remarkable. Many had difficulty looking at or talking to me, and some tried to avoid me altogether. I went to my attending to ask for guidance. He advised me to wait until after lunch to resume my patient duties. In the meantime, he would speak with the nurses and patients.

The solution was to tell the patients that I had been injured in a skiing accident. I guess such a nasty facial injury could not occur in basketball. Really…? Oh well, it worked, and I could continue the rotation until it was completed.

After four weeks, the packing was finally removed. It was one of the best days of my life. I could breathe! The only downside was that I occasionally smelled something terrible for a few minutes. It smelled like something dead. These events gradually decreased in frequency but continued for at least a year. I never knew the cause, but I always suspected that a small piece of packing had somehow been left behind…

PSALMS 38:5 My wounds fester and are loathsome because of my sinful folly.

ECCLESIASTES 10:1 As dead flies give perfume a bad smell, so a little folly outweighs wisdom and honor.

A Patient Who Could "Bring the Sun Down"
(I don't know if we are helping these people…or simply slowing them down with drugs…)

As mentioned previously, we all became a little depressed during our rotation at Dix. I was never sure if it was the older buildings, the large number of mentally ill patients, or the (sometimes) unusual staff. Perhaps it was that, in previous rotations, we had become used to seeing a patient, listening to their complaint, making a diagnosis, and treating the problem.

Psychiatry was a different ball game. Often, patients do not have a complaint. Friends, family, and even strangers bring them in because they are not acting, behaving, or speaking "normally."

Making the diagnosis can also be problematic—usually, no blood test or scan points to a specific disorder. Diagnosis is made based on cataloging of the patient's behavioral abnormalities and comparison to various described abnormal mental conditions – schizophrenia, manic-depressive, major depression, etc. Many of the diagnoses overlap or are "fuzzy" around the edges; therefore, transitioning from one expert to another can result in a spectrum of diagnoses.

Then comes treatment. Until the 1960s and 70s, pharmaceutical treatment was minimal. Time-consuming counseling and psychotherapy done by a limited supply of fully trained practitioners were the mainstays of treatment. Patients were often institutionalized "for their safety and the good of society." Electroshock therapy and even surgical manipulation of the brain were sometimes done in severe cases. The introduction of effective antidepressants and anti-psychotics revolutionized treatment but, unfortunately, led to the rapid closure of many mental health clinics. The medications did help, but they did not "cure." To a certain degree, they masked the symptoms of the underlying disorder. This can be readily appreciated when some patients stop taking their medications.

I recall riding the bus to Raleigh one morning and hearing Jack, a fellow third-year student, lament the fact that we didn't seem to be making a difference in helping these patients. We all agreed to varying degrees with what he was saying. However, at that point, most of us had already picked up patients who were already in the system, which might be why we could not appreciate the improvement that had already occurred. This was brought home to Jack when he got his first acute admission.

The North Carolina Highway Patrol brought in the thirty-two-year-old truck driver. He was driving his big rig along Interstate 40 when he pulled into the median, got out of his truck, and began preaching. This gradually drew several spectators who had stopped to see if they could assist, and the Highway Patrol soon followed them. When questioned about who he was and what he was doing, he responded that he was "Half Jesus Christ." He had been told to stop the truck and deliver his message. That is just the response that gets you a ride to a mental health clinic. Since Dorothea Dix was a couple of miles away, he got the quick trip.

Jack presented his patient at professor rounds, and everyone agreed the presentation was classic for schizophrenia. I asked why schizophrenia would present in a thirty-two-year-old (apparently normal to that point) truck driver, and I was told, "That's when it sometimes happens." Well, there is a cause-and-effect statement you can take to the bank...feel the fuzz. The decision was to begin treatment with haloperidol (Haldol) and continue counseling. Jack would frequently update us on what he considered his star patient. The Haldol had quickly stabilized his thought processes, and the talk of being half Jesus had subsided rapidly.

About two weeks before the end of our rotation, we were told that we needed to start preparing our patients for our departure. During our rotation, we had become a primary component of the team, and leaving could be upsetting, even traumatic, for some patients. We were instructed to begin explaining that we would be transitioning to a new set of students who would join after we left.

Of course, Jack wanted his star patient to know how proud and pleased he was regarding his progress and recovery. He also wanted some insight into the initial presentation. He shared a story about the interaction on the bus returning to Chapel Hill.

Jack said he told the patient that he was pleased with his progress and would be leaving. He also said he would like to ask a few questions to better understand some of the things the patient had been saying upon arrival.

Jack said, "When you first came in, you said you were half Jesus Christ. What did you mean by that?" The response was, "I'm not really sure."

Jack continued, "OK. You were also saying that you had special powers. Can you tell me what you meant?"

Patient, "Like, what kind of power?"

Jack, "Well, you kept saying you could 'Make the sun come down.'"

At that point, Jack noted that the patient's whole demeanor changed. He looked around and then told Jack, "Come with me." He took Jack down to the main hallway parallel to the front of the building on every floor. High-arch windows extending almost to the ceiling were located at the end of these hallways. He walked Jack to the window, where sunlight streamed in, creating a bright, arch-shaped pattern on the floor. He placed Jack to the side and stepped into the middle of the sunlight. Looking up and out the window, he closed his eyes, and with his arms held down but away from his body, he clenched every muscle in his body. He stood silently and motionless (except for the mild rocking due to the apparent strain) for about 30 seconds. Then he relaxed and opened his eyes.

He looked directly at Jack and said, "Don't you tell a single soul that I can do that…"

As he told the story, Jack became increasingly sad and crestfallen. His star patient had not improved as much as he had thought. He was better and less out of control. However, underneath the new, calmer exterior, not all was well.

Later, as a medical resident, another resident introduced me to what became one of my favorite axioms. "There's a shade for everyone in the 'Haldol forest'…" Unfortunately for Jack, his patient could still bring the sundown from the comfort of the shade.

1 SAMUEL 16:7 "…The Lord does not look at the things people look at. People look at the outward appearance, but the Lord looks at the heart."

Question of CO leak on the Bus Ride to Raleigh
(or… was it depression…)

Fall in the Piedmont of North Carolina, and particularly in Chapel Hill, is a beautiful time. The days remain warm until Thanksgiving, and the trees progress through various beautiful shades of yellow, orange, and red. So, it was for the group of third-year medical students who dutifully caught a van in Chapel Hill each morning and rode over to Raleigh (about 23 miles) for their psychiatry rotation at Dorothea Dix Hospital. We were happy to do a rotation with limited call and all weekends off ("Does it get better than this in third year?!"). Early in the rotation, we were all loud and talking during the ride to Raleigh, but we would all be quieter in the afternoons.

Oh, we were just tired in the afternoon. Well, wait a minute. We did not work that hard. Scut work was minimal, with only a few blood draws, procedures, or IVs to insert. The notes were straightforward. The admissions were somewhat limited, rarely exceeding one per day. The day itself was short, starting at about 8:00 AM and concluding at 4:00 PM. What did we have to be tired about…?

As time went on, even the morning rides became quiet. Now, we had no excuse or explanation. What was going on? Perhaps there was a problem with the van's exhaust system. Possibly, carbon monoxide was seeping into the van and causing our malaise. That could explain things.

We debated this possibility for a while, and then someone had the bright idea of asking the driver if he was having difficulty concentrating, increased fatigue, or trouble staying awake. Even more simply, had he noted any difference between this rotation and the previous ones he had driven? Was the van now different?

His response was – no, no, no, and no difference…

Gradually, what was happening became clear to us. Jack, who was the most severely affected, was the one to suggest the cause. We were all becoming depressed. It was undoubtedly situational depression, but it was depression nonetheless. Dorothea Dix was a depressing place. We went there each day and met people who were physically well (at least most were), but were obviously unwell. Unfortunately, we appeared to be very ineffective in making them better. The medications we used seemed to suppress some of the symptoms, but they did not appear to "cure" anything. Indeed, if the medicines were stopped, the symptoms seemed to return with a vengeance.

We were supposed to be doctors. Why could we not help these folks?

The other depressing part was that if we dug deep enough into our psychological status, we could begin to see hints of some of the same tendencies being played out by our patients. It was all somewhat unnerving and depressing. We had come with the expectation of an easy rotation. It turned out that psychiatry was not it...

LUKE 4:23 Jesus said to them, "Surely you will quote this proverb to me: 'Physician, heal yourself!'

Third-Year Pediatric Rotation
(NC Memorial Hospital)

An eleven-year-old boy with papilledema
(Why I could not be a pediatrician)

As mentioned, we went through the five basic clinical rotations during our third year. I was leaning toward internal medicine when I began, but I had not committed and was open to other options. By the time I finished my third year, I felt I would have been comfortable in OB/GYN, Medicine, or Surgery. Due to my desire to "fix the problem," I thought I was less suited for a Career in Psychiatry. The one specialty I knew I could not do was Pediatrics. Don't get me wrong, I love children, and I think Pediatricians are one of God's great gifts to the world. My problem is that I have trouble dealing with seriously ill children.

Adult patients often have a history of contributing factors that led to their illness. They smoke. They drink too much alcohol. They overeat. They don't exercise. They do something stupid and get hurt. Even if they do none of these things, and they are the victim of bad genes or a bad infection, at least they get to live to be an adult.

Most of the time, children have done nothing to bring on the terrible things that happen to them. They are innocents. They are full of potential. They do not deserve to have terrible medical problems. The unjust nature of their predicament becomes even more apparent when you are around them as they navigate these problems. They can have a deadly disease, but if you can relieve their pain and increase their energy level, they are up and playing. Watching children with shunts in their heads and venous ports playing reveals the power of the human spirit. It reflects all that is good. Why should they suffer? Why can't I fix it?

The following story describes the event that made me acutely aware I was not strong enough to be a pediatrician.

It was Spring, the end of the third year was in sight, and I was on my last clinical rotation. I could write good notes, I was good at procedures, and I was learning differential diagnosis. However, with all these "skills," pediatrics was a whole new ballgame. First, the youngest patients could not even talk. The next group could speak, but sometimes had difficulty describing their symptoms. The most reliable information typically came from parents; moms were almost always the best source. In addition, pediatric patients come in all sizes and all degrees of maturity, so writing for medications meant knowing their weights and ages. It was going to be more of a challenge than I had anticipated. Treating children would not be like treating "little adults."

The pediatric service I was on was bustling. The NC Memorial was a public referral and teaching hospital for much of North Carolina. Therefore, outside pediatricians referred most admissions, and many cases were complex diagnostic or therapeutic dilemmas. Since the residents tended to cover multiple services on the day we had primary call, my resident was typically on the move.

Judy was excellent. She was intelligent, dedicated to her patients, and willing to mentor medical students. We got along well, so after a couple of weeks, she would occasionally let me be the first team member to see a patient. One busy Thursday, I got to be the first to see a twelve-year-old male referred for diabetes insipidus. DI is a disorder where the patient urinates frequently without having high blood sugar. The hallmark is the patient's inability to concentrate urine.

I met the patient and his mom and was immediately impressed. The young man was an all-star Little League pitcher and was very well-spoken. He had no complaints. "I just have to go to the bathroom all the time." His mother was a very articulate teacher and widow. Her son was an only child. She stood by his bedside during the entire interview and physical.

I typically did a quick history of the present illness (chief complaint – when did it start and what has happened since it started) and then continued the history during my physical exam. Being an engineer at heart, I am rather methodical – I start at the top and work my way down. Looking into the boy's eyes, I saw something I had only seen in books. At least, I thought I was seeing what I had read about and what I had seen in books. It looked like he had papilledema. This means that the area in the back of the eye, where blood vessels and the optic nerve pass through, was either flat or even pushed forward. I looked in the other eye and thought I saw the same thing. I looked again, and this caught Mom's attention. She asked, "Have you found something?" I said I was not sure, but I would have the resident physician look.

I found Judy and told her I thought the patient had bilateral papilledema.

"What are his other symptoms?" she asked.

"No headache, no weakness, and his vital signs are normal," I responded.

"I will be right there."

Judy arrived with an ophthalmoscope in hand. She introduced herself to the patient and Mom and looked into his right eye. She straightened up, turned to me, and said, "I agree with your assessment." She then turned to the patient and his mother and said there was evidence of increased intracranial pressure on his eye exam and that we would need a scan to define the cause. After answering a few questions from Mom, Judy went to arrange a CT scan. I finished my history and exam, and then began my admission notes. About an hour later, radiology called the patient down for his scan.

About 45 minutes later, Judy was called down to review the scans, and she let me accompany her. It was not good. There was a mass in the center of his head, and from the location, it was postulated that it was a pinealoma bigger than a golf ball. The recommendation was for the placement of a shunt and monitor to relieve the increased pressure pending surgery for diagnosis. A neurosurgical consultation was conducted, and the patient underwent an intraventricular shunt procedure. Something unexpected happened (I never heard what), but the patient returned to us with a shaved head, a burr hole and shunt on the right side of his head, and rather dense paralysis of his left arm.

He was a left-handed pitcher.

His previously articulate mother could barely speak. She stood stoically by the bed. Most of her world was lying in that bed, and things were not going well.

The diagnosis was confirmed, and radiation was initiated. The paralysis was no longer complete, but his left arm remained weak.

Every time I went into that room, I was overwhelmed with questions that could not be answered. Why this child? Why this widow? Why can't we fix this?

Judy must have picked up on my mood, and I told her I had decided that pediatrics was not for me. She said that I should not let one case have such an impact. "Hey, this is a tertiary care center, and even here, we rarely see this type of tumor. You might be in pediatric practice for 40 years and not see another primary brain tumor." Well, OK. Perhaps I was being rash, but there was no doubt that this type of event was something I never wanted to deal with again.

After radiation was started and the shunt was removed, the patient was discharged to continue treatment.

I went on to another pediatric service, where I spent several days per week assisting in the clinic. A week into the rotation, I was in the pediatric screening clinic, which is similar to the medical screening clinic, where I saw non-acute pediatric problems that had presented to the emergency room. I saw a 15-year-old female who came to the ER for a headache. Since she did not have a fever, she was sent to the screening clinic. A bright freshman in high school, she was looking forward to the summer, but she had developed daily headaches that seemed to worsen in the morning. I began my examination at the top. This time, I knew what papilledema looked like. I knew what I was seeing and what it probably meant. She was admitted. This time, the diagnosis was worse – astrocytoma…a malignant, primary brain tumor.

Alright. Enough. I am just not strong enough to take care of children with lethal diseases. God bless the Pediatricians and all they do.

Everyone should hug their children daily and tell them they love them. There, but for the Grace of God, go each of us.

PSALMS 127:3-4 Children are a heritage from the Lord, offspring a reward from him. Like arrows in the hands of a warrior are children born in one's youth.

DEUTERONOMY 7:13 He will love you and bless you and increase your numbers. He will bless the fruit of your womb.

MATTHEW 19:14 Jesus said, "Let the little children come to me, and do not hinder them, for the kingdom of heaven belongs to such as these."

Third-Year OB/GYN Rotation
(Wake County Memorial Hospital)

First Pregnancy, No Prenatal Care
(an explosion...and a "good catch")

I did my third-year OB/GYN rotation at Wake County Hospital in Raleigh, North Carolina. Some classmates did not like doing rotations outside of NC Memorial because it meant getting up even earlier than usual and catching a bus to an outlying hospital. I loved it because I like being busy and learning hands-on. The upside for the OB rotation was that at Wake, you would get to deliver many more babies. Indeed, while some individuals who stayed at NC Memorial for their rotation got to deliver one or two babies and "assist" on several more, I delivered more than 15.

Chapel Hill is a relatively affluent, small town. Most pregnancies are followed by private doctors and delivered outside NC Memorial. When I was there, if a patient was delivering at Memorial, the odds were high that they had a complex or complicated pregnancy. A medical student never does such deliveries. Consequently, the residents often competed with the students for deliveries at Memorial.

Private practice doctors primarily ran Wake in the daytime, but the resident staff was in charge at night. Additionally, Raleigh was a significantly larger city with a more diverse population. Therefore, at Wake, seeing a woman walk in off the street with no prenatal care already in labor was not an uncommon event. Medical students and house staff teams often accomplish these "walk-in" deliveries. You would not get that type of opportunity at the University Hospital.

Delivering babies is fun. The mother does all the work (and feels all the pain), but when the baby arrives and you place it in her arms, all is forgiven, and you are thanked even though you did very little. Therefore, I enjoyed OB. After my first five uncomplicated deliveries,

I was getting a little cocky. "Hey, I can do this." But God has a way of putting you back in your place, and he did so dramatically during my sixth delivery.

It was about 8:00 PM when the rather large 19-year-old female arrived in the emergency room in labor. She was quickly moved to the labor and delivery suite, where Linda, my resident, and I met her for the first time. She was relatively quiet for a young lady in advanced labor, and she did not complain while admitting she had had no prenatal care. She first sought care when her water broke, and her contractions became regular. Her demeanor was even more amazing, given that this was her first pregnancy.

Upon examination, she was already 20% effaced, and this condition progressed rapidly over the next couple of hours. Perhaps the absence of complaints and the routine nature of the labor lulled me into a state of uber calm, but the situation changed quickly when it came to delivery.

"OK, give me a good push," I instructed, and the patient willingly obliged. Before me was a beautiful infant head with a full head of dark hair.

As I prepared to suction mucus from the nostrils and turned to get the rubber bulb, I said, "Just hold tight for a second."

I'm not sure exactly what happened - whether she misunderstood me or thought I said "push"- but regardless, it was like an explosion.

Out came a complete baby and what must have been several liters of amniotic fluid. I was drenched. Linda, who had been standing behind me to look over my shoulder, was drenched. The baby flew through the air. Luckily, I caught the brand-new little boy. The nurse from the nursery was standing to my left, ready to take the child. She, too, was a little wet, and her eyes were wide open as I turned and handed her the infant with the cord still attached.

It was quiet for a moment, and then Linda said, "Nice catch."

I gathered myself enough to cut the cord and deliver the placenta, and then I had a seat.

The words of a phrase often voiced by my mother rolled across my memory: "God takes care of fools and children..." In this case, he had taken care of both.

I completed my OB rotation without major incidents and was able to deliver nine additional babies. At no point in any of those deliveries did I ever let my hand leave an already delivered baby's head...

JAMES 3:5 Likewise, the tongue is a small part of the body, but it makes great boasts. Consider what a great forest is set on fire by a small spark.

Third-Year Surgery Rotation
(NC Memorial Hospital)

Pre-oping One of Bucky's Babes
(a failed gastric bypass…maybe not)

I started my third year on Surgery. I had three one-month services during my 12-week rotation. The first was neurosurgery, and my attending was the chief of the neurosurgery department. Rounds could be very intense. The second was vascular/trauma and was amazingly busy. This is the service that did the amputations, vascular repairs, and vascular bypasses regularly and took care of all trauma arriving at or transferred to NC Memorial. Once again, it was a hectic service where you started your pre-rounding at 5:00 AM, allowing you to begin your rounds at 5:30 AM (and rounds were typically completed on the run), so you could be in surgery by 6:00 AM. Your day would end when it ended, typically between 6:30 and 9:30 PM. My third rotation was a general surgery rotation, where the incident in this story occurred.

Although not the epidemic that it is today, obesity was clearly a problem in the 1970s. Gastric bypass was a relatively new procedure reserved for the most severe cases of obesity. The patients had to be morbidly obese with a Body Mass Index (BMI) of >40. For a normal six-foot-tall person, this would mean weighing at least 300 pounds. They also had to have failed at other attempts at weight loss. In 1978, Dr. Joseph Buckwalter was the primary expert and proponent of the procedure at UNC. At the time, most of the patients were younger, middle-aged females. Some members of the surgery house staff had tagged these ladies as "Bucky's Babes," and, as you can imagine, given the predominantly male nature of the surgery program, the name stuck.

As a medical student on the surgery service, my main jobs were to do "scut" work, to write progress notes (that were good enough only

35

to require the resident to write "agree with above" and sign their signature), and to show up for rounds with some idea of what was going on (so I could have a chance when the "pimping" of the medical students started). The pimping game would not stop until a question was asked that no one could answer. That could not happen on the first question because the Attending physician might think the resident and intern were not teaching you anything (which was sometimes the case). That would end poorly for everyone except the attending physician. You would appear to be someone who should not have been admitted to medical school, and the intern and resident would likely be reprimanded for not adequately preparing the students for rounds. This, of course, would piss the house staff off, and your life on that service would spiral downward. It required a delicate balance to play the pimping game to everyone's benefit. You did not have to appear to be a genius, but you could not look totally unprepared.

So, what is "scut?" It is work that must be done, but most people do not want to do it. Surgery house staff want to eat, sleep, and do surgery. They do not want to write pre-op notes, draw blood, check labs, etc. That is busy work. Where is that medical student? While all this is true, I thought that doing scut work was not bad for medical students. It is beneficial to be able to write a clear and comprehensible note. Drawing blood from a wide range of patients, including those with large and small veins, the elderly, and the young, allows you to become very skilled at a necessary task. By the time I finished my third year, I could "get blood out of a turnip." If you're proficient with your hands, you'll have the opportunity to perform more advanced procedures, such as lumbar punctures, chest tubes, central line placements, and even pacemaker insertions. Hey, you began to feel like a real doctor!

I was asked to "pre-op" one of Bucky's Babes on this occasion. I arrived to draw the blood, make sure the EKG and chest x-ray had been done, and write the appropriate "pre"-pre-op note. Reading through the chart quickly led me to the conclusion that this case was somewhat unusual. The patient I was preparing for surgery had already had her gastric bypass. Apparently, she did well initially and lost almost one hundred pounds. Then, her weight stabilized and began to increase. How could that be? The gastric bypass converted the stomach from a "roomy" sack capable of containing the ingested material from a generous meal to more of a tube (or pouch) that quickly filled up and prompted the patient to stop eating due to "fullness" – early satiety. They would need to take more frequent small meals simply to maintain their weight. The planned surgery was intended to investigate why the procedure had "failed."

The patient was charming, talkative, and anxious to determine the cause of her weight loss reversal. We spoke as I prepared to draw her blood, and I noticed that she was sipping frequently from a large cup of soft drink. Initially, I reminded her she could have nothing by mouth after midnight. Then I noticed that she had two large 2-liter bottles of soft drinks on her bedside table. They were not diet drinks, so I commented that she must really like soft drinks. I asked how many of these beverages she drank per day. She said that she typically consumed two to three 2-liter sodas per day. This was in addition to her regular, frequent small meals.

I asked if she had always consumed such large amounts of soda. She said that before her gastric bypass, during her dieting days, she had been a fan of diet soda. After her bypass, she frequently experienced a slight "swooning" feeling after eating small meals. She had been told this was due to the rapid release of insulin when the meal passed quickly into the small intestine. The insulin would cause her blood sugar to drop, and she would get the weak feeling and the shakes. She began to treat these episodes with various colas, and she found them to be very effective at quickly relieving the symptoms. She also found the taste of the sugar-containing sodas to be much better than her previous diet drinks, and she gradually began to drink them on a chronic basis.

A quick calculation of the caloric content of 6 liters of soft drinks per day led me to believe that we might have found the cause of her weight gain. The lady had replaced large meals with chronic high-calorie liquids that did not give her early satiety. When I brought this point to the resident's and Dr. Buckwalter's attention, the surgery was canceled, and the patient was sent home with instructions to decrease her fluid intake and switch to low-calorie beverages. Dr. Buckwalter's surgery had not failed! Perhaps I was not a genius, but the remainder of that rotation went well for me.

MATTHEW 15:11 What goes into someone's mouth does not defile them, but what comes out of their mouth, that is what defiles them.

III. RESIDENCY AND FELLOWSHIP – (NORTH CAROLINA MEMORIAL HOSPITAL)

I always took away more than I brought
(a little lady and four big sons)

When I began my fellowship in hematology at the University of North Carolina's North Carolina Memorial Hospital in Chapel Hill, I knew I wanted to pursue a career in academic hematology. I had no intention of pursuing a career in oncology, and I had no desire to work with oncology patients. The program, however, was a combined one. If I did three years, I would be board-eligible in both Hematology and Oncology. If I did two years, I could choose which one I wanted to test in. Oncology is hard. Oncology is psychologically draining for me. I do not like my patients to die, and oncology patients at that time (and still today) do it on a regular basis. I have trouble with this. I like my patients. I get attached, and I have a difficult time dealing with their death. They become more like friends. Professionally, this is probably a terrible mistake on my part, but I cannot (or will not) change who I am. This brings us to the subject of the Hematology/Oncology (Hem/Onc) clinic during my fellowship.

The Hem/Onc clinic, even in places like Chapel Hill, which is renowned for its hematologic expertise, is primarily focused on oncology. There are simply more patients with oncology conditions than there are patients with von Willebrand disease. For this reason, I always dreaded going to clinic. As the year progressed, however, my attitude began to shift. I began to realize that these patients had looked the lion (or tiger) in the eye, and they were never the same. They either had made their peace or were in denial and desperate to have any and all therapies, effective or otherwise, to avoid or delay death. Fortunately, most of my patients fell into the former category.

The fact that these patients were, daily, dealing with potentially deadly problems gradually had a significant effect on my attitude. I could be heading to the clinic, mad that my experiment had failed, upset that my manuscript had received a bad review, and terribly upset that our grant would not be funded. And then I would walk into the clinic. I would spend the next four to five hours dealing with people who had and were looking death in the face. Many of these patients viewed things with a much more discerning perspective than I could muster. I remember thinking multiple times as I took that elevator out of the basement, "Hey, I don't really have any problems." Whatever I brought into the clinic paled compared to what these special people were dealing with. One patient exemplified this point more effectively than any other.

I picked up her chart and began to read about my new patient, who was being referred to me for advancing breast cancer. She had been diagnosed approximately two years earlier and was being referred now with massive metastatic lesions in her liver. When she came through my door, she did not even look sick. If I had not seen her CT scan with metastases the size of grapefruits in her liver, I would have never believed she was in such trouble. She was a petite, elderly lady in her early seventies. She may have been a hundred and ten pounds soaking wet. She was brought to the clinic by her son, who must have weighed 240 pounds. He was probably in his forties, was going bald, had a little middle-aged spread, had a soft smile, and was usually quiet. I would always see the patient, talk with her, formulate a plan, explain it to her, and then call her son to go over the plan with him.

The lady had already had significant amounts of hormonal manipulation, so we began with a single-agent treatment with Adriamycin. I explained that this might cause her hair to fall out, and the patient smiled, saying it was gray anyway and that she had been thinking about getting a wig. The Adria worked! The metastatic lesions dramatically regressed. The therapy continued to be effective for about seven months, and then the tumors began to expand. So, we switched to tamoxifen, an estrogen antagonist. Once again, the metastatic lesions regressed, and we got another six months. When they returned, we went to 5FU and got another four-month response. As we continued down this road, I met the patient's other three sons. All were big guys, and all were relatively quiet. It was also evident that all were absolutely devoted to this little lady. I never got the impression that they were in a hurry to get out of the clinic - that they had "something better to do." They just took off work and brought their mother to the doctor. And they did not complain. They were also very polite and patient with our clinic, which was not always the most efficient, and they were always attentive to their mother.

After the third response (even though I admit the responses were getting shorter in duration), I began to think that anything I did would work. So, when the lesions came back, I once again tried hormone therapy. This time, the liver lesions did not respond. In fact, there were new ones, and the old ones were getting larger. I remember so well sitting at the little desk that folded down out of the wall, staring at what was, by this time, a large clinic chart, thinking to myself that there were no more rabbits in the hat. The lady sat quietly beside me as I tried to find the words to tell her I had no more treatment to offer. After a few minutes, she reached over and put her hand on my arm, and as I looked up into her face, she said, "You know, you really have done a good job." I could not speak. Here was this lady who was dying, and she was trying to comfort me! She wanted me to know that it was not my fault. What a moment. It touched me in a way that I cannot fully communicate. I went out to talk to her son, who was a little less stoic but who expressed no anger or frustration that the "University Hospital" had not been able to save his mother. This mother had done her job and was leaving behind several exceptional men who would make this planet a better place.

As I caught the elevator up and then the bus home, I thought about this special lady and her devoted sons. I realized I always took more away from that clinic than I took to it. I could go to that clinic filled with worry about multiple "problems," but four hours later, I would realize that my life was blessed beyond reason and that I had no "real" problems. Sometimes, I am such a slow learner.

EXODUS 20:12 Honor your father and your mother, so that you may live long in the land the Lord your God is giving you.

2 CORINTHIANS 1:4 Who comforts us in all our troubles, so that we can comfort those in any trouble with the comfort we ourselves receive from God.

Shooting the Bed Tower
(he has not bled enough yet...)

As will be obvious elsewhere in these stories, I spent much of my ER time as a solo Doc in the Chatham County Hospital in Siler City, NC. However, I also spent a significant amount of time in the emergency department at N.C. Memorial Hospital in Chapel Hill, N.C. I spent a month there as a medicine intern (you get to see the patient first as the intern), a month as the medical admitting resident (you make the decision as to who gets admitted and who goes home), and multiple visits as consulting resident from various services for all kinds to specific diseases and problems (consults give advice, but do not take the patient). Finally, all medical residents took night calls in the ER, serving as nighttime admitting residents. All in all, a significant (although not of the same order of magnitude as Siler City) emergency room experience.

**NC Memorial Hospital Circa 1982 – Bed Tower on Left.   UNC Hospitals Today –
Memorial Is to the Far Left.**

By the time I was well into my second year of residency, I had become more comfortable in the ER than most of the house staff. However, with confidence comes the risk of becoming cocky. This was made clear to me one evening when there was actual gunfire at the hospital. Now, do not get me wrong, gunplay and gunshot wounds were not a common occurrence at NC Memorial. Chapel Hill is a very liberal, live-and-let-live environment. It is nothing like some other hospitals I have worked in along the I-95 corridor in Richmond, VA, or New Brunswick, NJ.

As usual, the ER was busy this Friday evening, but it gradually slowed down, and by 11:00 PM, we had either admitted or discharged most patients. At this point, the sound of a single gunshot echoed off the buildings that surrounded the small parking lot and ambulance entrance. Someone came running in to say that there was a car sitting in the lot and that someone in that car had just fired a pistol. Call security!

In less than a minute, two security guards arrived. The path from the ER to the loading deck involved two sets of motion-activated double sliding glass doors. They were situated at right angles to each other. In the past, I had considered this an awkward arrangement. You had to come through the first set, make a ninety-degree right turn with the gurney, and then come through the second set. Once through the second set, you had access to the receiving desk. You had to go past that desk, and the receptionist could open yet a third set of doors that once again required a 90-degree turn, this time to the left to allow access to the ER proper. Therefore, there was no direct sight line from outside the building to the inside of the ER. Suddenly, this evening, this seemed like an acceptable arrangement. From my vantage point within the ER, I watched intently as the security guards went to work. One immediately left to call the police, and the other stood safely inside the second set of doors. OK. Now what? "Now we wait."

I am not a particularly good "waiter." The car reportedly faced the hospital bed tower across the hall from the ER. I thought I might be able to see what was going on by going into the ground-floor clinic and peeking out one of the windows (preferably one far away from the car) to see what was happening in the parking lot and car. When I did so, I could clearly see the car, and there was a single hole in the windshield. I did not see any movement, but I could see what appeared to be a man slumped across the steering wheel. I watched for a few more moments and confirmed that there was no movement.

Now, I was concerned that perhaps the driver had shot himself. It had been a few minutes since the gunfire and the first frantic report. Possibly, there had been another shot that we had not appreciated. I asked the guard for a status report, and he informed me that the police had been notified and were en route. Now I was concerned that whoever this was either was bleeding to death or had suffered a wound severe enough to require immediate treatment. I decided to take another look. Still no movement. Well, I decided to go and look more directly through the outer doors. I moved through the first set, and they closed behind me. I moved along the wall to the second set so as not to activate the overhead motion detector, which would have led to the doors opening. I looked around the corner, and to my dismay, the doors separated and opened. When this happened, I clearly saw the silhouette in the car move. Well, if he is bleeding, he has not bled enough! I quickly stepped back, and at that moment, two police cars pulled into the drive.

To my surprise, they did not have flashing lights on and left room for the offending car to back up. This is precisely what the car did, and then it sped away with the two police cars in pursuit, now with full lights and sound! They were able to stop the car a few blocks away. Their plan had been better thought out than mine...

I later found out that the individual in the car was a lower-level hospital administrator who had been fired earlier that day. After having a few drinks and thinking the situation through, he decided the best thing to do was to come back and shoot the bed tower...Well, in hindsight, that was much better than shooting a person or himself. I

45

am not sure what the charge was for shooting a hospital building, but I am sure this turned out better than could have been anticipated. No one died, and the security patrol and police did their job efficiently. I had a greater appreciation for the architecture of the ER, and I learned once again that sometimes you need to be patient.

PROVERBS 2:11 Discretion will protect you, and understanding will guard you.

PROVERBS 22:3 The prudent see danger and take refuge, but the simple keep going and pay the penalty.

Shrimp, Swollen Lip, and Difficulty Speaking
(*some reason for concern...*)

I spent a considerable amount of time in emergency rooms during my residency and fellowship, and I must admit that one can occasionally be slightly overconfident in one's abilities. This story is about one of those times.

It was a tranquil Friday evening in the NCMH emergency room. It was only 10:00 PM, but the surgery intern had already disappeared, and all the curtains were pulled back, revealing a neat line of empty gurneys. As I was leisurely finishing the note on my last patient, a well-dressed older couple appeared at the intake window and were brought back into the emergency room. It was summertime, and these lovely people had been to a nice restaurant with friends when the wife noticed swelling of her lower lip. She had a known allergy to some seafood and must have somehow come into contact with the shrimp cocktail being eaten by the lady next to her. The husband kindly explained that perhaps the forks had been switched somehow. In any event, the swelling had progressed to difficulty speaking, and her husband had brought her to the hospital.

On exam, the lady's lip and tongue were swollen. Although she was breathing normally, she could not speak and needed acute care. Hey, I got this one. "Bring me the epinephrine."

I had the lovely lady sit back on the gurney while I prepared to give her the injection that I was sure would immediately begin to alleviate the problem. Given the degree of swelling, I put in an IV to allow intravenous injection of the adrenaline and have access to other medication if needed. While administering a slow epinephrine push, I had the opportunity to speak with the well-dressed and articulate husband. As we chatted, I told him how glad I was that he had brought his wife to the ER when he noted a problem. His response was: "Well, after her heart attack last month, I thought I had better not take any chances..."

Oh my God...I am pushing intravenous epinephrine on an elderly lady less than a month after a myocardial infarction!

"Nurse, please place a cardiac monitor on this nice lady."

OK...mild tachycardia...no ST segment abnormalities (the ST segment goes down with ischemia and up with infarction)...

The lip and tongue swelling began to subside, and the tachycardia associated with acute epinephrine infusion began to fade. All went well, and the lady handled my cardiac "stress test" with no apparent problem. When she could talk, I asked about any chest pain, and she said that she had not really had any pain, just the swelling.

After keeping the lovely couple longer than I needed, I ran a twelve-lead EKG, removed the monitor, and let them go home.

Sitting in my chair writing my note, I wondered about this episode. Giving epinephrine to a patient four weeks post-MI is not without risk. Delaying acute treatment in a patient with swelling sufficient to cause an inability to talk might lead rather quickly to upper airway occlusion. If I had known about the recent MI, I might have hesitated about giving the epinephrine...

As I mulled over the options and potential consequences, a familiar phrase often used by my mother rolled through the recesses of my mind... "God takes care of young children and fools" ...

Well, I was not young, so my options were limited. It is always good to reevaluate your assessment of your capabilities occasionally and thank God that He still can use even an overconfident physician.

2 CORINTHIANS 11:17 In this self-confident boasting, I am not talking as the Lord would, but as a fool.

Together in Life, Together in Death
(Now they're bringing Jimmy in!)

Patients suffering from myocardial infarctions ("MIs" or "heart attacks") can present in all kinds of ways in the emergency room. Some patients have the classic signs and symptoms – crushing chest pain ("it feels like an elephant is sitting on my chest"), tachycardia (rapid heart rate), cold and clammy (cold sweats), shortness of breath, and nausea. Others will exhibit some, but not all, of the signs and symptoms. Some patients will "just not feel well" but lack specific symptoms. Others will have an altered pain pattern with pain in the jaw or pain radiating down their arm. Some patients will feel "weak" without the presence of pain. Others will have no symptoms and will be found to have suffered a "silent MI" with changes on their ECG (electrocardiogram) but no history of symptoms.

Having gotten to the emergency room in a talking, conscious state is an excellent prognostic factor for any heart attack patient. At that point, they will be given medications to limit the heart muscle damage and other medications to prevent cardiac arrhythmia. They will also be monitored for the occurrence of such arrhythmias. They will be appropriately treated to restore a normal rhythm if an arrhythmia occurs. Most people who die of a "heart attack" do so because of an arrhythmia that stops their heart from beating. Indeed, a patient can survive even a "massive" heart attack if arrhythmias are prevented or treated when they occur.

The patients with the poorest prognosis are those who have arrhythmia outside the hospital. They simply drop dead. Unless someone quickly restores their heartbeat, they stay dead. CPR can provide some blood flow, but does not typically restore the normal electrical activity necessary for a normal heart rhythm. To restore a normal, or at least functioning, rhythm, one needs to deliver a shock to the heart (cardioversion) that resets all the electrically firing cells back to baseline. When they start to fire again, the rhythm will be normal many (most) times. This is why CPR has changed from its previous pattern (back in the 1980s) of breathing and chest compressions to its current pattern of shock-shock-shock. This is why we see cardio-defibrillators (AEDs - Automatic External Defibrillators) everywhere – at work, in parks, and in malls. When someone has an "event" and is pulseless, the likelihood of survival is determined mainly by the ability to regain a functional cardiac rhythm that will drive blood through the heart and out into the circulation.

That is all well and good, but in 1982, there were no AEDs. The first group that might have this capability would be the first responders with the rescue squad. The first defibrillator near the patient was often in the emergency room. So, in the early '80s, it was not uncommon to have patients arrive at the ER after prolonged CPR but with no pulse or blood pressure. These cases had relatively poor overall outcomes. This story illustrates the situation well.

It was a typical Friday in early Summer in Chapel Hill. I was the admitting resident for medicine, serving as the primary doctor for all non-surgical cases and primary medical consultant for all cases. Fridays tend to be busy, but this one had not been too bad. Then the squaw box radio located at the ER intake desk began to explode. We had an incoming ambulance bringing a 56-year-old white male who had dropped at work. CPR, administered by a coworker, was in progress when the rescue squad arrived. The patient had virtually no electrical activity when the ECG leads were placed. He had been shocked twice at the scene without effect, and CPR was continuing during transport to the ER.

Upon arrival in the ER, it was quickly apparent that the gentleman was almost assuredly beyond our ability to resuscitate. However, one is never sure, and we made every effort to achieve a functional rhythm. We intubated and put him on high-flow oxygen as CPR was continued. Intravenous lines were placed, labs were sent, and electrical defibrillation was attempted on multiple occasions. At no time did we have even a trace of a rhythm. With body temperature

50

falling (despite the hot room) and pupils fixed, it was decided to "call" the code after 30 minutes.

It was now my job to tell the relatives that, unfortunately, we had been unable to resuscitate their loved one. The wife and two daughters had arrived and sat in a small waiting room across from the main ER doors. I entered, and before I could speak, they must have realized that I had no good news. My words confirmed their fears, and they had the anticipated emotional response. As I talked to the wife, a third daughter rushed into the room. She shouted, "Now they're bringing Jimmy in!"

I looked up, wondering who "they" were and who "Jimmy" was. It turned out that they were another rescue squad, and Jimmy was the son of the man who had just died. Jimmy was fishing when someone ran to tell him the news that his father had been rushed to the emergency room for a possible heart attack. Jimmy dropped his pole and began to run to his truck when he suddenly clutched his chest and fell to the ground. Jimmy was only 34, but he must have gotten every one of his father's high-risk genes. I asked the mom to excuse me and quickly returned to the ER.

Indeed, the squaw box confirmed that the son was en route. Unfortunately, the story sounded like a repeat of his father's case, but in this instance, the person delivering the message did not know CPR and had to rush to the car, drive to a phone, and call 911. The rescue squad found him pulseless, with no respirations, and no evidence of electrical activity. CPR was in progress, and early efforts at defibrillation were unsuccessful.

Unfortunately, the resuscitation effort in the ER closely mirrored that of his father. Despite our vigorous best efforts, we could never establish any electrical activity or rhythm. We called the code after about 40 minutes.

Now, it was my job to go out and speak to the same family to whom I had delivered the news of their husband's and father's death

51

about an hour before. I went directly to the mother, took her hand, and said I was sorry. The sobbing and shouts of "No, No, No..." were totally appropriate and expected, but they echoed in my head for months.

What had started as a reasonable Friday in the ER had turned amazingly draining.

The following Tuesday, one of the medical residents brought me a copy of a local newspaper. The obituary page had a big headline: "Together in Life, Together in Death." Below was a very nice story about how close the father and son were and how much they enjoyed fishing together.

I must admit that I read the article very carefully to ensure that the "treating" physician's name was not mentioned.

PSALMS 90:12 Teach us to number our days, that we may gain a heart of wisdom.

JOB 14:5 A person's days are determined; you have decreed the number of his months and have set limits he cannot exceed.

PSALMS 39:4 Show me, Lord, my life's end and the number of my days; let me know how fleeting my life is.

That BP Is Off the Wall!
(Does Electro Shock Therapy Cause High Blood Pressure...?)

As a resident, being a third-year house officer was not a bad job. You knew your way around the hospital. Your admission notes were short when you were on an inpatient service. Best of all, much of the time, you were on a consulting service where you had plenty of time to read and lots of medical students and fellows with whom to share the work. You also had an attending expert in the field who was the final authority and ensured things never went too far off the rails.

Subspecialty consults provided medical students with an opportunity to gain a deeper understanding of specific, specialized areas of medicine, including cardiology, endocrinology, nephrology, gastroenterology, hematology, oncology, pulmonary medicine, and rheumatology. They were also a time for medical residents and fellows to hone their diagnostic skills and prepare for the coming board examinations.

The consult services typically ran on a monthly basis. At the time of transition from one group to another, there would be a sign-off between the outgoing resident and the resident just coming onto the service. This was necessary because some patients would have incomplete evaluations, and the final recommendations could not be made until the results of laboratory assays, radiographic examinations, and other studies were back. This was the setting for one of the more unusual consults I was involved in while on Cardiology.

I got an alert regarding grossly abnormal urinary metanephrines and vanillylmandelic acid (VMA) assays. Well, that was unusual. Those are the kinds of tests ordered on the endocrinology service. Why was I getting the call? When I responded, I was told that these tests had been ordered by the cardiology consult team several weeks earlier. A little detective work revealed that the patient had been on the psychiatry service but had subsequently been discharged. I concluded that must have been why he was not on the list of patients that had been checked out to me at the beginning of our rotation.

After I found the chart, the reading was fascinating. The patient was a 27-year-old college-educated male who had been in good health until three months before seeking medical assistance for decreased appetite, decreased libido, and difficulty sleeping. When he developed auditory and visual hallucinations, he was admitted to a psychiatric hospital. His condition was diagnosed as psychotic depression, and he was treated with a series of antidepressants without significant improvement. His only medical problem appeared to be mild hypertension with systolic blood pressures ranging from 150 to 170 and diastolic pressures between 90 and 110 millimeters of mercury (mm Hg). Because of an inadequate response to antidepressant medication, the patient was transferred to N.C. Memorial Hospital (NCMH), for consideration of electroconvulsive therapy (ECT). At that time, ECT was commonly referred to as "shock therapy" in lay literature.

At NCMH, he was noted to be mildly hypertensive, and a psychological evaluation revealed an intelligent young man who admitted to one recent suicide attempt. Other testing was consistent with significant depression, and the decision was made to proceed with ECT.

The first episode of ECT was quite exciting for the anesthesiologist. After the routine cocktail of the time (0.2 mg glycopyrrolate, 50 mg succinylcholine, and 50 mg methohexital sodium), ECT was initiated, resulting in an immediate rise in blood pressure to 260/190 mmHg and a heart rate increase to 130 beats per minute. Well, that probably got someone's pucker factor up. Not only did the blood pressure spike to astronomical levels, but it stayed there for ten minutes. It was perhaps one of the longest ten-minute periods of that young anesthesiologist's career. An urgent (STAT) cardiology consult was called.

In the initial note, the cardiologist suggested initiating beta blockade for baseline blood pressure control, increasing

54

succinylcholine during subsequent ECT, and conducting urinary testing for metanephrines and VMA to exclude the possibility of a pheochromocytoma. Pheochromocytoma is a rare adrenal tumor associated with the secretion of molecules capable of inducing episodic symptoms, including hypertension. The 24-hour urine samples were collected and sent, and ECT was resumed with increased doses of succinylcholine.

ECT continued to cause spikes in blood pressure and heart rate. Still, the anesthesiologist was able to improve management by substituting atropine sulfate for glycopyrrolate and gradually increasing the methohexital sodium. Over the next four weeks, the patient received eleven additional ECT treatments, improving progressively his mood, appetite, and spontaneous conversation. During that period, the results of the urinary assays were returned to the psychiatric team. The results were so abnormal that the pathologist recommended repeating the tests after all potentially complicating medications had been discontinued. This recommendation was followed, and repeat urines were sent for testing. In the interim, the patient completed his ECT, was placed on oral antidepressants, and was discharged. The results of this second set of assays were what I had been called about.

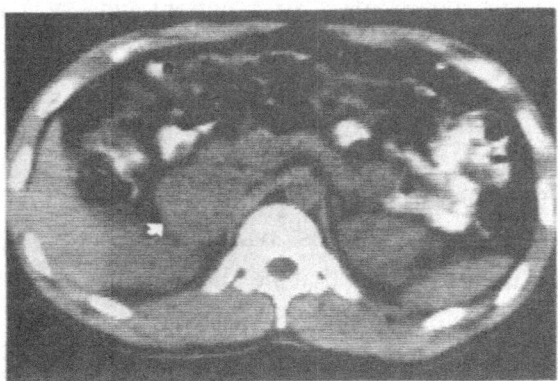

Abdominal CT scan shows large 5 cm soft tissue mass just superior and medial to right kidney (arrow).

The repeat assays were consistent with and confirmed the first set. The VMA levels were six times higher than the normal upper limits, and the metanephrine excretion was greater than nine times what would have been expected in a 24-hour period. The team and patient were notified, and arrangements were made for an outpatient CT scan. The scan revealed a mass above the right kidney. The urine and CT results were consistent with pheochromocytoma. The beta-blocker anti-hypertensives (which appeared to be working but could make things worse) were stopped, and alpha-blockade with phenoxybenzamine was started. The patient was admitted to the urology service, where an arteriogram was consistent with a hypovascular tumor, and a rather large 52-gram pheochromocytoma was removed at surgery. At two and three months of follow-up as an outpatient, the patient's blood pressure was 120/80 mm Hg off all blood pressure medications. His mental status was also improved on low-dose antidepressant therapy.

Having seen only one other case of pheochromocytoma in my young career, I searched the literature for evidence of ECT in patients with pheochromocytoma. I could find only two reports. The first was the tragic case of a 34-year-old female with an undiagnosed pheochromocytoma who died of cardiac arrest when given ECT. The second was a brief mention of a patient who was diagnosed with pheochromocytoma and who had apparently survived ECT within the previous year. Ours was the first undiagnosed pheochromocytoma to have survived an entire course of ECT.

The problem with diagnosing pheochromocytoma in our patient is the fact that many of his symptoms were consistent with his psychiatric diagnosis and that he did not have (or at least did not describe) episodic events that are typical of the tumor. Our gentleman did as well as he did, at least partly due to the advances in and appropriate application of good anesthesia. It was an excellent job by a frightened anesthesiology resident! My attending physician and I wrote a case report on this subject, which is noted below.

The citation for this published case is as follows:

M.E. Carr and J.W. Woods: Electroconvulsive Therapy in a Patient with Unsuspected Pheochromocytoma. Southern Medical Journal 78:613-615,1985.

James 1:2-3 Consider it pure joy, my brothers and sisters, whenever you face trials of many kinds, because you know that the testing of your faith produces perseverance.

A Raging Bull of a Patient on the Neurology Service
(Guards don't have to be large … if they know what they are doing)

In the early eighties, when I was a resident at NC Memorial Hospital, the Neurology service was jointly staffed by medicine and neurology house staff. The interns were all medical interns, and the remainder of the team consisted of a medical resident, a neurology resident, and a neurology attending. It was the responsibility of the medicine house staff to address the "medical problems," and the neurology team was tasked with managing neurological conditions and educating the medical house staff on basic neurology. All in all, it worked well. It was a relatively "cushy" rotation for the medical staff because you never really got "slammed" with admissions the way you would on a regular medical service. Occasionally, you could get some fascinating cases (myasthenia gravis, Guillain-Barré, muscular sclerosis, etc.), and occasionally, you would meet some fascinating people. This is a story that falls in the latter category.

As a public institution that deals with a diverse range of people, NC Memorial Hospital, by necessity, has a security team. In the late seventies and early eighties, they were rather nondescript in appearance. They wore gray jackets and pants and did not appear to carry a weapon, and I was always impressed by how small most of them were. Of course, I was taller at six feet and two inches than most, but many security personnel were in the five-foot-seven-inch to five-foot-eight-inch range. Having had a significant amount of military training, I often thought that these guys were probably not going to be able to help me much if they showed up without a weapon. One sunny morning, I found out I was mistaken.

In the early morning, we had admitted a thirty-something-year-old gentleman for episodes of altered mental status. He was a giant of a man – six feet five inches tall and weighing about 250 pounds. And…he was not fat. When I met him, he seemed completely normal.

However, his family stated that he had several episodes where he did not appear to recognize anyone. He would stare, not respond to questions, and did not speak during these spells. The episodes had started about two weeks prior and seemed to resolve spontaneously, but they were occurring more frequently and lasting longer each time. After each occurrence, the patient would be sleepy and have no memory of the event. His local physician had referred him to the neurology department at UNC, and given the increasing pace of events, he was admitted for evaluation.

I started an IV in preparation for planned CT scans and EEGs and told him that he was going to have a "busy day." He smiled and said he was hungry.

At rounds, the consensus was that this must represent some type of seizure activity. Since he had no prior history, new-onset seizures in an adult are worrisome for a brain tumor. Thus, the CT scan would check for a mass, and the EEG would investigate possible seizure activity. We have the patient, a potential diagnosis, and a plan.

All seemed right with the world, but it was not.

"Doctor, come quickly! Your patient has pulled out his IV, is going berserk in his room, and he is bleeding everywhere!"

That doesn't sound good, but it certainly gets your attention. Call security.

I ran down the hall to find the patient standing in his room, having turned over a chair and looking out the window. The nurse was correct. The IV was not attached, and blood was dripping on the floor.

As I entered the room, the patient turned and looked at me. He did not look happy, and he was holding his IV pole as a weapon in his left hand. I backed out of the room and shut the door. Luckily, he made no effort to follow me.

"Where is security?!"

About that time, the first of the small security guys came down the hall. I swear, I think he stood on his tiptoes to look through the door window.

As he was looking, I offered that perhaps he might need some help. Apparently, he agreed and began to talk into his walkie-talkie as he moved down the hall.

Hey, come back…you are better than nothing…

A few minutes later, a different small guard came down the hall. He, too, looked in the door window, but then he pushed the door open and started into the room.

He turned to me as he entered and said, "I know this guy."

I turned to the nurse and said, "Get me 5 milligrams of injectable valium."

The security guard spoke softly to the patient, who slowly turned to face him. The guard continued to talk without changing the tone or volume of his voice. The patient just stared at him. The guard waved me in with the hand he had behind his back.

Trying to be as "small" as possible, I reached down and reattached the IV. Luckily, it had not clotted off, and it began to flow. I slowly pushed five mgs of valium. Whether this was a seizure or mania, a little valium seemed appropriate. The guard continued to speak, and the patient continued his steady gaze.

After a few moments, the patient appeared to relax and waver a little. I retrieved the chair, and with the guard's assistance, we helped him take a seat. As we watched, the patient gradually came to himself and spoke the guard's name.

That security guard quickly handled a potentially nasty and dangerous situation. I was so glad he knew the patient and what to do. It was very impressive that he did not hesitate. He assessed the situation and acted. He might have been small, but he was also cool in a hot situation - well done.

The patient underwent a CT scan, which confirmed a two-centimeter mass, and an EEG revealed abnormal electrical activity. The tumor was removed, but it was a primary malignant brain tumor. I never knew how he did, but such tumors are not easily controlled.

Proverbs 15:1 A gentle answer turns away wrath, but a harsh word stirs up anger.

1 Samuel 16:7 But the Lord said to Samuel, "Do not consider his appearance or his height, for I have rejected him. The Lord does not look at the things people look at. People look at the outward appearance, but the Lord looks at the heart."

Doris von C and the Eye of the Beast
(*You need a haircut...*)

My mother taught me that it's essential to learn something new every day. Well, I picked the right profession because you can't help but learn something new every day as a physician. You learn from lectures and articles, but your primary teachers are the patients themselves. Occasionally, a patient touches you so profoundly that you are never quite the same. This is the story of one such patient.

I first met Doris on Ward Five West while interning on one of the medical services. She had leukemia. It was the most common kind (AML – Acute Myelocytic Leukemia) in adults. At that time at UNC, the head of the Department of Oncology, Dr. Bob C, was a world expert in leukemia treatment and had been an originator and primary proponent of high-dose Ara-C for treating AML. The therapy could be very effective in achieving early remissions. However, at some point months down the road, relapse was almost inevitable. The treatment was also very intense, with predictable drops in hemoglobin, white cell counts, and platelet counts due to suppression of the bone marrow. The drops in white cell and platelet concentration were typically severe enough to put the patient at significant risk for infection and bleeding.

Doris's favorite doctor in the world was Dr. Don G, an excellent hematologist and oncologist, and a great guy who would go on to head the bone marrow transplant team at UNC. He got a great start by taking care of these high-dose Ara-C patients who behaved in many ways like post-transplant patients. He was on the consult service when I began a medical rotation on Five West. I have forgotten the exact medical team, but it was a general medicine service, which meant we took all types of patients.

I had known Don for several years, having shared the same advisor/mentor, Dr. Jan Hermans, during graduate school. Don was a biochemistry student who studied physical chemistry. I was a biomedical engineering student who studied physical chemistry. It should be no surprise that Dr. Hermans was a physical chemist masquerading as a biochemist. Don had started his program several years before I did, but he had gone to medical school, followed by a residency at Massachusetts General Hospital in Boston. He returned to complete his dissertation while I was a student and postdoctoral researcher. Don encouraged me to pursue a career in medicine, and I eventually did. We continued to work together while I was in Medical School. Now, Don was on the faculty, and I was an intern. I suppose our history was why Don hand-picked me to take on Doris. I think he knew I would do my best to take care of her and that I would learn a great deal from her. That was the case, as I learned more from Doris than from any other patient during my residency.

The first time I met Doris, she had just begun her second round of high-dose Ara-C. She had a complete response after her first course, which lasted for 14 months. When the blasts (immature cells indicative of leukemia) reappeared, the decision was made to try another course. Her bone marrow had recovered entirely after the first course, but a second course was bound to cause complete ablation of her bone marrow, resulting in very low white cell and platelet counts. Of course, her hair would fall out, which was particularly devastating to Doris as she was a beautician.

Doris was always blunt. "So, you are going to take care of me?" All said with one raised eyebrow.

"Well, I am going to try," was my response.

"You better do better than try," she retorted. "At least try hard," she concluded.

This was the beginning of her ongoing attempt to keep me in line.

By day three, the battle had begun. Doris's granulocyte count rapidly fell and put her at risk for infection. She was placed in isolation, spiked fevers, and was followed closely by the Infectious Disease Consult.

Her platelet count fell, putting her at risk for bleeding, and predictably, she began to bruise at all her IV sites.

Doris questioned, "I look like a battered child. Are you beating me in my sleep?"

The hematology/oncology team continued to follow her, and her repeat bone marrow showed an ablated marrow. That was good in that the blasts were gone. That was bad because there were very few cells to produce red blood cells, white blood cells, and platelets. It was going to be a long struggle.

We began to do prophylactic platelet transfusions when her platelet count fell to less than 20 thousand. Despite this effort, she developed significant nose bleeds and was followed regularly by the ENT service. She also developed vaginal bleeding and was seen by the OB/GYN, who ruled out new sources of bleeding and then solved the problem by hormonally suppressing her menstrual cycle.

Doris's response: "Well, at least I won't get pregnant while I'm in here."

Days passed, and her counts remained low. She continued to spike fevers despite the use of broad-spectrum antibiotics. The infectious disease consult recommended prophylactic amphotericin-B, which caused her to have terrible shaking chills. When her chest x-ray showed possible patchy infiltrates, we fired our last shot and gave her granulocyte transfusions. These produced even worse rigors.

Doris's questions for me: "Do you know what you are doing? Can't you give me anything that won't make me feel worse?"

The continuous infusions of antibiotics and other medications, the daily blood draws, and the intermittent blood cultures wore out Doris' veins, and line placement became the purview of vascular surgery.

What else could go wrong? She developed herpetic cold sores that extended from her lips onto her face. She was seen by dermatologists, and I followed their recommendations.

Finally, after more than ten days, the white count began to recover slowly. At this point, she complained of abdominal pain. On examination, she had mild diffuse tenderness, questionable rebound (pain that occurs when you suddenly release hand pressure on the abdomen), and no bowel sounds. I called general surgery. Having worked with him as a medical student, I knew the surgery chief resident. He came, examined Doris, and stood silently at the end of her bed. He took me out into the hallway and said, "Although I think this may be a surgical abdomen, the risk of taking her to the operating room with minimal white cells and no platelets is just too high at the moment. I suggest we wait and watch. If something definitively declares itself, we will try to deal with it."

"So, what do you recommend?" I asked.

"I think you should continue the antibiotics and pray."

That was my plan even before surgery came by, so I continued that effort. By the following day, the pain had resolved, and Doris could eat a little lunch.

The white count rose slowly, but the platelet count remained low. Repeat bone marrow biopsies showed the absence of blasts but remained somewhat hypoplastic (empty). We were three weeks into this hospitalization, and as Doris improved, she began to inquire when she could go home.

My answer was always the same: " When you make a platelet." After the third time I said this, she responded, "Is that all you can come up with? You need to be more creative!"

It is day 25, and Doris still had fewer than 20,000 platelets. At this point, the blood bank knew Doris personally, and they were working diligently to obtain platelets that would survive the antibodies Doris was forming.

Finally, I had a pointed discussion with Doris one evening. I felt it was fair since she was constantly jabbing at me. "Doris, you have to make me a platelet tonight." She just looked at me and raised that eyebrow.

The next morning, her platelet count was 40 thousand! I could not believe it. The lines began to come out, and within two days, her count exceeded 100,000. She went home to her husband and two small children.

A few months later, Don called me to come down to the clinic to see someone. When I got there, there was Doris. She was full of life, and her hair was growing. She jumped up when she saw me, ran to me, and threw her arms around my neck. She did not spend a lot of time thanking me, but it was clear that she was glad to see me. She then introduced me to her daughter. It was one of the best moments of my life.

Unfortunately, the story does not end there. That remission lasted about eight months. By now, I was a JAR (Junior Admitting Resident), and I got a call from Five West. Doris was back in the hospital and not doing well. She was not expected to live more than a few days.

When I walked in, I could see that she was weak. She turned her head to look at me.

"I thought you had forgotten about me," she said in an unfamiliarly weak voice.

I took her hand and said, "Now, Doris, you know that is simply not possible."

I stayed for a few minutes and then offered to leave so she could rest.

She raised that eyebrow and motioned for me to come closer.

As I leaned in, she said, "You need a haircut."

As I left the room, I knew what a strong and wonderful person was lying in that bed. She had looked the Beast in the eye and was not afraid.

The world did not have enough Doris Von Cs, and it would lose one that night.

Matthew 7:20 Thus, by their fruit you will recognize them.

Galatians 5:22-23 But the fruit of the Spirit is love, joy, peace, forbearance, kindness, goodness, faithfulness, gentleness, and self-control. Against such things, there is no law.

Unloading the Emergency Room
with a Screening Clinic
(also known as the "screaming" clinic)

In the early 1980s, the emergency room was relatively small and always busy for a hospital of NC Memorial's size. Expanding the ER would require new construction, so it was decided to "unload" the ER by sending relatively non-acute patients to a medical "screening" clinic. This would be staffed by medical residents who assess the problem and typically arrange follow-up in one of the hospital's outpatient clinics.

This all sounded like a great idea, but word spread quickly to outside physicians, and the screening clinic promptly became a "dumping ground" for patients who had problems their local physician either did not feel comfortable dealing with or (more likely) did not want to deal with. The less pleasant the patient's demeanor with their local physician, the more likely they were to be referred to the UNC screening clinic. The trick was that the physicians did not refer these patients to physicians at UNC; they instructed them to go to Chapel Hill and "ask for the screening clinic."

For this reason, and possibly many others, the "screening" clinic gradually became known to the medical house staff as the "screaming" clinic. Each clinic was a new adventure, and Fridays were likely to have the most profound "dumps."

My most memorable day in the "screaming clinic" occurred when I was working with a Senior Admitting Resident (SAR) named John P. John was an excellent resident and, in his own way, had a good sense of humor, but his demeanor tended to be less pleasant in the screening clinic. This could be partially due to a prank played on him by a fellow SAR. Fred had somehow gotten a stack of John's business cards, taken them to the screening clinic, and placed them under a sign that said "Take One." Apparently, folks did, which generated several unwanted calls to John from folks he knew nothing about...

It was a typical busy afternoon, and I was sitting with my patient in an area closed off from other 'examining rooms' by a pull-around curtain like the ones used in the emergency room. I honestly cannot remember my patient's complaints, but I will never forget the conversation that came through the curtain from the next exam room. It was the good Doctor P, and he was speaking very loudly. Apparently, he figured the petite elderly lady he spoke with must be hard of hearing.

"Now, Ms. Smith, I see you have brought a bag full of medicines and a long list of medical problems with you today. I need to let you know that this is a screening clinic, and we will not be able to address all your problems today. I will review your medications to ensure they are appropriate for your problems. We will start with one problem today and then help you find the most appropriate clinic for follow-up. So, I want you to take a look at your problem list and pick one we can start on today."

There were a few moments of silence, and then, in a rather frail voice, I heard the lady say, "Well...I've been a little dizzy."

John's immediate response: "Pick another one."

A dizzy workup is an involved process at any age, especially in the elderly. John was not going to start a "dizzy" workup in the screaming clinic.

Listening to this from my side of the curtain, I got so tickled that I almost wet my pants. I had to excuse myself from my patient for a few seconds to regain my composure.

I still smile when I think of that moment, and if I tell the story, I sometimes laugh out loud.

ECCLESIASTES 7:8 The end of the matter is better than its beginning, and patience is better than pride.

EPHESIANS 4:2 Be completely humble and gentle; be patient, bearing with one another in love.

GALATIANS 5:22 But the fruit of the Spirit is love, joy, peace, forbearance, kindness, goodness, faithfulness, gentleness and self-control.

A Prank That Went Way Too Far
(the Friday afternoon dumping game)

Being the admitting resident was a busy, interesting job, but it was not one you wanted to do every day. As the admitting resident, you were the primary internal medicine doctor in the emergency room. As such, you saw all the patients with non-surgical complaints. You served as the supervisor and mentor for the medical interns, making all the decisions about who would go home and who would be admitted to the hospital. Additionally, you coordinated admissions from referring physicians.

Admitted patients would either go to one of the specialty wards, one of the general medicine wards, or one of the intensive care units. The residents "on call" for admissions would wear beepers (paging devices). When you decided a patient would be admitted, you would determine which service was up for an admission (the residents called them "hits"), and you would have them paged to come down and pick up their new admission. You tried to keep the services admitting in rotation so that no one group would get "hit" too much harder than another, but this was not always possible. Believe me, when you were on the receiving end of admissions, you kept track of how many admissions the other teams had so you could have an idea if you were next in line. This was critical because it allowed you to have some idea if you would be getting any sleep that night.

Residents were typically known to be "rocks," "sieves," or just "regular" in their admission habits. Most people were regular, and that was OK. However, house staff loved "rocks" and disliked ("hated" is too strong a word...) sieves. A rock would only admit truly sick patients and would make every effort to hold the middle-of-the-night admissions until the following day. A sieve admitted everyone. When a sieve was "on in the ER," everyone would have a busy night, and there would not be a lot of sleep for anyone.

71

While interesting, I hope that I have made it clear that being the admitting resident was not easy. What made the job even more complex was dealing with outside physicians who would try to "dump" their problem patients on the medical service of NC Memorial Hospital. NC Memorial was one of the largest tertiary referral hospitals in North Carolina. In the early 1980s, NCMH was the only public academic medical center serving patients who could not afford care, and it provided the lion's share of tertiary care for these patients. We did not turn people away because of money. There was no "wallet biopsy" before admission. However, we did not have unlimited bed space. Frequently, we were completely filled and were on "bed referral." This meant that a patient could not be admitted until someone was discharged, thereby opening a bed. This meant we would fill a bed as soon as it opened.

Outside physicians were aware of our situation, but some would avoid the problem of having their patients be on a waiting list by putting them in an ambulance and sending them to the NCMH emergency room. In these cases, you usually receive a "courtesy" call stating that the ambulance was en route with a patient.

In 1984, a notorious pulmonary doctor in Wilmington, North Carolina, was famous for the Friday afternoon "dump." If he had a patient who was either a financial burden or a challenge to care for, he could easily make his weekend better by referring that patient to NCMH. The fact that this physician was so well known with the house staff for this practice set the stage for one of the more notorious failed "pranks" during my time at UNC.

The UNC medical house staff came from all over the country. They were bright, dedicated, and generally enjoyed their work. They also had a good sense of humor and enjoyed a good joke or prank. Joe was one of the more gifted jokesters. He was married and had twin babies, and he worked and played hard.

One Friday, while working at Wake Memorial Hospital in Raleigh, Joe thought it might be fun to prank one of our more strait-laced senior residents who was in the NCMH emergency room as the admitting resident. So, about ten o'clock in the morning, Joe called the emergency room pretending to be the notorious pulmonary doctor from Wilmington. It was busy in the ER, so Joe left a message that he was sending a twenty-seven-year-old female for emergency cardiac catheterization and admission for worsening mitral regurgitation. The desk dutifully took the message, and Joe went on about his business at Wake. After letting the admitting resident stew for a few hours, he fully intended to call back around lunchtime and confess to the prank.

Unfortunately, Wake got very busy, and Joe did not call back. The note, which had been placed at the admitting resident's seat, was finally read about one o'clock in the afternoon and produced the appropriate "oh crap…is this a dump" response from the resident. He called Wilmington to see what the actual situation might be. Initially, he could not find the physician in question because he "had the weekend off…"

Oh, this is beginning to sound like a real dump.

The nurse said she would have the covering physician call back. About three o'clock, a physician from Wilmington returned the resident's call. When asked about the patient in question, he said he was not covering such a patient, but he thought the referring physician had a young female on his service earlier in the week. Perhaps he had arranged a transfer to NCMH before leaving for the weekend.

Well, the transfer now sounded legitimate.

There was a problem. The Cath lab, which had been busy all day, had already begun to let folks go home for the weekend. Getting home a little early was a rarity because the new lab director, Dr. P, was a workaholic. He had been hired to beef up the lab and did a remarkable job. They had turned into a factory led by a tall, thin guy always in green scrubs.

Now, the admitting resident had to let the cath lab know that a patient who might be losing her mitral valve was coming in for emergency catheterization. In addition, the cardiothoracic surgery team had to be made aware if emergent surgery was indicated.

When Dr. P received the news, he gathered a few people who had not left and called several who had departed, asking them to return to the hospital. And then, late on a Friday afternoon, they waited. The residents in the ER, the folks in the Cath lab, and the team on call for cardiothoracic surgery—all waited...

At Wake, about dinner time, things began to slow down, and Joe remembered his prank. He was not overly concerned because he knew no patient would show up, but it was only right to call the admitting resident to ensure all was okay.

That call got quite a response. Joe would have been called back to Chapel Hill on the spot, except that he was the medicine resident on call at Wake. He was instructed to report to the Department Chairman in Chapel Hill after completing his rounds on Saturday morning.

Whether he was busy that evening or not, I am sure Joe did not get much sleep as he saw his medical career flash before his eyes. The prank had backfired in an almost unimaginable way.

The good news was that although he suffered a significant tongue-lashing, there were no long-term consequences for him or anyone else. I am sure Joe learned a lesson that lasted a long while, but I doubt it stopped his pranks forever.

Perhaps the most impressive thing about the episode was that Dr. P did not explode. When he was told what had happened, he removed his scrub cap and smiled. I guess even a workaholic sometimes enjoys a prank.

1 CORINTHIANS 1:27 But God chose the foolish things of the world to shame the wise: God chose the weak things of the world to shame the strong.

ACTS 3:19 Repent, then, and turn to God, so that your sins may be wiped out, that times of refreshing may come from the Lord.

Mass Casualties from a Fitness Center
(Oh the humanity...)

Some people like to be dramatic, and some of those individuals enjoy being on the rescue squad. One of the more "dramatic" episodes of my career as a resident occurred on what I hoped would be a quiet Friday evening.

Over the "squawk" box that hung on the wall in the administrative hub (AKA "cage") of the emergency department, we began to get reports from a technician whose rescue unit had been called to a local fitness/athletic club.

"There are people down everywhere! They are all just collapsing!" He said, sounding like he was describing the crash of the Hindenburg: "Oh, the humanity..."

Sure enough, the ambulances shortly began arriving at the hospital. Intriguingly, instead of the usual one patient per ambulance, there were multiple patients in each. Then, cars loaded with people similar to those from the same facility began to arrive, carrying complaints similar to those.

The good thing was that, while some were still light-headed, most were coherent and felt they were improving. Another nice thing was that most of the patients were in their twenties and appeared to be in excellent physical condition. That's great. At least I would be starting with good protoplasm!

First things first. "When did you first start to feel sick or dizzy?"

The young, muscular male responded: "Well, I was having a really good workout, but then I began to feel a little nauseated. I was also a little more short-winded than usual, so I thought it was from the workout. So, I went and threw up and then went back to the weights. Then, I began to feel dizzy. Now, that was unusual! So, I asked the guy next to me, and he said he felt a little dizzy too."

"So, you were OK before you went into the club, and you are feeling better now that you are out?"

"Yeap."

OK, it's time to make a few radio and telephone calls. I had the clerk call the club and instruct everyone (including the rescue personnel) to be removed from the building. Some inhalant must have been (and perhaps still is being) released into the air.

"Did you smell anything unusual, like a gas leak?"

"No, nothing but sweaty people," came the response.

His exam was completely normal, and his only complaints were the same as those of all the other patients: shortness of breath and a feeling of dizziness. I drew a blood gas on my patient, and the pulsating blood was "cherry red." Diagnosis made—carbon monoxide. I told the clerk to have the fire department check for carbon monoxide.

They found it and the source – a poorly performing heater on a newly installed jacuzzi.

The patients continued to roll in. After a brief medical history to exclude significant underlying diseases, I started each new patient on oxygen via nasal cannula to displace the CO from their hemoglobin.

The problem was that the patients just kept coming. I had ten gurneys for acute patients, six holding beds for treatment, and one trauma room. The number of patients continued to rise—now there were more than twenty. I had the clerk call patient transport to bring extra wheelchairs to the emergency room. The patients just kept coming and eventually stopped at 34…

I could not have all these people in my emergency room; I might get someone who was acutely ill or injured. What should I do?

It was Friday night, and it was now about 9:00 PM. I thought the operating rooms would now be on skeleton crews, and the recovery room should be empty. I had the clerk verify that this was true, and then I asked permission to move my patients to recovery, where they would continue their oxygen therapy for a few more hours. I quickly wrote one-line admission notes for each patient and "admitted them to the recovery room for 3 hours of oxygen therapy to relieve symptoms of carbon monoxide exposure."

Patient transport began to dutifully move my "athletic patients" to the recovery room.

Once they were all gone, we had a few more (non-CO) patients, but the night slowed significantly by midnight. So, I went down to see how everything was going. It looked like they were having a party. They had formed a circle of wheelchairs and were talking, laughing, and enjoying some soft drinks supplied by the staff.

I had them all remove their oxygen and held them for a few more minutes to make sure no one had recurrent symptoms. I then wrote 34 discharge notes and let them all leave with a great story to tell their friends.

The following week, I received a letter signed by the Hospital Administrator and the Department of Medicine Chairman, thanking me for handling the "mass casualty" situation.

I think I might still have that letter somewhere.

ISAIAH 40:31 But those who hope in the Lord will renew their strength. They will soar on wings like eagles; they will run and not grow weary; they will walk and not grow faint.

PSALMS 150:6 Let everything that has breath praise the Lord. Praise the Lord.

IV. MOONLIGHTING –
(CHATHAM COUNTY HOSPITAL ER)

I would like to begin by sharing a few stories about my experiences working in the emergency room at Siler City, North Carolina. I started working in an emergency room as soon as I got my official medical license. I had just completed my internship at the University of North Carolina at Chapel Hill's North Carolina Memorial Hospital. I needed the money; at that time, $22 an hour seemed like a lot of money. From 1981 to 1985, I worked over 3,000 hours in the Siler City emergency room. All my shifts were either at night or on weekends because I was either a full-time medicine resident or a hematology fellow during that period. It was a great place to work because when you were there, you were the only Doc in the ER. There were excellent clerks, nurses, laboratory technicians, and pulmonary technicians, but you were the only Doctor. You made the diagnosis, you decided on the treatment, and you sewed up the wounds. Much was routine, but when something was out of the ordinary, you had to think quickly and occasionally trust your instincts. I often said that I learned as much in the Siler City ER as I did during my residency at NC Memorial, and I meant every word. The following are a few stories from that experience.

It could not have happened by chance
(skeet shooting, headache, and a bruise)

Occasionally, a series of apparently random events gets strung together to produce an outcome that borders on the miraculous. We often do not see the miracle until we have time to reflect on what happened.

When I was a chief resident in medicine at the University of North Carolina at Chapel Hill, a good friend from medical school invited me to give grand rounds at Rowan Memorial Hospital. He had joined the leading internist group in Salisbury, and I think he hoped I would consider joining them.

I was genuinely interested in blood clotting, so I thought it would be a good idea to put together a presentation on Disseminated Intravascular Coagulation (DIC). A primary presenting sign of this devastating problem is a skin lesion known as "purpura fulminans." The lesion looks like a bruise, but it is a full-thickness infarction of the skin caused by clots clogging the blood vessels in the region of the lesion—no blood, no oxygen, and the tissue dies.

I sought the assistance of an outstanding older Professor of Dermatology at UNC. Dr. Wheeler was a small man, very soft-spoken, but he was an excellent teacher and always had a wry smile. When I told him I needed a few slides for a talk on DIC, he took me into a small room entirely lined with cabinets filled with dermatology slides. He went straight to the appropriate cabinet and gave me several slides to copy for my talk. "No problem, glad to help."

I wanted to make a good impression, and I had not given very many presentations outside the friendly halls of UNC. So, I practiced the talk on several occasions. I went to Salisbury and gave the talk at lunchtime on a Monday. It went OK, nothing great. The following weekend, I was scheduled to work at the Chatham County Hospital ER in Siler City, NC. I was pretty much a fixture there by this time, having moonlighted there for four years. I worked the Friday night shift and had to be there by seven.

When I arrived, the place was packed. It was early May, and a virus was going around. I was up most of the night seeing patients with colds that I could only treat symptomatically. My shift was supposed to end at 6 PM on Saturday, but the person who was supposed to relieve me got sick. Could I stay on? Sure. Unfortunately, the second night was no better – cold after cold. By four o'clock in the morning, I was beat. I told the nurse I was going upstairs for a few minutes' sleep. As soon as I lay down, the phone rang. The nurse said she had a lady on the line that she thought I should talk to. A thunderstorm had come up, the lightning was flashing, and the phone crackled as I listened to the soft-voiced lady speak.

Her son had been skeet shooting the previous afternoon and came home late. When he got home, he seemed fine, but he awoke at two o'clock in the morning with a severe headache. He also had a fever and a bruise on his hand. He did not know how he got the bruise, but his mother thought it must have been when he was shooting. She wanted to know if she should bring him in to be seen in the ER. It was May in North Carolina, and that's already tick season, and there is a significant risk of Rocky Mountain spotted fever. I told her that anyone with fever, headache, and skin lesions needed to be seen by a physician. I knew I would leave in a few hours, so I told her to bring her son in. She asked if she could wait until the storm was over. I told her it should be OK, but to bring him in as soon as possible. I hung up the phone and lay my head on the pillow. The phone immediately rang again. "We got a drunk down here cut all to pieces." Great. No rest for the weary.

When I got downstairs, the inebriated fellow was so drunk that he slept while I sewed him up. I put in about 35 stitches on his arms, abdomen, back, and upper legs. Someone had given him a hard time, but they did not mean to kill him because all the wounds were rather superficial. As I finished the last closure, I remembered the lady had not brought in her son. I asked the nurse if she had seen or heard from the lady, and she replied that she had not. I decided to try to catch a shower but told the nurse to call me as soon as the patient arrived.

As I was leaving the ER, I noticed three people coming in through the ER entrance. We had the old double swinging doors that could be easily pushed open. Once inside, there was a gurney against one wall and the clerk's station on the other. As I turned to look, I saw a large man (at least six feet four inches and 250 pounds) on one side and a petite lady on the other. In between was a teenage male who appeared ashen. This had to be the boy. They came through the door and tried to lean against the gurney.

The boy started falling forward as the wife approached the clerk's window. Both the father and mother grabbed him in an attempt to break his fall. Since I was only a few feet away, I reached out to help. As the boy fell, he put out his hand to brace himself. There on the webbing of the right thumb was a 2x3 cm patch of purpura fulminans, just like in the pictures. I looked at the mother. "How long has he been sick?" "He was fine 8 hours ago. This was not Rocky Mountain spotted fever; it was too fast. It had to be meningococcemia.

I turned to the nurse and asked her to get me penicillin as quickly as possible. I turned to the parents and told them that their son was very sick and that we would probably have to move him somewhere else. The nurse arrived with the penicillin. We put in an IV and pushed the medication. It had been less than five minutes since his arrival. Within two minutes of the administration of the antibiotic, the patient began to seize. I gave 5 mg of valium, but it was no good. I gave five more. He was still seizing. Given the patient's relatively small size, I was hesitant to push more valium out of concern that I might suppress his respirations. I gave Phenobarbital. No effect. I gave a third dose of valium. The seizure had been ongoing for ten minutes, but it seemed like an hour. I remembered a new anticonvulsant, valproic acid, but I was unsure of the dose.

I ran to the phone and called the Chapel Hill ER, hoping to find someone who could provide the appropriate dose and mode of administration. It was about 7 a.m. on Sunday, and I knew the odds of getting a physician on the phone were slim. Amazingly, a neurologist was in the ER seeing a stroke patient and answered the phone. I told him my situation. He said that he knew the dose of valproic acid, but he suggested that I try the Phenobarbital one more time. I pushed the Phenobarbital, and like magic, the seizures stopped.

I told the parents that time was of the essence and we needed to move their son. They were reeling from what they had just seen and could not fathom that their son could have gotten so sick so fast. I told them Chapel Hill (NC Memorial Hospital) or Duke was their choice, but we needed to go quickly. The father wanted to go to Duke. I instructed the nurse to alert the ambulance and called Duke ER. I told them that I had a 16-year-old with meningococcemia who would need an intensive care unit. They said to bring him to the emergency room. My relief, a future chief medical resident at UNC, arrived, and we loaded the patient into the ambulance and began the trip from Siler City to Pittsboro to Durham—two-lane roads for most of the way.

The ambulance was flying with the siren blaring. About ten minutes into the trip, the boy stopped breathing. I was able to slip in an endotracheal tube and began to bag the patient. I do not know how that tube went in as we bounced around in that ambulance, but it did. As we approached the 15-501 bypass south of Chapel Hill, a little old lady drove slowly into town. There was a two-lane bridge just before the bypass, and immediately after crossing the bridge, one must make a quick right turn onto the ramp to the bypass. The lady must have seen or heard us coming. However, she stopped on the bridge instead of pulling off the road. There, she sat on the bridge in our lane. I do not know how, at the speed we were going, the driver managed to get around her and up the ramp. But - he did.

When we arrived at Duke, I think they thought we were probably going to be wrong about our diagnosis. When we rolled in with our intubated patient, who had now developed skin lesions on his neck, feet, and eyelids, they took him directly to the ICU. I rode the ambulance back to Siler City to pick up my car. By that time, Dr. Dave R had been inundated by inquiries about the case of meningitis and was writing prescriptions for rifampin as quickly as he could. He also took care of reporting the disease to the health department.

I drove home in a daze, feeling like a failure. I was convinced that the boy was going to die. The few labs we could draw in Siler City showed a sodium level of 118 and a platelet count below 100,000. He was already in DIC. I had spent the better part of 36 hours treating colds that I could do nothing about, and I was not able to save the one patient with a significant problem. I went home. I called Duke. The patient was alive but had gone into complete renal shutdown. I went to bed. I buried my head in my pillow and cried.

Amazingly, the kidneys began to function within two days, and he came off the respirator at the end of the fourth day. He went home on day eight. His only residual problem was a scar on his hand near the thumb and a scar on one of his feet from another area of infracted skin. It is good to have a 16-year-old heart. You can weather almost anything.

The patient's family was prominent in Chatham County. The father played football at Wake Forest, and they owned a tire store. The people at Duke told them their son was fortunate to have survived. Perhaps because of this, the patient's family continued to do things for me and my family for the remainder of our time in Chapel Hill. They came once, picked up my oldest son's car, and put four new tires on it. I'm sure the tires were worth more than the car. They gave us tickets to the governor's inaugural ball. They gave us tickets to concerts at the Greensboro Coliseum. But the best thing I ever received from them was a short letter two years later. It was from the mother who wrote that her son had turned eighteen years old that day and that she would always think of me on his birthday and be thankful that I was there when they needed me. I still have that letter, which is much more meaningful than any diploma or award.

When I had the chance to reflect on the sequence of events that led to a positive outcome, the hand of God became apparent. I got invited to give my first talk to an outside audience. I picked DIC as a topic. Dr. Wheeler handed me a picture that I memorized over the next two weeks, just like the lesion on the patient's hand. My replacement got sick, so I had to stay in the ER for another night. The penicillin was right in the emergency room when we needed it. The neurologist was in the ER at Chapel Hill and made the right call regarding Phenobarbital. Dave R arrived early so I could ride with the patient in the ambulance. The endotracheal tube went in. We were able to avoid the car on the bridge because no vehicles were coming in the other direction. Duke was ready to take the patient directly to the ICU. There's just no other explanation. God worked at multiple levels, times, and places to accomplish what happened. The patient's parents thanked me, but I played a small part. We all know who deserves the praise.

1 CHRONICLES 16:34 Give thanks to the Lord, for he is good; his love endures forever.

PSALMS 77:14 You are the God who performs miracles; you display your power among the peoples.

4th of July in Siler City
(Bubba gets the beer...We was already at the lake.)

It was sweltering on July 4, 1983, and the people of Siler City loved their holidays. This can make for a rough time in the ER when the good old boys get into their cups and start having a good time. Things started OK – Just the usual bumps, cuts, and bruises, but things began to go downhill late in the afternoon. As often occurs on these steamy days, the afternoon brought on a nice but brief thunderstorm.

It did cool things down a bit, but it set the stage for my first exciting patient of the day.

I suppose that out of respect for Uncle Sam, the 23-year-old male and his friends did not start consuming their favorite beverage until the afternoon. However, saving themselves that way brought on a real thirst, and they rapidly went through their case of beer. By three o'clock, they were in no pain but needed to resupply. What could fill the bill better than the old, reliable Seven-Eleven?

The storm had passed by this time, and the group headed off to the store in the pick-up – three in the front seat and my future patient, "Bubba," in the back. Before that short storm, it had been a while since the last significant rain. A considerable amount of oil had built up on the concrete in front of the Seven-Eleven. The water stood in large beads on the pavement as the boys drove in. Since Bubba was in the back, he was instructed to get the beer. Bubba was barefoot, and despite the cooling effect of the rain, the pavement was still rather hot. What better way to save your feet than to run across the parking lot to the welcoming front door of the store? Unfortunately, the pavement was slick, and Bubba's reflexes were slightly impaired.

Sitting beside the store's front door was an icebox for storing those wonderful 10-pound bags of crushed ice that convenience stores are famous for. This icebox had the typical galvanized-pleated-metal sheeting that is found on most. Unfortunately, someone (probably one of Bubba's associates) had hit it with a motorized vehicle. The box still worked, but the encounter had loosened one side of the sheeting and had caused it to separate from the main body of the box, starting about halfway down the side. By the time the sheet reached the ground, it was sitting about three inches out into the clear air of Chatham County. As Bubba's hot feet raced across the hot pavement toward the safety of the cooler surface at the front door, he slipped and skidded into the icebox. He fell backward, so he was moving feet first. His right foot avoided the collision. His left foot was not so lucky. Counting the big toe as toe number one, the metal sheet entered his left foot between the second and third toes. The remarkable clean incision that resulted extended into his foot at least one and one-half inches, probably to the base of the second and third metatarsal. This, of course, produced a significant amount of pain and not a small amount of bleeding. The pain was dulled by alcohol, and the bleeding was treated by wrapping the foot in material found in the back of the truck. Smarter heads prevailed, and Bubba was brought to the emergency room.

Thus, I was treated to my first fascinating story of the day. There wasn't much for me to do: clean the foot with betadine wash and soak, administer a tetanus shot, and send the group up the road to an orthopedic surgeon. The biggest problem was identifying someone who could be trusted to drive.

I had just finished eating and was enjoying the remnants of the day when my next interesting patient arrived. He was about 35 years old and somewhat sunburnt. His complaint was pain in his leg. When I examined the area of concern, I found a large, dark blue-purple flap of skin and fatty tissue almost completely severed from the lateral aspect of his left upper thigh. There was no active bleeding, and it was evident that this had not just occurred.

"How and when did you do this?" I asked.

"Well, I was getting the boat off the trailer at the lake this morning, and it slipped, and the propeller blade sliced my leg."

"You did this in the morning and did not come in until 8 o'clock at night?" I asked.

"Well, you see, the bleeding stopped, my wife wanted to ski, and we was already at the lake."

Well, that pretty much explains it. You can always treat pain with beer. So, after waiting all day, he brings me this dead piece of leg and wants me to "put a few stitches in it." I had to explain to him that I had four hours to close such wounds before the risk of infection was too great to allow wound closure. This was especially true since the wound had been exposed to lake water several times during the day. All I could do was clean the wound, give him a tetanus shot, put him on some antibiotics, and hope that there was enough blood supply to allow salvage of at least some of the skin flap. Otherwise, he would have required a significant skin graft. Follow-up was with my general surgeon friend in town.

I never knew how either of these two episodes eventually turned out, but I am sure they both had good scars to show and stories to tell. And so did I. Holidays are not dull in small towns if you know where the action is.

EZEKIEL 23:33 You will be filled with drunkenness and sorrow, the cup of ruin and desolation…

1 PETER 4:3 For you have spent enough time in the past doing what pagans choose to do – living in debauchery, lust, drunkenness,

PROVERBS 23:31-32 Do not gaze at wine when it is red, when it sparkles in the cup, when it goes down smoothly! In the end it bites like a snake and poisons like a viper.

MATTHEW 25:36,40 I needed clothes and you clothed me, I was sick and you looked after me, I was in prison and you came to visit me…The King will reply, 'Truly I tell you, whatever you did for one of the least of these brothers and sisters of mine, you did for me.'

The Scoop and Scoot Rescue Squad
(Stunned me pretty good...)

Rescue squads come in all sizes and capacities. The significant amount of training now required for EMT certification has led to a certain amount of uniformity. This was not always the case. The squads I became familiar with in Siler City varied in quality. Most were good to excellent. Some were a little too aggressive – "You want us to use the MAST trousers (oh please, please, please....)?!" [MAST trousers are an inflatable garment that fits over the legs and lower abdomen. Their role is to decrease blood loss from the lower extremities and help maintain blood pressure in patients who have lost a significant amount of blood and are at risk of developing hypovolemic shock.]

However, one Rescue Squad always impressed me with its lack of aggressiveness. They did what was known then as "scoop and scoot." They picked up that patient and took them to the hospital. No treatment. Just go. This approach has a certain amount of logic, but after watching this group in action, I was sure logic had nothing to do with it. I always felt that most of the guys on that unit wanted a "good look at the wreck."

With the above background, you can imagine my surprise one Saturday morning when the Scoop and Scoot Squad arrived with a bandaged patient. As if the bandage was not enough of a surprise, the placement was even more impressive. The patient's head was completely wrapped in a gauze bandage. He looked like a mummy. My first question was, "Which side is his face?" The straight-faced response was, " The side with the blood on it."

"What happened to this guy?"

"He fell out of his truck and hit his head on a stump." The same straight face uttered these words. Apparently, the fellow had fallen asleep driving home, run off the road, fallen out of his pick-up truck, and struck his head on a tree stump.

Well, now they had my attention. My curiosity was piqued. I leaned over the patient, who was lying flat on the gurney, and asked if he could hear me and talk. Some muffled response from underneath the gauze was the first reassuring moment in this unique encounter. I shouted that I would have to remove the bandage to see how he was doing. When I removed the bandage, I found the patient to be surprisingly alert. He had a jagged laceration that began on his forehead and continued between his eyes and across the left side of his face. The left maxillary sinus was fractured and open to South Chatham County air. I spoke reassuringly to the patient once again. I told him that I would try to be as gentle as possible. With the assistance of the squad, I put a neck immobilizer on and gently inquired if they had considered the possibility of a neck injury in this patient. The patient was breathing OK but was having some difficulty with speech. I inserted two fingers into his mouth, behind his upper incisors, and gently pulled them upward. His whole face moved. X-rays confirmed a Lafort III face fracture but did not show evidence of a cervical spine injury. The man had disarticulated his face – he had broken his face off his skull…

I knew we would not be able to handle this problem in Siler City, so I told the patient we would send him to another hospital. Before I put him on the road, however, I wanted to assess whether there was evidence of a closed head injury. I leaned over and asked if he had any idea how long he might have been unconscious after the accident. He focused on me but did not answer immediately. Then he said, "I didn't get knocked out… Stunned me pretty good."

It stunned him "pretty good." This man ran off the road, was thrown from a moving vehicle, hit his head on a stump hard enough to "break his face off," and it only stunned him pretty good – amazing.

His head was harder than that of some of the guys who worked on the Rescue Squad that picked him up…

LUKE 10:34 He went to him and bandaged his wounds, pouring on oil and wine. Then he put the man on his own donkey, brought him to an inn, and took care of him.

You're putting what up my nose!
(Fatback is not just for beans anymore)

I had seen the two elderly sisters multiple times in the emergency room. They reminded me of the two little ladies who sat on the back pew next to our family when I went to church as a child. Those two ladies from church were also sisters and were quiet like these two elderly women from Siler City. I remember asking my mother why the ladies' heads seemed to rhythmically bob to and fro as they sat and listened to the preacher. My mom would whisper in my ear, "It's the palsy. Sometimes older folks get it." Like my ladies in Siler City, they always wore hats with little flowers on them.

On this occasion, the problem was not aches or pains from her severe rheumatoid arthritis; it was a nosebleed. The smaller of the two ladies held a cloth to her nose, and the other explained that her nose had been bleeding for a couple of hours. Despite all their efforts, they were unable to stop the bleeding. When I looked, the blood was dripping from the left nostril and running down the back of her throat. I told her I thought I could help and began working my way through my tricks. First, I tried a little blue liquid containing cocaine as a vasoconstrictor. Usually, it worked, but not this time. Then, I tried an anterior gauze pack. It stopped the blood coming out of the nostril, but the blood flowing down the back of her throat seemed to increase.

Why was this lady bleeding like this? She had severe rheumatoid arthritis that was being treated with high-dose aspirin, using 16 to 18 tablets per day. This therapy was popular at the time and typically involved increasing the aspirin dose until the ringing in the ears became severe, and then backing off until the patient could hear again. This approach did allow a significant anti-inflammatory response, but it also produced a profound qualitative platelet disorder. This lady's platelets did not work.

I did not want to attempt a posterior nasal pack in this elderly lady. I had seen and helped place such packs by passing a Foley catheter into the nose, grasping the end as it entered the posterior pharynx, and pulling the catheter out of the mouth. At this point, you use a suture to attach gauze balls to the end of the catheter, and you then pull the Foley out of the nose and the gauze balls up into the posterior pharynx. One produces tamponade by applying traction to the sutures that protrude from the nostril. I did not want to subject this fragile little lady to such a thing.

I decided to send the lady up the road to NC Memorial Hospital's emergency room to be evaluated by an ENT specialist. I called to make the arrangements, and unbelievably, I spoke to an ENT resident who was attending to a patient in the ER. When I explained my situation and plan, he suggested placing a "fatback" nasal pack.

To those unfamiliar with "fatback," it is a salt-cured pork product sold as seasoning. It is used primarily when cooking beans and other vegetables. Sometimes, fatback is cut into thin slices and fried to yield grease for cooking and a crispy, salty treat for those of discerning taste. You might imagine my surprise when it was suggested that I push this material up a lady's nose.

"If you send her up here, we are going to put in a 'fatback pack.' So why don't you do it there?"

"How do you do it?"

"You carve a piece of fat about two centimeters square on one end that tapers to about 1 cm square on the other. The length should be about one inch longer than the nose. Avoid the peppered edge. Push the pack into the nose and hold it in place with a folded piece of gauze and tape. The bleeding should stop within ten minutes. Leave the pack in place for 12 to 24 hours and then let it slide out."

It did not sound too hard, so I explained the plan to the sisters. "Anything you think will help, Doctor." Problem: I did not have fatback in the emergency room. Solution: I called the patient's family physician, who said he had some at home in the refrigerator and would bring it by. This doctor was in his sixties, and his patients loved him for good reasons. In about twenty minutes, he arrived and decided to wait a few minutes to see what I would do. I followed the instructions and carved a piece of suitably shaped fatback. I put the piece in the lady's nose and secured it with gauze and tape. Like magic, the bleeding stopped. We all looked at each other. I told the lady to drop by the ER in the morning before I left, and I would take the pack out.

When the ladies came in, I removed the tape and gauze, and the fat back strip slid out. When I first put the pack in, it was cold from being in the refrigerator. When it came to body temperature, it had become much slicker, more flexible, and less adherent to the nasal tissue. It thus did not dislodge the clots that had formed. I turned to the nurse, gave her the paper bag containing the fatback, and instructed her to label it "for nose bleeds" and place it in the ER refrigerator.

About six weeks later, I worked at the Chatham ER on a Sunday night. A man in his fifties enters with a nosebleed. He was a chronic dialysis patient who had a history of recurrent nosebleeds. He had missed his routine Friday dialysis and came into my ER with a nosebleed. This was not the first time. In the past, he had required blood transfusions on at least three occasions for extensive nose bleeds. I went through my usual routines – anterior nasal pack, cocaine instillation, etc., without apparent benefit. At that point, I turned to the nurse and announced: "Bring me the fatback."

I explained to the patient the treatment plan as I was carving out the piece of fatback. I could see his pupils begin to dilate, and for a moment, I thought he would refuse this novel treatment. When I told him this would be what they would do in Chapel Hill if I sent him there, he agreed to try. Chapel Hill was where he had his routine three times per week hemodialysis. I placed the pack as before, and within five minutes, a brisk nosebleed had stopped. Now, I was genuinely impressed. I instructed the patient to ensure he made his appointment for his Monday dialysis session.

A literature review revealed reports from Iowa on the use of porcine fatty tissue materials to treat bleeding in patients with thrombocytopenia (an insufficient number of platelets). My patients both had sufficient platelet numbers, but their platelets did not function properly. In the first case, the dysfunction was caused by aspirin, which acetylates proteins in platelets, leading to decreased function. In the second case, the platelets are dysfunctional due to uremia, known as the uremic platelet syndrome. I wrote the two cases and published the experience in the Journal of Emergency Medicine. This earned me the enviable title of "fatback doctor," which I still carry with pride.

But, as is sometimes the case, the story does not end there. Several months after taking care of the gentleman with uremia, I returned to Siler City and was given some mail that had arrived for me from NC Memorial Hospital. When I opened it, I found a copy of a clinic note on the patient who had undergone dialysis with the nasal pack still in place. It was fun to read. The first part of the note was from the hemodialysis unit and read:

"Patient reports for routine dialysis with *something* in his nose. Sent to ENT for examination and removal."

Next, a brief note from ENT read: "Patient referred from dialysis unit with porcine fatty tissue pack in right nostril. The pack was removed without complication or bleeding, and the patient was returned to the dialysis unit."

Finally, there was another note from nephrology: "Patient returns from ENT clinic with 'thing' removed from nose. Dialysis completed without complication." The stamped dialysis note followed, indicating all appropriate times and volumes.

That note hung on the ER bulletin board in Siler City for several years, alongside a copy of the case report, which was published in the Journal of Emergency Medicine.

The citation for this published case is as follows:

M.E. Carr and D.A. Gabriel: Nasal Packing with Porcine Fatty Tissue for Epistaxis Complicated by Qualitative Platelet Disorders. The Journal of Emergency Medicine 3:449-452,1985.

LEVITICUS 17:11 For the life of a creature is in the blood, and I have given it to you to make atonement for yourselves on the altar; it is the blood that makes atonement for one's life.

LEVITICUS 17:14 Because the life of every creature is its blood. That is why I have said to the Israelites, "You must not eat the blood of any creature, because the life of every creature is its blood."

LUKE 8:43 And a woman was there who had been subject to bleeding for twelve years, but no one could heal her.

PSALMS 72:14 He will rescue them from oppression and violence, for precious is their blood in his sight.

Somehow, they know
(I thought it was a bag of trash…His brake light never came on.)

You may have heard that, somehow, patients know that they are going to die. There is a sense that they have, or a sixth sense that clues them in, or they have a vision of the events to come. I am not sure if this happens in every case, but I know it occurs in some instances. I tell my medical students that if they are dealing with a patient who says they think they are going to die, they better listen. If you are caring for a patient who says, "I'm going to die" or "I'm dying," they probably are. Whether you think they are sick enough or hurt enough to die becomes irrelevant at that point.

Two cases I saw in Siler City illustrate the point with crystal clarity. The first involved a little old lady and a young black man. It was a Friday night, around 11:30 PM. The rescue squad brought the young man in, and he was torn all to pieces. He had been run over and dragged for about 90 feet by the little old lady. She kept saying she "thought it was a bag of trash." Apparently, the young man was sleeping on the road.

When I first heard this, I thought it was not possible. Later, I was told that this scenario is not uncommon in the coastal plain of North Carolina. Sometimes, there are multiple deaths from people getting run over while sleeping on the road. Events typically unfold as follows. The boys go out on Friday or Saturday night and walk down to a local establishment or a friend's house for an evening of fun and relaxation. Of course, this almost always involves alcohol. As the night passes, they consume more and more alcohol. At some point, the boys decide, or are told, that it is time to go home. The walk home is always much longer than the walk to the party. The roads are poorly lit, and although the days are very warm, the evenings can get chilly with the constant brisk sea breeze. As the boys walk and talk, someone will suggest they stop and sit for a while. There is typically minimal

97

traffic; if a vehicle approaches, one should easily see it by the approaching headlights. The boys sit down and quickly realize that the pavement is warm. It feels good, so simply lying back after sitting leads to a significant amount of warmth on their backs. The combination of being tired, alcohol, and warmth rapidly puts them to sleep. Now, they do not see the lights coming. Due to the late hour, tiredness, perhaps a little extra speed trying to get home, the poor lighting, and the ever-present possibility of prior alcohol consumption, the driver does not see the boys until he is on top of them. What a completely avoidable, sad story.

When they brought the young man in, he had on MAST trousers. This is an inflatable garment that fits over the legs and lower abdomen. Their role is to decrease blood loss from the lower extremities and help maintain blood pressure in patients who have lost a significant amount of blood and are at risk of developing hypovolemic shock. They work by inflating air bladders (balloons) contained within the trousers. You can inflate the airbags on the legs and, if needed, a panel across the lower abdomen. In the early 1980s, some rescue squads always asked to put these on. Most of the time, they were not indicated, and stopping to put them on might delay transport to the medical facility. In this case, however, the trousers were undoubtedly indicated. The young man only said three things to me while I worked with him. First, he said, "Please help me." Then he said, "I'm really hurt bad." The last thing he said was, "I'm going to die…" I assured him that I would do whatever was possible to help him. He was certainly correct about being badly injured. He had multiple rib fractures, what appeared to be a displaced (out of alignment) fracture of his upper lumbar spine, a crushed pelvis, and one fractured femur. Multiple areas of skin were denuded. He was conscious but drifting in and out. He was hypotensive at 90 over 50, but his blood pressure went completely away when I briefly tried to deflate the abdominal panel of the MAST trousers to allow for a better assessment of his abdomen. This individual required a Class 1 trauma center and needed to arrive there quickly. I put in large bore IVs, got fluid running, pumped up the panels, and got him on his way to NC Memorial Hospital in Chapel Hill; he survived the trip but died several hours later despite acute stabilization surgery. He was found to have severed his left femoral artery. He had been entirely correct in his assessment of his injuries and his statement of his prognosis.

A second case from Siler City, illustrating the ability of patients to assess their condition, also involved motor vehicles. However, this time, the vehicle of interest was a motorcycle.

Communities adjacent to large military installations are great places to buy slightly used, high-end motorcycles. Young recruits with their first taste of money and raging testosterone rush out and buy a "really nice hog." The dream often ends poorly when they cannot make the payments or get shipped off to parts unknown, where their Harley is not allowed to follow.

Two early-middle-aged Michigan men, who had decided it was now or never to live their dream of owning a Harley, read in a biker magazine that Fayetteville, NC, home of Fort Bragg and the 82nd Airborne Infantry Division, was the best place in the world to get a deal on a barely used Harley. They contacted a used cycle dealer and arranged to buy two nice bikes. Since it was summertime, they flew down to Fayetteville to pick up the bikes, planning to ride them back to Michigan. They arrived on a Friday morning, made their way to the dealer, and picked up their Harleys. After some shopping and a fine local meal, they set off northward in the cool early evening.

If there is one thing a young man loves more than a new motorcycle, it is the company of a young female. This is the origin of another common occurrence in and around large military bases. Often, out of range of parental advice, these young couples rush into marriage only to find that a three-week courtship is typically insufficient to work out their system for handling interpersonal conflicts. This leads to a variety of dysfunctional relationships, many of which end up in divorce court.

A young couple had a rousing argument this Friday evening, ending with the wife stomping out the door to go home to her mother. She jumped in her car and headed North on the same two-lane road where our two Michigan friends proudly rode their new Harleys. Several miles up the road, the young wife began to have a change of heart and decided to go back home to her husband. Unfortunately, there can be long distances between places to turn around on these narrow rural roads. The young wife decided the best way to get home quickly would be to turn around. The road was too narrow for a U-turn, so she attempted a Y-turn. This maneuver involves turning to the left across the oncoming lane, stopping, cutting your wheels sharply to the right, backing up, and then pulling forward into the lane opposite your previous direction. It is not a particularly difficult maneuver and can be done safely if you are on a flat stretch of road with good visibility in both directions. Unfortunately, the distracted young wife had just gone over the crest of a hill when she decided to attempt the Y-turn. She did not see the lights of the motorcycles behind her. They did not see her slow down and turn after she went over the hill. When the two motorcycles crested the hill, they ran up on the car sitting sideways across the road. One motorcycle was riding behind and to the right of the lead bike. He was able to swerve to the right and barely miss the tail end of the car. The other motorcycle hit the middle of the vehicle. The trailing biker said he never saw a brake light from the first bike.

The ambulance transported the motorcyclists to the nearest emergency facility, Chatham County Hospital. While the lead cyclist had a variety of significant injuries, it was damage to his face and upper airway that was the most acute concern. I knew that I would not be able to care for this patient at Chatham; we had no ICU, but I needed to stabilize his airway before I could ship him elsewhere. Efforts to ventilate him with an ambo bag blew blood onto the walls through a hole just above his right eye. I made a pass at intubation, but the mandible was so severely destroyed that I had difficulty visualizing the trachea due to soft tissue cascading rearward. Our local surgeon passed by the ER as he was leaving after checking on one of his patients. He stepped in to see if he could help. With me holding and stabilizing the jello that had previously been this man's face, Dr K was able to get a tube into place. Within minutes, the fellow was en route to a trauma center. They were able to keep him alive for about five hours. During that time, I had the task of calling his wife in Michigan to tell her that her husband had been in an accident. I told her that it was a severe accident, that her husband was critically injured, and that he had been moved to a trauma center. You know the question that was coming: "Is he going to live?" I could truthfully say that I could not be sure, but that he had severe injuries.

Before he left to follow his friend to the trauma center, I spoke to his companion to get the telephone number. He told me that immediately after the wreck, the only thing his friend had said that was understandable was, "I'm going to die." Unfortunately, he was correct.

Somehow, they know.

ECCLESIASTES 3:1-2 There is a time for everything, and a season for every activity under the heavens: a time to be born and a time to die, a time to plant and a time to uproot,

PSALMS 90:12 Teach us to number our days, that we may gain a heart of wisdom.

PSALMS 39:4 Show me, Lord, my life's end and the number of my days; let me know how fleeting my life is.

JOB 14:5 A person's days are determined; you have decreed the number of his months and have set limits he cannot exceed.

The worst day to work in the ER
(She Just Don't Look Good...)

Occasionally, when telling stories of the ER, I will be asked, "What's the worst day to work in the ER? Is it Christmas, the 4th of July, New Year's Eve, or Thanksgiving...?" My response almost always raises eyebrows.

The worst day, at least for me, in Siler City was...*Mother's Day*.

It is always on a Sunday, so an ER doctor covers it in Siler City. I remember the first time I signed up to cover it. I thought this should not be too hard. It was a warm Sunday in early summer or late spring, with most people going to church and then visiting their mothers. It should be quiet. That was probably wishful thinking because that is not how it turned out.

The first ambulance arrived at about 1:00 p.m. No lights flashing, no siren blaring, just rolled up to the loading dock. The clerk brought the clipboard with the complaint, "She just doesn't look good." I thought that was an unusual complaint, but sometimes they "don't look good." I pulled back the curtain to see a lady in her early eighties surrounded by her daughter (who lived in Siler City) and her son, who had driven down the previous day from Pennsylvania. The lady was alert, had no fever, and was breathing without difficulty. I asked her what problem prompted her to come to the ER today. She looked at me, somewhat puzzled, and said she was unsure why she had been brought to see me.

Now concerned that I might be dealing with acute mental status changes, I turned to her children for assistance. The lady was a resident of a local nursing home. The daughter, who lived in town and saw her mother several times a week, did not notice any acute changes in her mother's speech, memory, or appearance. The son, however, was insistent that his mother did not look well, and he wanted her "checked out and treated." He had confronted personnel in the nursing home and had insisted that his mother be transported to the hospital

102

for evaluation. When I tried to pinpoint what changes he was most concerned about, he reverted to the "she just doesn't look good." Now I understand the "complaint" registered by the clerk on the intake form.

As I talked with the family, I found that the son, who lived in Pennsylvania, had not seen his mother for several years due to "work commitments and other obligations." Having not seen her for a while, he was concerned that her appearance had declined since his last visit.

I asked the family members to step out so that I could examine the patient. As I listened to her lungs and heart and felt for adenopathy, I asked the lady about decreased appetite, weight loss, and difficulty concentrating or remembering. And she denied any significant problems. She still read books, could walk to the dining room without assistance, and was not on any new, unusual, or "mind-altering" medications. All in all, she looked good for an 82-year-old, and I felt she could have probably been living independently if her children had not insisted that she move to a senior facility when her husband passed away.

I once again returned to the family and explained that I thought their mother did not seem to have an acute problem and that she appeared to be doing well for her age of 82. The local daughter nodded her agreement, but the son was not satisfied. "I know that something is wrong with her."

At this point, I knew this would not end to the son's satisfaction. I called the lady's family physician to inform him that his patient had been brought to the ER and that I thought she was okay. He said, "Well, I have not seen her in a while…so why don't you ensure she is not anemic and that her kidneys are working OK?" Well, at least that gave me something to do…

Of course, the labs were normal and unchanged from previous reports, and I relayed this information to the family. Once again, the son asked, "Well then, why does she look like she does?" At this point, I tried to state as gently as I could that we all gradually change as we age. This explanation was also unsatisfactory. I finally said that we had no reason to keep his mother in the ER or hospital, and it was appropriate for her to return to the senior center.

As arrangements for ambulance transport were being made, another ambulance arrived with another mother from another long-term care facility. The pattern quickly became apparent. I was dealing with children who had moved away, not been back in a while, and arrived at the nursing home on *Mother's Day* to find that mom had "changed." I have no doubt that there were probably some changes, but the significant change was that Mom was older, and the big problem was that the child had not been around to see the changes. I was also sure that in some cases, righteous concern and a desire to "make things right" were being substituted for guilt over not visiting.

My primary job in the ER was to take care of sick people, and I was pretty good at it. It was much more difficult for me to take care of guilt-ridden children. They certainly did not want to hear the truth. It made for a very long, tiring, and dissatisfying *Mother's Day* in the ER.

I never again volunteered to work in the ER on *Mother's Day*. Instead, I did my best to make sure I visited my mother.

EXODUS 20:12 Honor your father and mother, so that you may live long in the land the Lord your God is giving you.

1 CORINTHIANS 13:4-8 Love is patient, love is kind. It does not envy, it does not boast, it is not proud. It does not dishonor others, it is not self-seeking, it is not easily angered, it keeps no record of wrongs. Love does not delight in evil but rejoices in the truth. It always protects, always trusts, always hopes, always perseveres. Love never fails.

Scariest Case in the ER
(*You made me drive in 45 minutes for this…*)

One of the questions lots of people ask about my time in emergency rooms is, "What is the scariest thing you've seen in the ER?" My response usually surprises folks. Most think it is big-time trauma – bad car wrecks (having lived in Pennsylvania for 15 years, I know that up there, they are called "crashes"), gunshot wounds, etc. No, not really. After you have seen trauma a few times, it gets pretty routine. You ensure they have (and maintain) a pulse. You ensure they are (and continue to) breathe. You check for bleeding and ensure it has stopped. You ensure that no additional harm is done to the patient while you do what is necessary – stabilize that neck and spine. You assess whether the wounds are life-threatening and determine if the patient needs to be transferred elsewhere. It is a step-by-step process. You do not want to be "creative," you want to do what works. You reserve "creativity" for situations where your actions are not working. If the trauma patient is dead when they get to the ER, they typically stay dead. Caring for them is not too hard if they are not severely hurt. If they are alive but badly hurt, you are stabilizing in the ER and handing the patient off to someone else for definitive care. None of which is too scary.

"Well, if trauma is not that scary, it must be a bad heart attack…" Well, no, not really. Most massive heart attacks kill the patient on the spot, and there is not much for the ER doctor to do. If you are dead from a myocardial infarction (MI) when you get to the ER, you typically stay dead. If you are not dead, the job in the ER is to put you on medicines to reduce the amount of heart muscle loss (clot-dissolving proteins, etc.) and on other medications (antiarrhythmics such as lidocaine) to prevent the development of an abnormal heart rhythm. Such rhythms are common in patients suffering from acute MI, and they have the potential to stop the heart from beating. Once stabilized, the patient is handed off to a coronary intensive care unit for monitoring. Again, the treatment is a step-by-step process and is indeed pretty "cookbook." Do not get creative. Do what you should, and the patient will typically do well.

So, what is the scariest type of patient in the ER? In my opinion, it is a new asthmatic. These folks were well a few hours earlier, but now are sitting in front of you with diffuse wheezing, blue lips, rapid heart rate, and fear in their eyes. They are having great difficulty breathing, and if you do not do the right things, they could die. That is right. A person who was absolutely normal a few hours earlier could now die if you do not help. That's a pretty scary thing. The following case nicely illustrates this point.

Many of my most memorable cases occurred on a Friday evening. So, it was with this case. It had been a routine evening, with a couple of patients an hour, and it appeared to be slowing down after 9:00 PM. The visitors and most of the on-call staff had left for the evening, and I had settled in to watch a classic Clint Eastwood western, "High Plains Drifter," on the TV in the doctor's room.

I heard the curtain being drawn around the Bay 1 cubicle, and I knew someone had come in. The nurse brought me the clipboard, which read, "nineteen-year-old white male, new asthmatic." I went in to see the patient, and he was on the gurney with his sister standing beside him. He was so short of breath that he could barely talk. As I examined his chest, I asked his sister if her brother had a history of asthma, and she replied that to her knowledge, he did not. Her brother had been away from Siler City for several years but had come home earlier in the week to visit.

On exam, it was clear that the patient was having great difficulty moving air. His lips were blue, he had loud wheezing throughout all lung fields, and his heart was racing. He had no fever, and a chest x-ray did not reveal infiltrates. Infiltrates can be evidence of fluid in the air spaces (as occurs in heart failure) or inflammatory responses, as occurs in infection. A healthy nineteen-year-old would not have

106

congestive heart failure, so the absence of infiltrates ruled out pneumonia. I wanted a blood gas to evaluate the severity of his hypoxia, but the respiratory tech had already left for the day. So, I started oxygen at two liters by nasal prongs and figured he would perk up with therapy for bronchospasm.

If this is a new asthmatic, he should "break" when I give him a dose of epinephrine. It is called "breaking" because the loud wheezing will rapidly decrease, and the bronchospasm responds to the drug. Typically, the patient rapidly feels better, and although epinephrine is a cardiac stimulant, the recovery of the ability to breathe and exchange air tamps down the hypoxic drive on the heart. As a result, the heart rate quickly returns to normal as the oxygen level rises and the epinephrine, which is quickly removed from the blood, dissipates. Since his heart rate was already rapid, I put him on a cardiac monitor just in case.

So, let's give the epinephrine and make this young man all better!

But…that is not what happened…

After I gave him epinephrine, his heart rate increased to 200 beats per minute, and he broke into a cold sweat. The wheezing continued. I increased the oxygen to 4 liters per minute and waited. After five minutes, there was still no decrease in wheezing, but the heart rate fell below 200.

I decided to try a second dose of epinephrine. Again, the heart rate increased without improvement in his bronchospasm. He looked at me through dilated pupils, and I was not sure how high my heart rate had gone.

I had the clerk call the respiratory tech. When I spoke to him, he immediately said he had just gotten home and lived 45 minutes away. I told him I was sorry about that, but his guy had not come in until after he left, and he had remained "really tight" despite epi times two.

"Alright. Since this is the first time you've ever called me, I'm coming back. I'll be there as quickly as I can."

Knowing he was coming made me feel better, but the patient had not shown any improvement. I was a little perplexed why a new asthmatic would not respond to a bolus of epinephrine, but my perplexity did not matter. I needed to break this young man's bronchospasm. I put in an IV and started an aminophylline drip. Aminophylline is a potent bronchodilator and was a mainstay treatment for hospitalized lung patients. At that time, at least half of the patients in a pulmonary intensive care unit would be on an aminophylline drip.

As anticipated, the heart rate began to climb once again. What could I do next? Intubate a very awake patient? If I did, could I force air into his very tight lungs with an Ambu bag? I prayed.

After about 25 minutes, his bronchospasm broke. His color returned to normal, and his wheezing decreased dramatically. His heart rate fell below 150. He could talk.

I told him how surprised I was that it took such aggressive measures to treat his "new onset" asthma. He once again stated this was his first problem with asthma and that he was not on medications.

Then, the rest of the story came out. He had developed some wheezing the day he arrived at his sister's house. His sister was asthmatic, and he had started taking her medication as the wheezing got worse. By the time they came to my emergency room, he was fully tanked up on her bronchodilators! Well, that explained a lot!

About this time, the respiratory technician arrived to see my patient talking away and "looking good."

"You called me in for this...?" he said with a slight look of disgust. "This guy looks great."

"You should have seen him a few minutes ago" was my only defense. "I'm going to leave him on the drip and admit him overnight for observation."

"OK. I'm here. I will check a few patients before I leave and check in on your guy on the floor."

I wrote an admit note, and the young man was more than willing to stay and try to get a good night's sleep, which he had not had for the previous two nights.

About half an hour after the patient got to his bed, he began to wheeze and rapidly "tightened up." I was called to the floor, and beside the bed was the respiratory clerk. He drew a blood gas and an aminophylline level, and we increased the aminophylline drip. Once again, the bronchospasm broke, and the patient "pinked up."

The respiratory technician looked at me and said, "I would not have believed it if I had not seen it with my own eyes."

I responded, "I know. I was the same way."

I spent the rest of the night doing hourly checks on the patient as he slept through the night. Thankfully, he did not have any additional episodes of acute bronchospasm. I left at 6:30 AM to return to my regular job in Chapel Hill, and I placed the patient in the care of his sister's doctor, who graciously agreed to take over his care.

Epinephrine, aminophylline, and scary patients are all capable of increasing heart rates…

GENESIS 2:7 Then the Lord God formed a man from the dust of the ground and breathed into his nostrils the breath of life, and the man became a living being.

Constipation and a Breast Mass
(A misunderstood – perhaps nasty – aging celebrity)

When I worked in Siler City, it was a typical small Southern town. It had one primary industry, the Chatham dog food factory, and many friendly, ordinary people. Entertainment was where you found it, and celebrities were rare. However, there was one, and I met her in the emergency room.

Andy Griffith was an honored son of North Carolina. He grew up there, attended the University of North Carolina, and took that great accent with him everywhere he went. When I was growing up in the sixties, he had the number-one show on television for multiple years in a row. It was called "The Andy Griffith Show" about a small-town sheriff in Mayberry, North Carolina. Of course, Mayberry was fictitious, but the characters in the show would talk about real towns that were apparently near Mayberry. Mount Pilot (really, it's 'Pilot Mountain'), Raleigh, and Siler City were mentioned regularly. Most of the main characters in the show were males – Andy the Sheriff, Barney his deputy, Gomer a mechanic, Gobber - Gomer's cousin, Floyd the Barber, Otis the drunk, Andy's son Opie, and so on. The female roles were limited to girlfriends of the main characters, with one exception – Aunt Bee. Andy was a widower raising his son with the help of his Aunt Bee.

The role of Aunt Bee was played by Frances Bavier, who was born in New York City and was a professionally trained Broadway actress. While reportedly having a love-hate relationship with her role of Aunt Bee (it did not allow her to demonstrate her breath of talent, but it did win her an Emmy award for best supporting actress in a comedy), Ms. Bavier was the only character to remain with the show through its entire run and the sequel, Mayberry R.F.D., that followed.

Amazingly, this lady eventually retired to Siler City, NC. When asked once in an interview why someone who grew up in New York

110

would end up in a small North Carolina town, she replied that she always loved the country roads and trees.

In the early 1980s, when I spent many nights and weekends at Chatham County Hospital, I heard that "Aunt Bee" was living in Siler City. The stories that would follow this revelation were not particularly flattering. She had a reputation as a mean old lady who would bite your head off for no particular reason. Folks said she lived alone, had many cats, and was "just strange." I never attempted to verify any of this, but it was apparent that her presence did not enamor at least some of the residents.

My encounter with Ms. Bavier began on a relatively quiet Thursday evening. We had an early run of colds, cuts, and rashes, but that had all settled down. I was reading a medical journal in the doctor's office when I became aware of a conversation between the clerk and someone in the receiving lobby off the loading deck. The conversation got louder and more animated with time and questioning, and within five minutes, the patient was handed off to the nurse.

She picked up the chart, suppressed a frown, and went to see the patient. I heard the curtain pull around, and the young nurse said, "We need to check your blood pressure and temperature…"

The response was quick and jarring: "Why must you do that? I'm here to see the doctor!"

The nurse explained that we did vital sign measurements on all patients in the emergency room.

"Well, that's silly!" came the retort.

The interaction spiraled down from there…In a few minutes, the nurse appeared before my desk, tossed the chart down, and made no effort to hide her frown on this occasion.

She whispered through her clenched teeth, "That woman is impossible."

Well, now it was my turn. After the reception given to the clerk and nurse, I was slightly hesitant, but there was no other recourse. I gently pulled back the curtain and said, "Good evening, Ms. Bavier. I'm Dr. Carr. What seems to be your problem this evening?"

I was not expecting what came next. She brightened up, smiled, and said: "It is my pleasure to meet you, doctor, and I do hope you can help me with my constipation."

Well, that was nice! I said that I was sure that I could help with her constipation, but that I would need to do a quick physical exam to make sure we were not missing anything. She responded that she completely understood. There was not much that was unexpected about this older lady, but when I checked her heart, I noticed some asymmetry in her left breast. Further examination revealed a discrete, movable, but rigid mass in the left upper aspect of her breast. I asked if she had noticed this, and she said she thought it may have been there for a while.

Suddenly, all the questions I had been asking about changes in her diet, how much she drank, and how often she needed to use a laxative seemed to fade into irrelevance.

"Have you told your doctor about this?" I asked.

"Well, no. It does not seem to bother me. What I'm really concerned about is my constipation. Do you think it could be causing my constipation?"

Her chief complaint was clear, and I assured her we could handle the problem. I did suggest that while we were doing so, it might be a good time to take a closer look at the breast mass because I was concerned that it was probably malignant. She agreed to come into the hospital for laxatives and an enema, and her physician would see her in the morning before she left.

I found the nurse standing outside the curtain with a frown.

"Two things…Why was she so nice to you, and why in hell did you admit her!" The last phrase came through those same clenched teeth.

"Come with me to the office, and we will discuss while I finish my note and write her admission orders."

On the way to the office, I instructed the clerk to inform the floor that we had an admission. She also gave me a rather unpleasant look.

In the office, I explained that the admission was only partially for the treatment of constipation and obstipation. The other reason was to ensure that her physician was made aware of her probable breast cancer.

"Well, what about the 'it's a pleasure to meet you' stuff she laid on you after biting everyone else she met?"

My initial response was that my Southern charm had soothed the savage beast, but she was not buying that. I told her I was not entirely sure, but I think this was a lady who was used to getting her way, and the fastest way to do that was to find the person in charge as quickly as possible. She knew the clerk and nurse were only gateways to the physician, and she would not be held up or waste time there. If being nasty would expedite things, she would be nasty.

The explanation seemed plausible to the nurse, who prepared to roll Ms. Bavier to the floor.

About thirty minutes later, I heard shouting from down the hall, and soon, the ward nurse appeared at my door.

"Why did you admit that witch…?!"

But she was not a witch; she was just an older lady who was alone and trying to look out for herself.

Addendum: Ms. Bavier died four years later. The cause of death was reportedly congestive heart failure. The report did not state that she also had breast cancer. I never knew if she had ever had it treated.

JEREMIAH 17:10 "I the Lord search the heart and examine the mind, to reward each person according to their conduct…"

PROVERBS 21:2 A person may think their own ways are right, but the Lord weighs the heart.

1 SAMUEL 16:7 The Lord does not look at the things people look at. People look at the outward appearance, but the Lord looks at the heart.

Three Gunshot Wounds to the Abdomen
(He tried to commit suicide…I'll never tell who shot me…)

Gunshot wounds were not common in the Siler City emergency room, but I did see my share. What always struck me as odd was that the rescue squad rarely brought in these folks. The "good ole boys" were probably too embarrassed to admit they had managed to get themselves shot. The "bad ole boys" did not want the attention from the authorities that 911 would bring. So, most of the time, my gunshot wounds were brought by car or truck driven by a friend or buddy. This is such a case.

It was a typical, relatively slow Wednesday evening when the double, swing-both-ways doors to the ER were pushed open by a rough-looking fellow who was holding up his companion, who was covered in blood and moaning.

That sight got a shout out of the ordinarily calm clerk, and the nurse and I came running.

We quickly got the patient onto the gurney, always strategically placed inside the door.

As we rolled him into the ER's first (and larger) examination bay, I asked the patient how this had happened. He was in too much pain to mount a coherent response, so I turned to his companion.

"How did this happen?" I asked.

He tried to commit suicide was the short response.

The thought of trauma care somewhat enamors some folks, but the truth is that the early assessment and stabilization are relatively routine. You ensure they have a pulse, blood pressure, and can breathe. If blood is squirting from somewhere, you put pressure there and consider using a tourniquet. The tourniquet is placed somewhere between where the squirting is happening and the heart, preferably as close to the squirt as is feasible. If the blood pressure is low, you can use MAST trousers to push blood back into the body's core. You place large-bore IVs to allow for the administration of fluids, blood, and medication. If you have one, you call your surgeon because most folks will require some type of surgical intervention. If you do not have a surgeon, begin arranging for transfer or transport to a trauma center. It is all pretty rote.

This case was a little different. When we pulled back his blood-soaked shirt, our patient had three apparent entry wounds on his abdomen. Well, that is interesting for a "suicide."

This guy looked tough, but you would have to be quite a macho man to commit suicide by shooting yourself three times in the abdomen. You might shoot yourself once, but that would be very painful. It is hard to imagine one having the wherewithal to do it a second time, let alone a third…Also, gunshots to the abdomen not only cause a painful death, but it is generally not instantaneous.

Most suicides by gunshot involve wounds to the head – one bullet and a quick death. This guy would have had to hate himself to want to suffer the way he was suffering. I had significant doubts about the accuracy of his friend's report.

Given his appearance, the patient was amazingly stable. His blood pressure was stable, and his pulse was strong. His lungs were clear. I had seen enough. Three entry wounds and no exit wounds meant the patient had what we used to call "acute lead poisoning," or there were three bullets somewhere in his belly—time to ship him somewhere else.

The trauma center in Chapel Hill was willing to take him as soon as the ambulance could get him there. He could be there quicker by ground than by waiting for a helicopter (we did not have a landing pad).

As I prepped him for transport, I once again had the chance to ask him how he had been wounded. This time, as his head rolled from side to side, he simply said: "I'll never say who shot me."

Well, in that case, I did not need to know. Off he went to Chapel Hill.

When I returned to my regular job at UNC, I stopped by to see how my patient had done. It was amazing. They removed three 22-caliber slugs from his abdomen and closed 27 separate holes in the bowel. However, after being shot three times, he did not have involvement of a major blood vessel, nerve complex, kidney, ureter, or other critical structure. What a fortunate man.

I know that if I were ever shot in the abdomen, the bullet would go either straight through the aorta, killing me in a few minutes, straight into the spine, leaving me a paraplegic from the waist down, or it would do both...

I told him he was a very lucky man, but he did not appear to be impressed. When you have friends like his, you are either lucky or dead...

1 CORINTHIANS 15:33 Do not be misled: "Bad Company corrupts good character."

PROVERBS 13:20 Walk with the wise and become wise, for a companion of fools suffers harm.

PROVERBS 22:24 Do not make friends with a hot-tempered person, do not associate with one easily angered.

PROVERBS 1:11 If they say, "Come along with us; let's lie in wait for innocent blood, let's ambush some harmless soul;

V. ACADEMIC MEDICINE IN RICHMOND, VA

McGuire VA Medical Center

When I moved to Richmond, Virginia, in 1985 to take a job as an Assistant Professor of Medicine at the Medical College of Virginia, I was initially based at the McGuire VA Medical Center. The VA Hospital had been in Richmond since 1946, but the new Hunter Holmes McGuire VA Medical Center had just recently opened when I arrived. Everything was brand new. The architectural design made the interior resemble a ship. As you walked in the door, two parallel walkways resembled the promenade deck of a ship. In the center, structures housed a store, offices, and other facilities. As you moved farther into the hospital, the ceiling was raised over an open cafeteria area, and along the sides were walkways of the second floor with rails like you might see on a ship. Toward the back was the administration area, which looked out over the open area in a manner reminiscent of a ship's bridge. Well done.

The hospital staff were civilian federal employees. I gradually realized that what you get with federal employees seems uniform across multiple agencies (except for the military and law enforcement). They typically fall into three categories. One-half are dedicated, hard-working individuals who do all the work at the facility. Another 30% come to work daily and do as little work as they can get away with, but they feel they have done their job by showing up. "Hey, I came to work, so pay me."

The remaining group requires close attention. These are the folks who are obstructionists. No matter what you ask for or about, the answer is always some form of NO. "We can't (or don't or won't) do that here." "That's not possible." "We've never done that (and we never will)." "I think there are regulations against that (if there were regulations against it, they would quote them...so, when you heard this one...it meant they were just making it up...).

Initially, I couldn't figure out why these individuals (who appeared to be otherwise capable) would behave in this manner. I eventually came to the conclusion that there were two things this behavior avoided. First, if new things were allowed, it might cause more work for them. Second, if someone new comes in and starts doing innovative things, it might make them "look bad." Obviously, both of these events should be avoided at all costs.

Part of breaking into the VA culture was settling in, during which you gradually could classify folks into their appropriate categories. Having done so, you could smile at those who came for paychecks, work with those who did everything, and avoid (if possible) the obstructionists.

I began as a six-eighths VA employee. That meant I spent three-fourths of my time at the VA and one-fourth at the University Hospital (MCV – Medical College of Virginia). My commitment gradually changed over the first ten years, so I spent one-fourth of my time at the VA and three-fourths at MCV. All in all, I must say that I thoroughly enjoyed my time at McGuire. I made many friends, and the patients shared a bond that made them more of a family than at other treatment facilities.

Hepatic Insufficiency, Lactulose, and a Poor Response
(*Your job is to give this patient his meds...*)

As I mentioned, there are good, not-so-good, and bad Federal employees. This episode illustrates the latter category.

I would serve as an attending physician on one of the medical services at the VA for one to two months each year. These were typically good months. Having a team of eager third-year medical students and typically very good medical interns and residents was fun. Having a team of such talent made the job easy. We would round (walk from patient to patient for updates on their status) on the patients previously admitted to our team. Then, we would have sit-down rounds on the new patients, during which the students would present their new patients, and the resident would outline a proposed treatment plan. My job was to tease out the points of the case that would make it a learning (and hopefully memorable) experience for all. I always tried to do this in a way that moved above simply "pimping" the students and house staff.

Most of the support staff (ward clerks, etc.) and nurses were good to excellent. However, there was one ward that had a bad reputation—4D. Once, a sick patient begged me not to admit him to 4D: "Put me anywhere but 4D...they will kill me up there." I was able to accommodate his wishes, but I must say that his insistence piqued my curiosity.

A few months later, I was attending on 4D. All seemed to go well the first couple of days, but then we got a patient with acute-on-chronic hepatic insufficiency. Such patients are not uncommon at a VA, and the cause is virtually always either years of alcohol use/abuse or untreated hepatitis C. Either way, the result is the same – cirrhosis.

The liver is an excellent protein factory, toxin filter (and eliminator), and a significant immune organ. The absence of the liver is incompatible with life, and we have not produced an artificial liver to replace even part of the liver's multiple functions. While there are dialysis machines to keep folks alive while awaiting a kidney transplant, these do not exist for patients with liver failure. They must go on the transplant list and be lucky enough to get a matching liver, or they will die from a lack of liver function.

Cirrhosis is a scarring process. Liver cells, hepatocytes, are capable of dividing and thereby replacing themselves. Therefore, some hepatocyte turnover and renewal are standard in the human liver. This renewal process can be replaced by scarring in various disease states, such as alcoholism, chronic hepatitis, or diabetes. The scars are fibrotic material produced by the liver's attempt to heal itself. As more liver cells are replaced by scar tissue, the ability of the liver to perform its normal functions gradually declines.

In cirrhosis, the ability to make plasma proteins declines. Many of these proteins are essential for stopping bleeding, and their absence puts the patient at risk for bleeding. Other proteins, such as albumin, are necessary for maintaining normal fluid balance; when they are absent, fluid leaks out of the blood vessels and into the tissues, causing swelling.

In cirrhosis, the ability of the blood to flow normally through the liver is impeded by the presence of inflexible scars. This increased resistance to flow causes backup of blood, increased pressure in, and subsequent swelling of the liver (portal) veins. These distended or "varicose" veins are more fragile and prone to rupture. They extend up into the stomach and esophagus, and then back through the pancreas to the spleen, causing it to enlarge. The result is an increased risk of life-threatening bleeding into the esophagus and stomach.

Thus, as cirrhosis gets more severe, the patient will get a variety of symptoms, including GI bleeding and swelling of the abdomen (ascites) and of the lower extremities due to decreased protein production and pressure on the large abdominal blood vessels.

In the end stage of cirrhosis, liver function is so impaired that the body can no longer handle the breakdown products of normal metabolism. This is particularly the case for protein. The nitrogenous byproducts of protein breakdown continue to circulate and will cause the patient to become somnolent (sleepy) and less alert. At the very end stage, even eating as much protein as is contained in a typical hamburger will be enough to put the patient in a virtual coma - "hamburger narcosis."

At this point, the only chronic treatment is protein restriction and whatever can be done to limit additional hepatotoxin exposure (stopping the alcohol and avoidance of any medication or substance that is known to be hepatotoxic). When these measures are ineffective in these typically non-compliant patients, the treatment involves inducing diarrhea by removing any additional protein from the gastrointestinal tract.

So, our patient arrived on the ward in a minimally responsive state but with an apparent previous history of similar events. The student presented the case, and the resident outlined the appropriate plan to treat the patient with lactulose (a laxative that draws liquid into the gut and produces watery diarrhea). It is not a pleasant treatment for anyone involved, but it can be very effective. Patients typically wake up soon after the diarrhea begins.

The patient had been admitted on a Sunday night, and lactulose was started after rounds on Monday. On Tuesday morning, we found the patient still minimally responsive. I also noted the absence of recorded stooling on the chart (which could also be verified by the lack of stool odor in the room). I had the resident check the dose, which appeared to be correct. We asked the nurse if the patient was getting his lactulose, and she assured us he was. She also showed the resident that the meds were signed off on the medication cart.

When I checked later in the day, there was still no stooling, the patient was still asleep, and the meds were cleared and signed off as "given" in the chart.

On Wednesday morning, the situation remained unchanged. I once again asked the nurse about the medications. I was becoming increasingly blunt, and she was becoming more defensive. I decided to take another tack. I spoke to the resident and informed him that I thought the patient was not receiving his medication. I talked to the medical student following the patient and instructed him that administering the patient's lactulose dose would now be his responsibility.

The not-so-sweet smell of success permeated the patient's room on early morning Thursday rounds. By the afternoon, he was awake and talking. He was still not the sharpest knife in the drawer, but he was improving. By Friday, he was ready for discharge.

At this point, I once again confronted the nurse with what I thought was clear evidence that not only had the patient not been receiving his lactulose but that the medical record had been falsified to indicate that he had. She did not deny my accusation; she became red-faced, turned, and walked away.

I was later called to the administrator's office to address a complaint of my verbal abuse/harassment of a staff member. Now, I knew where the nurse had headed when she walked away. I explained my position and was told that we had a nursing shortage and that any such future interactions would not be tolerated. I responded that my first responsibility was to the patient and that I would probably behave similarly in a similar situation.

In this case (in my opinion), a nurse who did not want to deal with the diarrhea and associated smell and frequent bed changes required with lactulose therapy had decided to avoid the problem by preventing the administration of the medication that would induce it.

We needed to find other solutions if we were so short of nurses that we were willing to tolerate lying, falsifying medical records, and inappropriate medical care that put patients at risk.

PSALMS 34:13 Keep your tongue from evil and your lips from telling lies.

PROVERBS 12:17 An honest witness tells the truth, but a false witness tells lies.

JOB 40:21 You, however, smear me with lies; you are worthless physicians, all of you!

PROVERBS An honest witness does not deceive, but a false witness pours out lies.

ISAIAH 32:7 Scoundrels use wicked methods, they make up evil schemes to destroy the poor with lies, even when the plea of the needy is just.

A Friday Afternoon Transfer from Beckley and a Needed CT
(*You do your job ... I will do mine*)

One might think I did not enjoy my time at the VA Medical Center in Richmond, but that would be incorrect. There were dedicated, well-trained, intelligent people working there who did their jobs and delivered high-quality care to our patients. I truly enjoyed their companionship. However, like everywhere else, some folks did precisely what was required (or less) and thought that was all that was necessary. I can tolerate such individuals when I don't have to interact with them directly, but occasionally, they push too many buttons. I tend to be very direct on such occasions, and hospital authorities have advised me that I might have overstepped my bounds. This is one of those cases.

It was a Friday afternoon, and I was attending on one of the medical wards. I received a call indicating that a patient was coming to us from the VA in Beckley, West Virginia, for acute treatment of brain metastasis and cerebral edema. It was about three o'clock in the afternoon, and this was my first notice about the patient.

When I checked further, I found the patient had known lung cancer and had presented to their emergency room the previous evening with an increasing headache. The patient gave a history of worsening early morning headaches consistent with brain metastasis. Since they had no radiation therapy facility, and it was almost the weekend, they decided to treat him with steroids (Decadron - to reduce cerebral edema) and ship him to Richmond. They had not done a CT scan since it would have delayed transport, and they knew we would likely perform a baseline scan upon his arrival at McGuire.

OK, although the information was late in coming, it all seemed reasonable, and no matter what, the patient was in an ambulance on the way to Richmond.

I contacted the radiation therapy department. They had left for the day but said that they would come in and treat as soon as brain metastases were documented on CT. The next call was to radiology.

By now, it was about 5:30 in the afternoon, and when I got someone to answer the phone in radiology, I found that the person covering radiology had left a little early because "it was really quiet here today." I said that I understood, but it looked like we would need a CT to document brain mets in a patient coming from Beckley.

The clerk said he would call the radiologist.

About 20 minutes later, the clerk beeped me, and when I called, I was informed that the radiologist was at home and would prefer to come in the morning to do the scan.

I informed the clerk that we needed the scan this evening so that the patient could be treated acutely with radiation therapy. I also mentioned that radiation therapy was ready to treat as soon as we had a confirmatory CT scan.

The clerk said he would relay this information to the radiologist. I said I would be happy to speak with the radiologist to explain the situation.

At this point, I got a call from the emergency room announcing the arrival of our patient from Beckley. About ten minutes later, I got a call from the radiologist.

The conversation started well enough, as I explained the patient's situation and included that he had now arrived at McGuire. I indicated that radiation therapy was standing by to treat him as soon as we had the CT scan.

It soon became apparent that this fellow did not want to come in on a Friday night. He asked, "Do you know that he has cancer?" I responded that the records he arrived with indicated that he had stage four lung cancer.

126

He then asked if he had a fever. I responded that the patient was afebrile.

He then suggested that I treat the patient with steroids and that he would do the scan "first thing in the morning."

I responded that the patient was on steroids and that the sooner he was treated, the better. I also reminded him that the patient was transferred expressly for acute radiation therapy and that the RT team was ready to treat him this evening.

He continued to push for a delay until the following day.

At this point, I had had it. I was going to be there most of the night; the RT team was coming in from home, and the medical service would care for the patient through the night, but this guy was giving me a hard time when he should do the best thing for the patient and come in and do his job.

To move things forward, I employed a tactic I knew would be effective.

I said, "In my medical opinion, this patient needs a scan tonight. If you are unwilling to come in to perform the scan, I will try to find someone else."

The response was, "I never said I would not come in."

I probably overstepped my bounds, but I could not help myself. I responded, "I do not need you to tell me how to care for my patients. You do your job, and I will do mine. Come in and take my picture..."

Well, he came in and did the CT scan and documented the brain metastases we all knew would be there. He would not speak to me, but I did not care. The radiation therapy team began their therapy within the hour.

On Monday afternoon, I received a letter from the hospital director indicating that my behavior during the incident was not as professional as expected.

OK. I should have bit my tongue.

However, the patient got his CT scan and treatment for his brain metastases that night.

I would try to do better. However, your top priority as a physician should be doing what is in the patient's best interest. In this case, I did not feel that the patient was receiving the necessary care. Having to argue with a fellow physician who was trying to avoid a little night call was not something I thought I needed or wanted to do.

1 PETER 2:15 For it is God's will that by doing good you should silence the ignorant talk of foolish people.

1 PETER 3:17 For it is better, if it is God's will, to suffer for doing good than for doing evil.

ROMANS 7:21 So I find this law at work: Although I want to do good, evil is right there with me.

ROMANS 7:19 For I do not do the good I want to do, but the evil I do not want to do – this I keep on doing.

PROVERBS 1:3 For receiving instruction in prudent behavior, doing what is right and just and fair.

A Clinic Patient with Acute Pain and Decreased Hearing in His Right Ear
(*Is that blood behind the eardrum...*)

I met some wonderful people at the VA Hospital in Richmond. The older World War II and Korean veterans were my favorite. They were humble and grateful for the care they received at the VA. They rarely complained about waiting for their appointment or in line at the pharmacy.

The younger veterans were much more likely to complain about things – having to wait (for anything), the quality of the food, the size of the hospital store, the coffee in the cafeteria...They also had a much more entitled attitude. "The government owes me..."

I suppose some of the difference was due to how they were greeted when they came home. The World War II veterans had saved the world from tyranny and came home to a joyful nation that welcomed them with parades.

The Korean veterans (some of whom were also WW II vets) had fought in a savage but smaller and shorter war and had stopped the communist advance in Korea. However, the war seemed to come to a halt with an armistice, and the American public welcomed the soldiers home with little fanfare. After all, it was not a "victory."

The Vietnam veterans fought in a meat grinder war, which was not popular and basically ended in defeat. Not only did they not come home to parades, but some groups depicted them as war criminals. Simply wearing the uniform was enough to make them targets for abuse. They had done their duty. They had answered the call just as their fathers had. They went when others did not. Yet, when they returned, much of the public turned their backs on them. The government owed them, and they were entitled to better treatment than they had received.

One little fellow comes to mind when I reflect on the WWII vets. I followed Jim for mild pancytopenia. He was slightly anemic, his white cell count was on the low end of normal, and his platelet count (the small pieces of cells that help stop bleeding) was always borderline low. I watched Jim for the entire time I was at the VA. His counts would move up and down a little, but stayed the same. He did not seem to get infections or complain of low energy, weakness, bruising, or bleeding.

Jim did not complain about anything. He was pretty much on his own. Jim had no local family and lived in an adult home, where they took part of his social security for payment, and he lived on the rest. He got enough to eat, but he was always thin. He suffered from arthritis in his knees and walked with a slight limp, but he had no complaints.

It was always a pleasure to see Jim because he always met you with a huge smile—one of those ear-to-ear smiles that cannot be faked. He was one of the nurses' favorites and certainly one of mine.

So, when Jim came in one Friday morning, and his smile, although present, was not as broad as usual, I immediately became concerned. When I asked how he was doing, he said he had some pain in his right ear and thought his hearing had decreased. He thought his left ear was fine.

OK, let's take a look. If there is a unilateral complaint (only on one side), I always start with the normal side to understand what "normal" should look like. The left ear canal had a little wax but was otherwise normal. The right ear canal was normal, but I saw only blackness instead of a whitish tympanic membrane (eardrum) at the end. On closer observation, it was not black. It was dark brown.

My first thought was that he had bled into his inner ear, and I was seeing blood behind his eardrum. Why would he have bled…? Was his platelet count suddenly lower? By now, his labs were back, and his platelet count was where it had always been.

I asked about trauma to the ear or that side of his head. Jim said he could not remember any recent trauma, but he did say that his ear was hurting when he woke up the day before.

It did not make sense. I took another look.

This time, I saw something different. I saw what appeared to be a serrated edge. What could that be? I refocused my otoscope, and this time, it came into focus.

I knew what that was. It was part of the hind leg of some insect!

Well, I knew what to do. Jim required an urgent visit to the ENT clinic.

Instead of trying to arrange this via nurses and clerks, I picked up the phone and asked to speak to any ENT doc who might be in the clinic. When I got a doctor on the phone, I explained that I had a patient with ear pain and a large insect deep in his right ear canal. I was told they would see him as soon as he could get to the clinic. I walked him over.

I returned to my clinic to continue seeing patients. After about 30 minutes, I got a call from the Doctor in the ENT clinic, who told me that he had removed a cockroach from my patient's ear. The patient reported that his pain had already been reduced significantly.

When Jim returned to my clinic, the old grin was back. We figured the insect must have crawled into his ear while he was sleeping.

"We have had some trouble with them where I live," Jim admitted.

If multiple people live in that facility, they need to take measures to address cockroaches and other insect infestations.

"Jim, they need to treat for bugs. I will write a note that I want you to deliver to your landlord. This should not happen again," I explained.

Jim assured me he would deliver the note, but he "did not want to be a burden" to anyone.

I could not believe his attitude. He was paying to live in a room and was "entitled" to have it free of disease-spreading insects.

Jim had never been a burden to anyone, and I was sure he never would be.

ROMANS 5:3-4 Not only so, but we also glory in our sufferings, because we know that suffering produces perseverance; perseverance, character; and character, hope.

JAMES 1:4 Let perseverance finish its work so that you may be mature and complete, not lacking anything.

TITUS 2:2 Teach the older men to be temperate, worthy of respect, self-controlled, and sound in faith, in love and in endurance.

PROVERBS 17:22 A cheerful heart is good medicine,

Appearances Can Be Deceiving
(*A large ring and no wrinkles...*)

When I first started working at the McGuire VA Medical Center in Richmond, Virginia, in 1985, there were still a significant number of World War II and Korean veterans who were patients there. Vietnam veterans were gradually replacing them. I always tried to keep an open mind about what these folks had been through and how it might have affected them, but, like most people, I usually make my initial assessment based on my first impression. Although I was mostly accurate, there were times when I was caught off guard. The following are a couple of examples.

Most of my veterans came to the clinic in nice, clean, but rather casual apparel. Therefore, when someone came in with a suit and tie, it tended to catch your attention. Early in my time at the VA, a relatively short but well-dressed gentleman in his fifties came to my clinic for follow-up on a low white blood cell count. When your white blood cell count is low (<3000), it catches people's attention because if the neutrophil count (which is part of the white blood cell count) falls below 500, the patient is at an increased risk of serious infections.

When I spoke to this fellow, he had no infections and was doing well. After following him for a few months and seeing a very stable, although somewhat low, white count, I decided he had benign neutropenia, which is not uncommon in black Americans. I told him that I thought he was in no real danger but that I would be happy to follow him in the clinic on a six-month or yearly basis "just to make sure the count did not fall."

He was okay with that idea and asked if we could follow him on any "general medical" problems since he did not have a "private" physician. I told him I would be pleased to do so if he would let us know if he developed any problems, concerns, or symptoms. I also indicated that we could (and probably would) refer him to a general

133

medicine clinic if he needed routine follow-up for nonhematologic conditions.

He said he was "fine with that, but did not want to have to go to multiple clinics" unless necessary.

That seemed fair to me, so we saw each other regularly every six months.

During one of these visits, I noticed a large ring on his right hand—more prominent than a high school or (most) college ring. Finally, my curiosity got the best of me, and I asked about the ring.

He was more than happy to show it to me. It was a player's ring from Super Bowl II! That's right, I was taking care of a former professional football player. He played defensive back for several years with the Green Bay Packers! I was floored. I was half a foot taller than he and certainly outweighed him. I am sure he could outrun me and was a better athlete, but he looked too small to be a professional football player...Not only was he a player, but he had played on one of the best teams ever to play the game! He was not a full-time starter, but he said he played virtually every game and got to play a couple of series in the Super Bowl.

Wow, just wow — and he never mentioned this during his previous visits. I would never have known if I had not asked about the ring. I told him I had been a huge Packer fan and watched that game on our family's black-and-white television.

I then told him that it was an honor to shake the hand of a Green Bay Packer who played in a Super Bowl. He simply smiled at the comment. If it had been me with the ring, I would not have been able to have a five-minute conversation without bringing up Super Bowl II.

He was amazingly humble, and I often wondered why he did not have a "private" physician. I later learned that many players from that era did not make vast sums of money or have significant retirements.

The second fellow to catch me off base was Roland. Roland was a Korean War veteran whom I followed for polycythemia. Unlike the previous patient, he did not have too few blood cells; he had too many. His white count and platelet count (small pieces of cells that help stop bleeding) were relatively normal, but his hemoglobin was greater than 18, and his total red cell count was high. In my memory, I paired him with the previous patient because Roland also typically came to the clinic in a suit or a sports jacket.

There are several concerns about polycythemia. First, since it is a stem cell disorder (stem cells are the cells from which all types of blood cells originate), there is a low-level risk of evolving into a malignant process, such as leukemia. Second, if the platelet count is very high, there is an increased risk of thrombosis (clots forming when you don't want/need them). Third and most worrisome is the risk of excessive strain on the heart if the blood viscosity (thickness) gets too high. Blood viscosity affects the blood's ability to flow. The higher the viscosity, the more difficult it is to push blood through the vessels. The heart's job is to supply the force needed to push the blood; if more force is required, the heart must work harder. Since the percentage of red blood cells in the blood is the primary determinant of blood viscosity (the higher the percentage, the higher the viscosity), having too many red blood cells is a problem.

If there are too many red cells, let's eliminate a few. That makes sense; therefore, phlebotomy (the process of drawing blood – "blood-letting") has been the mainstay of therapy for the last hundred years. You take out blood rich in red cells; the body quickly replaces the plasma, and the percentage of red cells drops. The body will also replace the red blood cells over time, so you must have regular blood tests. Initially, phlebotomy is relatively frequent, occurring every couple of weeks or monthly. However, as the patient becomes iron deficient, the body's ability to make red cells is retarded, and the frequency of phlebotomy can be reduced to once every three to four months. I would see Roland several times per year and would remove a unit of blood.

So, what did we do with the blood? Well, Roland liked and grew roses. Roses like and need iron. Red cells are a great source of iron. Roland would come to the clinic, have his blood drawn, take the bag with him when he left, and go home and put it at the base of his roses. He also told me that for the first couple of weeks after "treating" his roses, it would "help keep the deer away from his roses." It worked for everybody!

Roland was also unique in several other aspects. First, he was the only patient I ever had who had undergone "Plombage." Plombage was an early treatment for cavitary tuberculosis of the upper lobe of the lung. The therapy consisted of surgically opening the involved side of the chest and placing inert objects into the upper chest, thereby collapsing the involved upper lobe. The thought was that collapsing the involved lobe would lead to more rapid healing and scarring of the diseased area. The most common objects used were ping-pong balls. This surgical treatment of TB was practiced from the 1930s to the 1950s, before antibiotic treatment for TB had been developed. The best therapies included rest, good nutrition, and isolation.

You can imagine my surprise when I first examined Roland and asked about the impressive surgical scar on his right upper back, and his response was, "That's where they put the ping pong balls to treat my TB..."

In many cases, the ping pong balls were left in the chest. In Roland's case, they had been removed, and the chest X-ray was not nearly as exciting as it could have been...(QJM: An International Journal of Medicine, 2017, 191).

Lastly, did I mention that Roland looked like he was in his late forties or early fifties? He had a full head of dark hair and virtually no wrinkles. Despite his appearance, his chart confirmed that he was in his early seventies. I was always amazed. I thought, "his guy must have a great set of genes."

One visit, while we were catching up on his activities, my curiosity got the better of me, so I had to ask: "Roland, how old was your father when he passed away?"

Roland looked at me, a little puzzled, and responded: "What makes you think he is dead?"

Well, that answered that question. Roland had a fine set of genes!

So, I had two older combat veterans who came to the clinic in suits. One was a professional football player who played in a Super Bowl. The other had lived with ping pong balls in his chest, had survived TB, would probably outlive me, and grew roses using his blood as fertilizer.

In the age of social media, where everything is immediately shared, my admiration for these humble men who had endured the hell of war continues to increase. Such amazing stories would not have been shared if my curiosity had not gotten the better of me.

1 Samuel 16:7 But the Lord said to Samuel, "Do not consider his appearance or his height, for I have rejected him. The Lord does not look at the things people look at. People look at the outward appearance, but the Lord looks at the heart."

A Paratrooper with Multiple Vertebral Fractures after a Normal Landing
(*When do you stop therapy...*)

Occasionally, you take care of a patient who has a lethal disease or illness, but you have such success with your therapy that you get lulled into believing that perhaps, just perhaps, you might beat the odds this time. This story is about such a time.

John L was a young man with a young wife and young children. He came to me directly off active duty in the Army. He had been stationed at Fort Bragg, North Carolina, where he served as an airborne soldier in the 82nd Airborne Division. Unfortunately, he landed normally after a routine training jump, only to have several vertebral bodies in his spine collapse. He was taken to Womack Army Hospital, where his spine was stabilized, and a diagnostic evaluation revealed that he had multiple myeloma.

Multiple myeloma is a malignant disease of plasma cells. Plasma cells are specialized cells that produce immunoglobulins (IgG, IgM, IgA, etc.), playing a vital role in the normal immune response. The antibodies that plasma cells produce against various viruses and bacteria are crucial for preventing recurrent infections by pathogens to which we have been previously exposed. The immune system recognizes and attacks a pathogen with a response targeted to the pathogen by immunoglobulins. In multiple myeloma, a plasma cell becomes independent of the normal response and begins to produce an increasing number of identical copies of itself, spontaneously and continuously. Since plasma cells typically have long lifespans, the dividing cells form plasma cell tumors that weaken bones and fill the bone marrow cavity. They also produce large amounts of useless myeloma immunoglobulin. Since the cells originate from a single abnormal malignant cell, they are termed "monoclonal" (derived from a single clone of cells). The immunoglobulin produced by these cells is thus also identical. When one looks for immunoglobulins in the plasma of patients with myeloma, instead of finding a broad spectrum of proteins, one primarily sees a spike of a single protein, termed the "monoclonal spike."

The weakening of bones leads to fractures, as occurred with John. The filling up of the marrow spaces leads to crowding out of normal cells and eventually to low red cell, white cell, and platelet counts. The useless immunoglobulin can cause problems by making the plasma more viscous or by interacting with other cells, leading to cell and tissue damage. Replacing normal plasma cells with dysfunctional ones increases the risk of infection.

At the time John presented with the disease, we had a combination chemotherapy that would dramatically reduce the number of malignant cells and reduce the amount of monoclonal immunoglobulin circulating in the blood. The therapy, a combination of a steroid and a chemotherapeutic cytotoxic agent, could be given orally and was generally well tolerated. Unfortunately, it was known that, despite the therapy's apparent effectiveness, it was not curative. If you stopped the treatment, the myeloma would come back. If you continued the therapy, eventually, it would become ineffective, and the myeloma would reappear and advance. In either case, the patient would die within a few years of complications of their myeloma. Since many patients with myeloma are elderly, the lack of curative potential did not seem such a terrible deficiency. However, John was in his late twenties with a wife and young children. We did not want to consider a couple of years of life as an option.

I had read that a group in Seattle had reasonable success with the potential for curative results in young myeloma patients by performing bone marrow transplants. With a transplant, you can give levels of chemotherapy that could not be given without a transplant. Cytotoxic therapies will kill the rapidly dividing cells of the bone marrow. If you kill too many marrow stem cells (as can happen with high-dose treatment), the marrow will be depleted (ablated), and it will not recover due to the absence of stem cells. If the marrow does not recover, the patient will eventually die from a lack of red blood cells, white blood cells, and platelets, as well as the complications these deficiencies cause. You can replenish the marrow and rescue the patient by supplying bone marrow stem cells from a donor's marrow. In simple terms, that is how the bone marrow transplant works.

In John's case, we would harvest marrow from a genetically compatible donor (close enough to John's genotype to be accepted by John's immune system while not being toxic to John), treat John with high-dose chemotherapy to kill the myeloma, and then rescue him by giving him marrow cells from the donor. The procedure is not without risks, and in the mid-1980s, the mortality related to the transplant was between 5 and 10 percent.

I had started John on the combination chemotherapy, and he was tolerating it well with an excellent response. I told him that, while things looked promising, we could not expect a cure or long-term survival (lasting more than a few years). I explained the option of bone marrow transplant and the increased possibility of prolonged survival and perhaps a cure. He listened carefully.

I did not want to sugarcoat the risk, but I thought he needed to know that our options were limited.

I then had John bring his wife in so that I could explain the situation to her. She, too, listened in silence. I offered to answer questions and suggested they discuss the possibility, letting me know if I should proceed.

Two days later, John called and said that he would like to pursue the option of a transplant.

Great!

Now, it was off to the phone to discuss this with the VA administrators to see if it would be covered. I also called the physicians in Seattle to see if they could take a veteran from Virginia.

Amazingly, the stars seemed to align. The VA would cover the expense because this was considered a service-connected illness. The team in Seattle said they would be glad to take our patient if he had a compatible donor. They also said they would coordinate his care with the VA Medical Center in Seattle!

Wow, that went much better than I anticipated!

Next, could we find a donor? Due to a relative shortage of African-American bone marrow donors in the National Registry, the best chance would be to find a close relative.

I began the process with a simple question: "John, do you have relatives who might be willing to be tested for bone marrow compatibility?"

He immediately provided the names of siblings and close relatives from three different states: Georgia, Virginia, and Michigan!

"Could you call them and ask if they would be willing to discuss this option with me?" I continued.

"Yes, Sir," was the immediate response.

The next day, I had the phone numbers and began calling and explaining the situation to various relatives. The response was unanimous—they would "do anything to help John."

OK, I have potential donors. How do I get the blood samples to see if any are suitable matches?

I decided that a little "family reunion" would allow for the rapid collection of samples and provide the opportunity for these fine folks to see John.

John liked the idea. The blood draws would need to be done in the VA clinic, but when could we arrange to have all those people in the clinic without disrupting the schedule? In addition, most of these folks worked, and some would have to travel significant distances.

The solution was to have them come to the clinic on a Saturday morning. It was not hard to find a volunteer nurse to help with the blood draws, and the pathology lab said it would be open and agreed to process the samples for shipment (on the weekend!). Now, all we had to do was bounce the idea off the relatives.

Not only did they think this was a good idea, but they were also excited.

Three weeks later, on a Saturday morning, I had nine of John's close relatives in the VA oncology clinic for blood draws. It was like a party, and I let them linger for a while since there were no other patients to see that morning. I'm sure the "party" continued at John's house after they left the clinic.

I continued to treat John with melphalan and prednisone for the next several weeks as we waited for the results regarding a potential match. He continued to do well, and to my amazement, we not only found a match, but we found two!

Calls were made to both to explain in greater detail what donation of marrow would entail (a minor surgical procedure involving multiple needle aspirations of their hip bones), and both wanted to be donors.

I'm back on the phone with Seattle with the news that the patient was willing, and we had two potential donors. Within a few days, we had secured potential dates for John to be in Seattle.

Final arrangements involved John flying to Seattle one week before his donor to allow the transplant team to perform final evaluations. It was an exciting and happy moment when we met John in our clinic the day before he was to fly to Seattle. He was excited and, for the first time, a little nervous.

Everything seemed to be going according to plan until I got a call from John saying he was coming home.

What had happened to change his mind...was there a problem...did we not have him well prepared...these thoughts raced through my mind.

"They are kicking my family out of our housing. I have to come home to take care of them," John explained.

How did this happen...? When John was medically discharged from the Army, he was transferred from Fort Bragg in North Carolina to Fort Lee in Virginia. Fort Lee is located in Petersburg, which is close to Richmond. He had been given base housing on Fort Lee during final evaluations and out-processing. This arrangement also facilitated his treatment at the VA Medical Center in Richmond. Apparently, there was a time limit on how long this arrangement could continue, and that limit had expired. So, someone calls John's wife and tells her she must vacate housing immediately. She calls John in tears and tells him what she has been told. John's decision is immediate, and he tells his medical team that he is leaving.

It was incredible that after all the effort...having so many dominos fall in order...the whole process was derailed by someone who probably had no idea of the current situation...someone doing their job and checking a box...

I tried to tell John that we would try to handle the situation from our end, but he would have none of it.

"It's my family. I'm coming home," was his final word.

John handled his housing problem, but I could never get him to go back to Seattle. The chemotherapy continued to be effective, and he was pain-free and asymptomatic. Doing so well made the risk of the procedure (5-10% mortality) suddenly appear much greater. Multiple conversations about the lethal nature of his disease failed to be effective in having him reconsider.

Time passed. John continued to do well. There were no new bone lesions, and his spine had healed entirely. Even the M-Spike went away. It was already well beyond two years.

We performed a bone marrow examination, and no increased plasma cells were observed, nor were any abnormal plasma cells noted.

What do we do now? What were we treating?

"Doc, if you can't find the myeloma, maybe it is gone. Can we stop this chemotherapy?" John asked.

"John, I know you feel good, and I am pleased you are doing so well, but I know from experience and the medical literature that the myeloma is almost certainly there even if we can't see it. I cannot make you take the chemotherapy, but I think it is what is keeping the disease in check. I recommend we continue it," was my response.

He agreed, and we continued the meds for an additional six months. At that point, he decided that he had had enough therapy.

From that point on, we watched him closely every month. Sure enough, the M-Spike reappeared, and chemo was minimally helpful this time. Radiation was required to treat the bony tumors that began to appear in critical areas, and narcotic pain meds were needed to cover the pain. It was an agonizing downhill course that ended in pneumonia and the death of one of the finest young men I had ever met.

I was asked to speak at a ceremony in the VA Chapel to commemorate John's life. I carefully wrote out my remarks and got up to the podium to read them. As I tried, tears began to roll down my face, and it was challenging for me to speak. By the time I finished, I was almost sobbing.

I couldn't shake the feeling that I had a chance to save this young man and failed.

Time and distance have eased that feeling, but as I wrote this story, I realized that I still feel that way — it is a regret I cannot overcome.

EZEKIEL 21:6 Therefore groan, son of man! Groan before them with broken heart and bitter grief.

PSALMS 31:9 Be merciful to me, Lord, for I am in distress; my eyes grow weak with sorrow, my soul and body with grief.

ROMANS 9:2 I have great sorrow and unceasing anguish in my heart.

ECCLESIASTES 1:18 For with much wisdom comes much sorrow; the more knowledge, the more grief.

MICAH 4:6 "In that day," declares the Lord, "I will gather the lame; I will assemble the exiles and those I have brought to grief."

JEREMIAH 46:11 "Go up to Gilead and get balm, Virgin Daughter Egypt. But you try many medicines in vain; there is no healing for you."

Medical College of Virginia (MCV)

How Do You Operate on the "World's Worst Bleeder?"
(*Can we use this stuff to fix my knee...?*)

An Introductory Note About the Hemophilia Treatment Center:

While on the faculty at the Medical College of Virginia (MCV), one of my favorite jobs was working in the hemophilia center. As a "benign" hematologist and having trained at one of the world's foremost hemophilia centers, I expected to spend time there. Unlike UNC, where the Hemophilia Treatment Center (HTC) was situated squarely within the Department of Medicine, at MCV, the center was housed in the Department of Pathology and directed by the Chief of the Coagulation Laboratory. The Physician in charge of the clinic was a Canadian. He had a lifelong interest in patients with bleeding disorders and had developed expertise in caring for their complications. Although he treated patients, he did not have a faculty appointment in Medicine.

When I first moved to Richmond, I was not involved with the hemophilia center, but I became increasingly involved after being asked to assume the role of director of the coagulation special studies laboratory. That was an interesting transition. The physician previously running that lab was a hematologist in the Department of Medicine who had a joint appointment in pathology. In a way, he was the converse of the Physician running the Hemophilia Center, a hematologist based in pathology. Unfortunately, my predecessor had a run-in with the Chairman of Pathology, which resulted in his dismissal from both Pathology and Medicine.

When I took the job in the Special Studies Laboratory, I got a joint appointment in Pathology. That was a nice bonus, and I got along well with the Chairman. After a few months, he indicated that he would appreciate it if I could have more input in the care of patients in the Hemophilia Center. I said I would be happy to and met with the center director.

I also hit it off with the center director, and from that time onward, I saw patients on a routine basis in the Hemophilia clinic. I also saw patients on the Clinical Coagulation Consult Service, which I started through the hematology division of the Department of Medicine. Once again, this approach worked for everyone, as it relieved the Hematology Consult team of the burden of these patients and allowed for close coordination with the main and special coagulation laboratories.

This seemed to be a good marriage of efforts for everyone, and we continued along that path until my Pathology Hematologist colleague retired. At that point, I took over the full reins as Director of the Hemophilia Treatment Center.

The center was a stepchild in the School of Medicine and the Medical Center. The staff, who were excellent, were housed in a group of offices in the oldest part of the hospital. The clinic met once per month and used space borrowed from the pulmonary service. Funding was received in small amounts from the State of Virginia, the Centers for Disease Control and Prevention (CDC), and the National Institutes of Health (NIH). The hospital tolerated us but did not fund our efforts. The primary reason for this situation was that hemophilia was a money loser for the hospital. If you do not generate revenue for the hospital, it is not easy to obtain funding from the hospital...

At one time, this was pretty much the situation for all HTCs. However, the situation changed in 1992 when the federal government established the 340B Drug Pricing Program. The 340B program required drug manufacturers to provide outpatient drugs to eligible healthcare organizations and covered entities at significantly reduced prices. HTCs were eligible to participate in this program. Plasma-derived factor concentrates and the (at that time) newly developed recombinant protein clotting factor preparations were expensive, and

147

all hemophilia patients needed and used them on a chronic (lifelong) basis. If an HTC set up a 340B program where the drug company supplied the concentrates at one price and the insurance companies reimbursed at a higher price, then the HTC could use the money derived to support its functions. Many HTCs quickly took advantage of this opportunity, and some rapidly transformed into business enterprises. Many flew under the hospital's radar and used the funds to expand their services, staff, and facilities. In some cases, when the hospitals became aware of the potential to dip into this new pool of money, some centers stepped out of the medical centers and became "free-standing" business entities.

At MCV, we were initially reluctant to adopt the 340B model for two primary reasons. First, we would rather continue to spend 100% of our time caring for patients than have to spend time running a "business." Perhaps just as (probably more) important was that we were sure the hospital would quickly take a large share of any money derived from the endeavor.

In MCV's defense, it should be noted that MCV took care of a large part of the indigent care patients for the state of Virginia. Indeed, in the 1990s (and likely still), MCV cared for more than 50% of all intensive care indigent patients in the state. Because of this significant burden of unreimbursed care, MCV constantly ran on fumes. So, if the smell of money was noted, it was to be expected that the medical center would find it.

Having painted a rather bleak picture, I must say that working with the amazing, gifted, and dedicated staff, as well as the very special patients we served, was one of the most rewarding highlights of my life. The nurses and social workers took a direct interest in each patient, despite having the opportunity to work in better conditions and earn higher pay elsewhere.

The patients were dealing with a lifelong, inherited disease that required diligent attention. They could bleed significantly from

148

minimal trauma, and even worse, they could bleed for no apparent reason (i.e., spontaneously). Some bleeds had the potential to be lethal (bleeding into the head, for example), and all bleeding had the potential to cause severe acute pain and chronic long-term complications. These patients and their caregivers learned to live with needles and pain, and despite this, they were typically a pleasure to be around. You would see all these patients on a recurrent basis, and you would come to know about their struggles and triumphs. The connections you made went beyond a normal doctor-patient relationship. I missed them when I left.

Now, on to the patient!

Before 1982 and after 1990 (arguably during this period, HIV and AIDS were the most significant complications), the development of an "inhibitor" was the most dreaded potential complication to develop in a patient with hemophilia. An inhibitor is an antibody that some patients develop during treatment with a factor concentrate. If it develops, the antibody binds the infused clotting factor, limiting its ability to work. Infusing the clotting factor does not help if the antibody level is high. If this happens, the ability to stop or prevent bleeding by infusing the missing clotting factor is lost. So, if the patient is bleeding, we cannot stop it with standard treatment methods, such as factor infusion.

These antibodies were first identified in the 1970s, when the use of factor concentrates became widespread. The hallmark of their appearance was the failure of factor replacement to stop bleeding in a previously responding patient. Laboratory tests were developed to detect and monitor these antibodies, and physicians did whatever they could to stop the bleeding. In some, but not all, patients, very high levels of clotting factor were effective. In the patients where this did not work, using plasma concentrates containing multiple clotting factors and low levels of activated clotting factors appeared to work to some degree in most patients. These concentrates were felt to bypass the need for FVIII during clotting.

The most effective way to treat patients would be to eradicate the inhibitor by inducing immune tolerance. The patient would again tolerate and respond to factor replacement if this could be accomplished. Various regimens utilizing continuous exposure of the patient's immune system to the clotting factor were developed. They were time-consuming (taking up to 18 months to work), costly (requiring a factor valued at more than $1 million), and were successful in only about 60% of patients. The need for improved methods to treat bleeding in inhibitor patients persisted.

In 1983, Ulla Hedner, a Swedish physician, published an amazing paper describing the use of FVII isolated from plasma to treat bleeding in a couple of patients with inhibitors to FVIII. Apparently, FVII was activated to FVIIa during the purification process, and the resultant molecule could produce clotting in the absence of FVIII or FIX. Thus, FVIIa might be a reasonable way to prevent bleeding in patients with inhibitors. Unfortunately, FVII is only present in very small amounts and would require processing large amounts of plasma to purify enough for patient treatment.

When the AIDS crisis accelerated the development of recombinant clotting factors, a Danish pharmaceutical company produced recombinant FVIIa. Once it was demonstrated that it could be infused safely without causing thrombosis, it rapidly became a mainstay for treating patients with bleeding disorders. In 1999, "NovoSeven" received FDA approval for treating bleeding in hemophilia patients with inhibitors. This brings us to a patient I followed in the clinic at MCV.

Steven was a 32-year-old engineer, intelligent, well-educated, and well-read. He had a good job, hemophilia, and a high-level inhibitor of FVIII. He developed the inhibitor at age 13, and it rapidly climbed to greater than 30 Bethesda Units, causing him to suffer numerous joint bleeds that were difficult to treat. All options for treatment were suboptimal. Attempts to use porcine (pig) FVIII were unsuccessful because Steven's antibody to human FVIII cross-reacted with porcine FVIII. Factor Eight Inhibitor Bypassing Agent (FEIBA) was somewhat effective but required a higher dose and more extended treatment periods than usually needed.

While in college, the patient read exhaustively regarding his condition. He discussed with me the option of immune tolerance induction (ITI), but he was hesitant to move forward with the attempt until he could get his inhibitor level below 10 Bethesda Units. He had read that the lower the level when the therapy was initiated, the greater the probability of success. He was also aware that his inhibitor level

151

would increase every time his immune system saw FVIII. Since he had read that FEIBA contained low levels of FVIII, he was hesitant to use it for anything less than a massive bleed. Instead, he used immobilization and ice and put up with the pain. Not a very pleasant lifestyle for a young engineer…

Then came the day I was called to the emergency room to see Steven because of a massive left knee bleed that resulted from an attempt at "tubing" behind a boat in a local lake. I was not the first consult called. When I arrived, I found an orthopedic resident who had seen the massively swollen knee and had attempted to evacuate blood from the joint with a needle. While he was able to pull off a syringe full of blood, he had created a hole that was now dripping blood.

I asked the resident if he was aware that this patient had been diagnosed with hemophilia and had a high-level FVIII inhibitor. He said he had seen the diagnosis in the chart. I asked him to step out briefly and informed him that it was not usual practice to put needles into the joints of hemophilia patients, and certainly not hemophilia patients with high-level inhibitors. I suggested that he discuss the topic with one of the excellent attending physicians in the department, who regularly helped us manage the severe joint issues in some of our hemophilia patients. I then returned to the patient.

After putting a pressure bandage on the puncture site and initiating ice therapy, I spoke to the patient and confirmed that he twisted his knee while "tubing." I told him that the X-ray did not show evidence of a fracture but that the knee looked "terrible" and that this episode would not be handled by ice alone. He agreed to treatment with FEIBA, and I admitted him to the hospital. Three days of treatment with FEIBA were unsuccessful in improving the situation.

Although I had not used it before, I decided to try recombinant FVIIa, which had recently received FDA approval. I gave one dose and then, two hours later, a second dose. The oozing from the needle puncture site stopped after the first infusion, and the patient reported that he felt the bleeding had stopped entirely after the second dose. Given the massive nature of the bleed, I administered a third dose to make sure.

Steven was waiting for me the following day when I arrived on rounds. "What was that stuff you used yesterday?"

I provided him with a brief description of NovoSeven and its proposed mechanism of action. He listened quietly and then asked: "Could we use NovoSeven to cover me so I can have my knee replaced?"

It was a great question. This had been Steven's goal for years. He would get his inhibitor level down below 10 Bethesda Units, have the inhibitor eradicated by ITI, and then have his left knee replaced. Did I mention that Steven was an engineer…

There was no doubt that the knee needed to be replaced. He had terrible bone-on-bone arthritis and deformity that limited his ability to walk.

I looked at him and said, "You know, Steven, total knee replacements have not been attempted in patients with inhibitor levels as high as yours—even with NovoSeven. Also, rFVIIa is very expensive, and I would use a lot of it."

He responded, "Dr. Carr, it works great for my bleeding. I want to give this a try."

Steven had an excellent job with good medical insurance, so I said, "Steven, if you can get pre-approval for the knee replacement and associated clotting factor use, I'll talk to the surgeon."

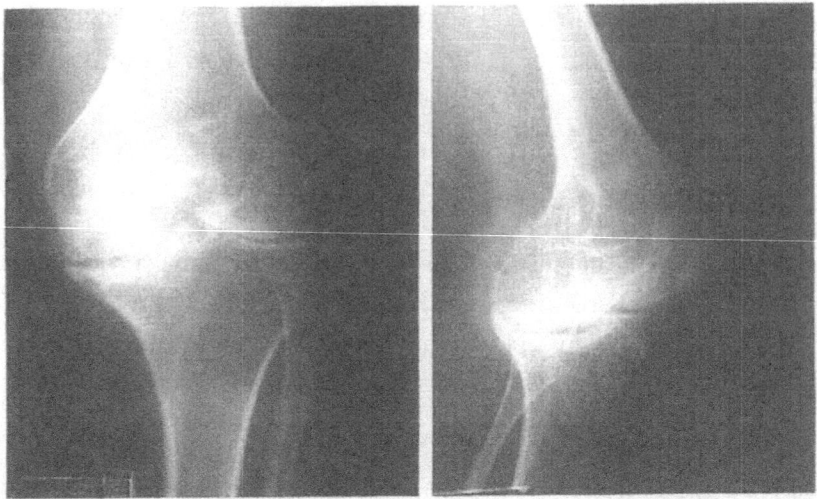

Later that day, I discharged Steven, and two days later, he called to say that he had pre-approval authorization for his left total knee replacement. I could not believe it.

The ball was in my court, so I spoke to Dr. Tom L, who regularly treated our patients' terrible joints. We had a standing agreement—it was my job to control excess bleeding due to hemophilia, and it was his job to perform the surgery. We felt everything went better when everyone did what they were best at. It seems like a simple idea, but it is too often ignored.

I have to say, however, that Tom L was no routine surgeon. He was one of the best orthopedic surgeons I ever knew. In addition, he was not afraid of my bleeding hemophilia patients, nor the fact that most of them were hepatitis C positive, and many were HIV positive. I had great respect for the man.

Dr. L listened to my story and said, "You tell me that you will control excess bleeding from his inhibitor, and I will do your surgery."

I responded, "I will do my best."

He said: "That is good enough for me. Let us get it scheduled."

Well, this was going to be exciting! I read all I could find on the use of rFVIIa in surgery and devised an aggressive plan of every two-hour dosing during the procedure and for the first three days post-procedure. Frequent dosing was necessary due to the short half-life of rFVIIa. The level of rFVIIa would drop by 50% in two hours, and I did not know if less than 50% would be enough. I dosed the patient intravenously with 85μg/Kg of rFVIIa just before surgery, and he was in the hands of the surgeons.

Dr. L had also been reading and decided that speed and expertise would be the best approach. Therefore, the surgery was done by a combination of Dr. L and the chief of orthopedic surgery, Dr. John C. While Tom would routinely complete a total knee replacement in my hemophilia patients in under three hours, this time, it was completed in about an hour and a half.

The surgery itself was relatively bloodless. This is largely due to the placement of a tourniquet above the knee, which restricts blood flow and keeps the surgical field relatively "dry." The fact that the surgery was completed in one and a half hours was remarkable, but it did lead to excitement when the tourniquet was released. I immediately got a call that the bleeding was "marked and diffuse" and had resulted in the re-application of the tourniquet.

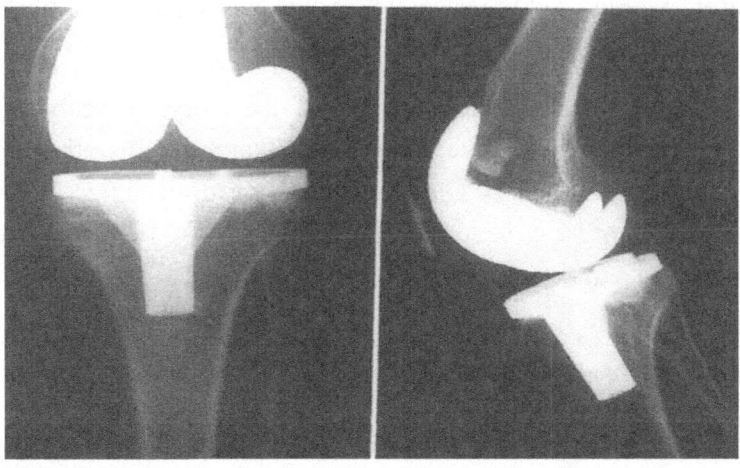

It had been almost two hours since the last rFVIIa dose, so I recommended giving another dose before letting the tourniquet down. Thankfully, this worked.

The post-operative period was remarkably uneventful. He was dosed with rFVIIa every 2 hours for the first 48 hours of the post-operative period. After 48 hours, the infusion interval was increased to every 4 hours for an additional 48 hours. This interval was increased to every 6 hours and continued until he returned to the clinic. He began rather aggressive physical therapy (PT) and suffered one episode of PT-associated bleeding. The bleed responded promptly to a single dose of rFVIIa. By two months, the patient was back at work intermittently using crutches. By four months, he was no longer using crutches, was ambulating much better than before the surgery, and was very satisfied with the results. When I asked if he had any recommendations for improving the process (remember, he is an engineer), he stated that he would have preferred to start the aggressive PT even earlier when the rFVIIa dosing was more frequent. "Knowing the level is up gives me more confidence to push the envelope safely."

Since there was a lack of information regarding the potential use of rFVIIa for major orthopedic surgery in a patient with a high-level inhibitor, we reported the case, which was subsequently published in the International Journal of Hematology.

However, that was not the end of the story. A year after his surgery, Steven asked if we could do the same for his other knee. I smiled at him and said, "Did you know we used almost a million dollars' worth of NovoSeven for the first surgery?" He responded that his insurance had covered it.

"Well, here's the deal…you get prior approval for the surgery, and I'll talk to Dr L.

Three days later came the call. "I have pre-approval!"

The rest of the story ended with his second knee replacement, during which we gave him rFVIIa just before tourniquet removal and started aggressive PT while the patient was still in the hospital. The result was excellent, and we saved almost $250,000 in rFVIIa use over the first surgery.

Most impressively, we changed the life of a 33-year-old engineer who could now walk with virtually a normal gait and no pain. He had not been able to do that for 20 years.

The citation for this published case is as follows:

M.E. Carr, T.P. Loughran, J.A. Cardea, W.K. Smith, J.G. Kuhn, M.V. Dottore. Successful use of recombinant Factor VIIa for haemostasis during total knee replacement in a severe haemophiliac with high titre Factor VIII inhibitor. International Journal of Hematology 75:95-99, 2002.

PHILIPPIANS 2:4 Not looking to your own interests but each of you to the interests of the others.

LUKE 6:31 Do to others as you would have them do to you.

If You Can Prevent Bleeding in Children, Why Not in Adults...?
("You know Dr Carr - No one likes to bleed..."- Terry, AIDS and lessons learned)

Terry was one of my favorite patients. In fact, he was one of the best people I have ever met. He was from Virginia and had severe hemophilia. He was probably in his late thirties when I met him, and he already had the ravages of bleed-induced arthritis. His elbows were basically frozen, and he walked with a significant limp due to advanced, deforming arthritis of his ankles and knees.

I am sure he must have hurt every day when he got out of bed, but he never complained of joint pain. He rarely complained at all, and he always had a fantastic smile. A big smile that seemed to take up more than half his face. He also always seemed to have a little devilish twinkle in his eye. That twinkle always seemed to get even brighter when he was about to tell you a story, and Terry was full of stories.

In addition to terrible arthritis, Terry carried the burden of both hepatitis C and HIV exposure. We were able to control the HIV with a multi-drug regimen of anti-viral medications (HART – Highly Active Retro-viral Therapy), so Terry did not have to worry too much about infections (I think he already had more than his share).

The hepatitis C, which put Terry at risk for cirrhosis and liver cancer, was a much more difficult problem. Our therapies were, to say the least, poor. We initially tried interferon therapy. That just made everyone sick. They had terrible flu symptoms. Your body makes interferon when you have a viral infection like the flu, and many of the symptoms associated with the flu are due to the immune response, including interferon. Now, imagine instead of the normal levels of interferon produced by the body, we give you "industrial strength" doses. The symptoms were terrible. In addition to the acute symptoms after each dose, it became apparent over time that there was a significant risk of inducing severe depression. The therapy would continue for months; ultimately, less than 20% of patients would clear the virus. What a "great" treatment...Terry took it and did not clear the virus.

Later, investigators developed "pegylated" interferon. The addition of polyethylene glycol (PEG) to the interferon molecule extended its half-life, allowing for a reduction in the frequency of injections. The pegylated interferon also appeared to have fewer flu-like symptoms, but it continued to be a "tough" therapy. The result: about 30% could clear the hepatitis C virus...

Subsequently, one of the new antiviral drugs, ribavirin, was added to PEG-interferon, and as a result, up to 45% of patients were able to clear the virus. Still, therapy was challenging, but now, at least, the result approaches the potential of a coin toss...

Terry continued to harbor the hepatitis C virus until the development of HARVONI® (ledipasvir/sofosbuvir). Suddenly, we had an oral medication that would "cure" most patients (>95%) in ten weeks. It was like a miracle, and Terry's hepatitis C was history!

So, where did Terry get all those terrible viruses...? Was he some drug addict or sex fiend? No. We, the physicians taking care of him, gave him these infections...We did not mean to. The viruses were in the clotting factor concentrates we used to treat and prevent his bleeding episodes.

The development of factor concentrates was one of the triumphs of hemophilia therapy. The earliest therapies involved the transfusion of whole blood. When the ability to separate blood into plasma and red cells evolved, simply returning the plasma appeared to be effective. During World War II, the need for plasma to be readily available led to the development of freezing techniques, allowing plasma to be stored until it was needed. The use of fresh-frozen plasma (FFP) led to the observation that precipitation sometimes formed when the plasma was thawed. Additional work revealed that specific proteins precipitated when the plasma was cooled. This material, known as cryoprecipitate, was subsequently found to be rich in clotting factors. Cryoprecipitate rapidly became the new treatment for hemophilic bleeding, allowing treatment with much smaller volumes of these concentrated clotting proteins.

By the 1960s, biochemists had gotten very good at purifying proteins. So, if one could start with a material rich in the proteins one wanted to isolate, one should be able to make a relatively "pure" concentrate of that protein. Thus, plasma-derived concentrates of FVIII and FIX were made and approved by the FDA, and we entered the first "Golden Age" of hemophilia. The hallmark of this period was the realization and subsequent demonstration that one could prevent bleeding by giving clotting factors on a regular basis. Since manufacturers could produce concentrated precipitates of clotting factors, which could be stored and later dissolved when needed, trials soon proved that administering FVIII three times a week could dramatically reduce the number of bleeds. It was also demonstrated that if bleeding to the joints could be stopped, the joints would remain normal.

It was amazing. The curse of spontaneous bleeding could be avoided. Young patients who had not developed arthritis learned to do their infusions and began living much more "normal" lives.

The hint of problems began to appear during the glow of that first golden age. Some of the patients got hepatitis. The diagnosis of hepatitis was still in its infancy. We knew that you could get hepatitis from food – Hepatitis A, and we knew that you could get non-A Hepatitis (OK – "hepatitis B") from close personal (OK – "sexual") contact. Now, we were seeing a new (non-A, non-B) hepatitis in patients who received blood transfusions. This new virus seemed to stay in the blood supply. Since it took 1000 donor samples to make one FVIII vial, virtually every FVIII concentrate was contaminated.

Therefore, almost every hemophilia patient using factor concentrate had been exposed to the virus.

When the magnitude of the problem was realized, steps were taken to identify "clean" donors and to find ways of eliminating the virus from the concentrates if it were to enter. Various filters and solvent/heat treatment of the concentrates were tried. While some viruses could be removed or inactivated, the non-A, non-B (subsequently designated Hepatitis C) virus was amazingly tolerant of these procedures. As a result, the heat-treated products never reached the clinic.

One of the great tragedies of this story was not revealed until a new series of retroviruses emerged in the early 1980s. These new viruses attach to the human T-cell lymphocytes, which are critical for preventing and controlling infections. Initially found primarily in the blood of gay males, they were subsequently found to be rapidly spread via the sharing of needles, so IV drug addicts were also significantly exposed. By the time the concern was raised about potential contamination of the blood supply, the epidemic was already on, and virtually a whole generation of hemophilia patients were exposed to HIV. The subsequent AIDS epidemic was devastating to this group of patients. Virtually every one of these individuals was prescribed their concentrate by their physician. I still carry shared guilt over this terrible time.

The irony was that HIV is sensitive to solvent/heat treatment. If that procedure had been in routine use in the early 1980s, we might have spared hemophilia patients from the AIDS epidemic...

Looking back, I see multiple silver linings from that terrible experience. First, the blood supply has become much safer due to the screening of donors and blood products.

Second, the ability to make recombinant proteins was pushed to the forefront. The ability to isolate and sequence the genes for clotting factors had been developed. Now, the ability to make the proteins by putting the gene into living cells grown in solution allowed the production of pure proteins that had never been in another human. These proteins should be free of human viruses and other small pathogens (even ones we have not yet discovered).

Third, anti-viral medications were developed. Most people do not realize that we had no effective treatments for viral infections in the early 1980s. They did not exist. The only option was to try to prevent viral infections via vaccinations. If you did not have a vaccine, you were in real trouble. That is why public health officials always pushed for 100% vaccination of the population; if you are not vaccinated and you get the disease, treatments are supportive at best.

Out of the AIDS epidemic, the first genuinely effective medications arose, and this occurred at a rapid rate. Building on these initial drugs, newer compounds have been developed with direct antiviral activity. This is one of modern medicine's largely underappreciated miracles.

It is a good thing that the new anti-viral drugs were developed so quickly and proved to be effective because, despite the ongoing efforts of lots of very bright people, we still do not have an effective vaccination for HIV.

Sorry for the prolonged digression from Terry's story, but this is, to a large degree, the life he led.

So, Terry survived the AIDS crisis, and his HIV status was stable on medications. The recombinant clotting factor developed during that time quickly dominated the clotting factor market in the United States. Many treating physicians were just as traumatized by the events as were the surviving patients. Although significant strides were made in the purification and viral deactivation of plasma-derived concentrates, for a considerable time, many healthcare providers were hesitant to take a chance on the next unknown pathogen.

All the new "safe" products ushered in a new golden age of hemophilia treatment. Prophylaxis became the standard of care for younger patients. During the initial part of this new "era," younger patients were rapidly converted to prophylaxis, and older patients remained on "on-demand" therapy. On-demand therapy meant that they only used factors when they thought that they were having a bleed.

There were several reasons why the older patients were on this route. Some did not want to stick themselves if they were not bleeding. Some were concerned about exceeding their lifetime cap of factor payments. At the time, some insurance plans determined the amount they would pay in factor reimbursement over the patient's lifespan. By treating less, hemophilia patients with this type of coverage felt they were "saving factor." However, the main reason physicians did not push hard for adult prophylaxis was that data showed that if a patient had already experienced several bleeds into a joint, the ability of prophylaxis to slow or prevent arthritis was likely compromised. If this were the case, since most severe adult hemophilia patients had already bled into their joints, the great "preventive" benefit of prophylaxis was felt to be lost.

Terry was a worker and was very much engaged in the hemophilia community. He typically worked for companies delivering supplies, services, and products utilized by patients with hemophilia. His personality, ease with the public, and obvious knowledge of and experience with hemophilia made him a "natural." Since the hemophilia community – comprising patients, family members, physicians, other healthcare professionals, product suppliers, researchers, and pharmaceutical companies – is relatively small and tight-knit, I often saw Terry at hemophilia-related meetings. He never failed to shout my name when he saw me; it was always great to see him. He also frequently came to hear me speak on various topics, such as prophylaxis.

One day in the clinic, he was more reserved and quieter than usual. Finally, he asked me, " Why don't you recommend prophylaxis for older adults like me?"

I was a little surprised by the question, but I went through my usual spiel about how most of the benefit was lost due to the existing damage.

He responded, "Are you saying that prophylaxis will not prevent bleeding in me because my joints are already bad?"

"Well, I'm not saying that…I'm just saying that the benefit might not be as great…"

He responded, "You know, doc…no one likes to bleed."

The truth and clarity of his statement were undeniable.

Instead of another canned response, I said, "Terry, let's look at how often you infuse and how much factor you use."

Sure enough, he was using enough factor on demand that putting him on a standard prophylaxis dose three times per week would not increase his factor use. So, that is what we did.

In two months, Terry returned and reported minimal bleeding and that his knees felt better than they had in years. He was delighted. I was very humbled. Why had I not thought of that before? Well, at least I listened.

MATTHEW 7:12 So in everything, do to others what you would have them do to you, for this sums up the Law and the Prophets.

JUDE 1:23 Save others by snatching them from the fire.

VI. MILITARY MEDICINE
OPERATION DESERT STORM
(LANDSTUHL ARMY MEDICAL CENTER)

I wanted to be in the desert, but I ended up in Germany when the 56th Station Hospital was activated. The 56th had a lot of remarkable reserve soldiers, but unfortunately, much of its full-time staff was not very good. In fact, some were terrible. So, when the great mobilization for Desert Shield and Storm occurred, the 56th, as a unit, was found wanting, and this led to only some of the personnel being deployed, while many had to spend time in the States doing backfill for those sent downrange. In this aspect, I was lucky. I accompanied approximately 150 56th unit members to Germany. When we arrived in late January of 1991, we were sent to army hospitals all over Germany. The evening we arrived at the Replacement Company in Frankfurt, Germany, I was asked where I wanted to be. I said, "Send me to the busiest place you have because I do not sit around well." I had assignment orders to Landstuhl Army Medical Center (LARMC) within minutes. Upon arrival, I became a member of the Medical Service and was assigned to the Burn Unit. The following are stories from that period, specifically the first half of 1991.

Just give me a minute to pray
(without fingers, you use a Ouija board)

When I joined the 56th Station Hospital in 1987, it had never been activated (called to active duty). That all changed when Saddam Hussein decided to annex Province 13, otherwise known as Kuwait, in 1990. I knew when I heard the tanks were in Kuwait City that this was going to be a war involving the United States, and I was right. Perhaps because the 56th Station Hospital was one of the poorest-run operations in all of the reserves, we did not get activated until December of 1991, less than a month before the start of the ground war.

It may seem strange, but once you are activated, most people want to go where the action is. I certainly did, but it was not to be. The 56th, with over 400 personnel, was mobilized to Fort Eustis for in-processing before deployment. We had been there for four days when the air war started. Suddenly, we were called into formation, and a list of names was read. One hundred and forty of the four hundred would catch a plane in six hours for Europe, and the rest would remain at Fort Eustis to await orders for stateside deployment. I was in the 140 who were going. I still remember seeing the looks in the eyes of those who did not get on the buses that night. No one wanted to be left behind.

Within a few hours, we slept on cots at Andrews Air Force Base, awaiting transportation to our destination. For the first time, we were informed of our destination. We were headed to Europe, where most of us would work in hospitals in Germany. This disappointed those of us who wanted to go to the desert.

When we got to the receiving station at Frankfurt, the people asked me where I wanted to go in Germany. I replied that I wanted to go where I would be busy. They had an immediate response. "You're going to Landstuhl." LARMC – Landstuhl Army Regional Medical

Center – was the largest US military medical facility in Europe and would serve as the primary Corps support medical facility for the war. If I were not going to be in the war, at least I would help take care of those who were.

At Landstuhl, I was assigned to the newly evolving Burn Center. Before the war, there was no burn center at Landstuhl. That all quickly changed. The Germans came in and put in several miles of new wiring in a week, and the former labor and delivery and neonatal intensive care unit became the LARMC burn unit. It had three small operative suites and 38 monitored beds for burns. During Operations Desert Shield and Storm, the LARMC burn unit was the largest in the world - larger even than the Brooke Army Medical Center (BAMC) burn center. I was assigned as an internist in the Burn Center, where I met many extraordinary people.

It takes eight people to care for one burn patient. Our burn unit was never full during the war, which was good. Thirty-eight (beds) times eight is a large number. Undoubtedly, more significant than the number of staff we had in the burn center. We once had up to fourteen patients and were plenty busy.

Perhaps the burn patient I remember most was a tanker I helped care for during the early stages of the ground war. To understand his injuries, you need to know a little about the new tanks and the personnel working there. The first bit of information is not new. The way people die in tanks is still pretty much the same as the way they died in the early tanks. They either die from the blast when the tank is hit, or they burn up when the fuel in the tank catches on fire. Since fire is such a problem, tankers wear burn suits. These suits should protect them long enough to allow them to escape from the tank. There is a suit, a hood, and gloves. Even though the Abrams M1A1 tank is air-conditioned, it still gets hot in the desert heat. Therefore, the tankers take off that hood because it makes them even hotter. The Abrams tank is also high-tech equipment, featuring numerous dials and switches. The gloves impede functioning, and so they come off as well. The remainder of the suit is typically left on. So, when the tank gets hit and catches on fire, the soldier suffers severe hand and head burns.

I helped take care of one such patient. He was 19 years old when I first saw him. I was struck by how much his head looked like a bowling ball. It was black from the burns and round from the edema. His hair, most of his eyebrows, and a lot of his ears were also burned away. His hands were also severely burned, and he was left with only the proximal digits of each finger. He had also suffered significant pulmonary injuries and had been intubated in theater to protect his airway. He had been shipped quickly, so he arrived in our unit within 48 hours of his injury. He was on antibiotics, and cultures were pending. He had received a lot of intravenous fluids but nothing of nutritional value since his injury. He could not eat, there was no feeding tube, and intravenous hyperalimentation had not been started. This is not surprising since he had spent much of his time in acute care facilities or evacuation aircraft.

A check of the culture results revealed the growing organism was resistant to his antibiotic. Within six hours of switching to Augmentin, he was afebrile. The pulmonary docs came in and performed a bronchoscopy to assess the status of his upper airways. The chest x-ray was normal (no pneumonia or apparent inhalation injury). His blood gases were good on room air. If he did not have significant erythema or swelling in his upper airways, he could be extubated, making him much more comfortable and allowing his GI tract to be used for nutritional support (i.e., we could feed him).

The bronchoscopy was quick and went well. I was left with the instruction to extubate the patient. This all sounded good to me, but when I went to tell the patient we would remove the tube, he suddenly became somewhat agitated. Since he could not talk, the nurses had rigged up a board with letters resembling a Ouija board. By attaching a wand or stick to the patient's forearm, he could point to the letters, spell out words, and thus communicate. In the corners were the words "yes" and "no," which sped up the process of answering questions and removed any doubt about his intent. I called the nurse and asked that she bring the board.

While the nurse was getting the spelling board, I once again went over what we were going to do – deflate the balloon on the trach tube and then quickly pull it out of his throat. I emphasized that this was a good thing and that the bronchoscopy indicated that it was safe and appropriate to do at the time. He was utterly focused on me as I spoke. His pupils were slightly dilated, but when the board arrived and I asked him if he understood, he pointed to yes. Then, he began to spell something out. I followed closely and repeated his words to ensure I had it right. With great determination, he spelled out –GIVE ME A MOMENT TO PRAY… So, I did. And I said a little prayer, too. I am sure to that young soldier, that tube was one of the things that had kept him alive, and he wanted all the help he could get if he was giving it up. When he opened his eyes, he nodded that he was ready. I let the balloon down and pulled the tube out. Within half an hour, he had had his first drink of water and was trying to talk.

Due to the ten-day evacuation policy, we had ten days to return the soldier to duty, or he would be sent to the States. This young soldier was going to need months of therapy and recovery time. So, he was put on a plane, and I never saw him again. Unfortunately, this was the case with virtually all our patients. A year later, I did see this young guy on TV. It was the anniversary of the end of the ground war, and they were interviewing this young soldier who had been wounded during the war. It was my guy. They had done an excellent job of skin grafting and restoration of his eyebrows and ears. Although he would never be the same, he seemed to have a very positive attitude. I was probably one of the few watching the TV who knew for sure from what well that young man was drawing his strength. God had kept him in the palm of his hand, and I prayed that God would make his life as complete as possible and more blessed than most.

PSALMS 5:11 But let all who take refuge in you be glad; let them ever sing for joy. Spread your protection over them, that those who love your name may rejoice in you.

1 KINGS 8:28 Yet give attention to your servant's prayer and his plea for mercy, Lord my God. Hear the cry and the prayer that your servant is praying in your presence this day.

2 CHRONICLES 6:19 Yet, Lord my God, give attention to your servant's prayer and his plea for mercy. Hear the cry and the prayer that your servant is praying in your presence.

EXODUS 21:13 However, if it is not done intentionally, but God lets it happen, they are to flee to a place I will designate.

What was the cause of this polyuria?
(Trash burns and an urge to pee)

During Operation Desert Storm, I was activated with the 56th Station Hospital. I was deployed to Landstuhl Army Regional Medical Center (LARMC), the primary Medical Corps support facility for the conflict. I was assigned to the burn unit. We had three Internists, two plastic surgeons, a general surgeon, some wonderful nurses, and many support personnel. Before Desert Storm, there was no burn center at LARMC. In preparation for the conflict, labor and delivery and the neonatal intensive care unit were closed and transformed into the Burn Center. The patients were assigned physicians in the German healthcare system (they were put out to bid on the economy), and the Germans came in and installed four miles of new electrical wiring in about two weeks. Suddenly, LARMC had the largest burn unit in the world. We had 38 monitored beds for burn patients and two operatory suites in the unit.

During the early Desert Shield part of the conflict, we never got more than four patients at a time. This was beneficial because caring for one burn patient requires the assistance of eight people. We would have been overwhelmed if we had ever had 38 patients. We were well-staffed, but you do the math. When one of Saddam's SCUD missiles hit a Reserve Unit from Pennsylvania deployed to northern Saudi Arabia, we were sure we would get some burn patients. However, all died in the theater from their wounds and burns, and we did not get to help. We did get a steady string of trash burns and tanker injuries. The episode I will talk about now involved the former.

Trash burns occur when people burn trash. In the army, it is not trash; it is human excrement. I am sure many people have seen the film clips of Vietnam with the black smoke billowing up in the background. Well, a lot of that smoke was burning excrement. Many latrines are above ground, with seats positioned over tubs where the excrement is collected. The tubs are typically large oil drums cut in half, allowing for a wide opening that enables them to slide easily under the seats. When they get full, someone pulls the tub out, pours diesel fuel on the contents, and sets it on fire. This job is unpleasant and is routinely given to people who have not been performing well or have committed some infraction. These individuals are not at the top of the pecking order for multiple reasons.

Typically, the diesel fuel comes in five-gallon tanks. Things go well initially, but things can drift off course when the tank gets dry. Soldiers should receive more diesel fuel, but they may settle for whatever is closest if they are somewhat lazy. Unfortunately, sometimes, this is gasoline (MOGAS). If you have ever tried to start a fire with diesel fuel, you will realize that it requires effort to get it started. That is not true with gasoline. Remember, you can make bombs with gasoline (the Molotov Cocktail, for example). So, the soldier comes back and begins to pour on the gasoline, and it either spontaneously ignites from the smoldering remains of the previous fire or explodes in their face when they throw in the match. This has been happening for years, and it occurred during Desert Storm. The burns are always the same, involving primarily the face and hands.

I cared for several such patients in Germany, but one stood out. He had been stationed in Germany when his armor unit had been deployed to Saudi Arabia for Desert Storm. The evacuation policy for LARMC during the conflict was to hold no patients for more than seven days. If we could return them to duty in seven days, they would return to Saudi Arabia. If we could not, they went to the States. No burn patient will return to duty in seven days, so the decision was made not to perform skin grafting in Germany. This was later modified to allow us to graft patients who came from Germany. We took care of them, and then they went to their prior station in Germany.

This staff sergeant had a trash burn and underwent skin grafting in Germany. His story was a little different in that he was trying to help one of his troops with the foul duty when the accident happened.

The situation was made worse because aviation fuel was used instead of gasoline in many instances. That stuff burns with a clear flame (remember the burning Indianapolis 500 drivers who do not appear to be on fire because the flames are not visible) and is more explosive than gasoline (remember 9/11). He had suffered burns to his face, hands, and forearms.

Since the Sergeant was from Germany, his grafts were placed at Landstuhl. He had his forearms wrapped in bandages to keep the grafts from lifting off due to swelling. He also had both arms held up in a traction device to reduce dependent edema (swelling). The reason I remember him so well is that, for the first three days after his skin grafts, every time I went to see him, he had to pee. I began to wonder about the cause of this polyuria. We were giving him a significant amount of fluid because of his burns, but his electrolytes were OK. However, I could count on it. The response was always the same whenever I asked if he needed anything – "I need to pee." On the third day, it occurred to me. I was the only male involved in his care. He had many wonderful nurses and aides, but all were female. With his hands held up in the air, he could not use the urinal by himself. He was too embarrassed (or shy) to ask for the help of one of the females, so he held it until I came in. Finally, I figured it out and arranged for a male orderly to intermittently check on the patient when I was unavailable.

Sometimes, we become so engrossed in the numbers that we overlook the obvious. I did for three days. I do not think that grizzly old soldier would have ever told me what was happening, but he certainly taught (or re-taught) me a lesson I have tried not to forget.

I forgot to mention that his wife was also in the military and was deployed to the desert while he was in the burn unit. There are many reasons I love soldiers.

PSALMS 72:12 For he will deliver the needy who cry out, the afflicted who have no one to help.

173

JOB 36:15 But those who suffer he delivers in their suffering; he speaks to them in their affliction.

Headaches and Drug Abuse?
(A little case of reserve abuse)

During the early part of my deployment to LARMC, there were so many reservists at Landstuhl that it was difficult to notice any differentiation between the active and reserve components. Everyone was pretty much treated equally. Immediately after the ground war, some units started to return to the US. Since we were one of the last units to arrive, we were also one of the last to leave. First, we had to take care of all the patients from the war. No problem, everyone wanted to do that. Then, we were told that we had to wait for everyone who had deployed to the theater to return to Germany. Again, this was entirely reasonable. Next, we had to work our way through the backlog of patients (primarily dependents and retired personnel) who had been waiting to be seen. This requirement was less clear, as many of the backlogs had existed even before Saddam attacked Kuwait. However, no problem. Reservists are accustomed to the real world, and we rapidly processed the entire backlog within two weeks. At that point, the last of the large units left for home. We had gone through March and April and were now entering May. Next, we could not leave until all personnel stationed in Germany had had a chance to take some time off, as all leave had been canceled following the Kuwait invasion. Hey, now, wait a minute. Why was that my job? When I got home, I wasn't going on leave; I was returning to a job that would put me more than a year behind.

As we got into May, I began to get a few "coded" messages from friends that we would be leaving soon. I went to my service chief and said they needed to start looking at the call schedule because I might be leaving soon.

"We will look at the call schedule when you have the tail number on your plane." This meant that nothing would change until everything was in concrete. The tail number on your plane indicated that you had a seat on a flight departing on a specific day. Until I had that, no changes would be made. On May 7th, I received the final confirmation and returned to say that I would be leaving. The response was to change the call schedule, so I was on the following six nights in a row. This was done so I could get all my call done for the month before I left. This is not the response I had been expecting, but at that point, my response was: "OK, your ballgame and your ball, but I'll be gone soon."

As it was, being on call made the time pass more quickly. I thought I was through when my beeper went off at 0630 on my last call night. I was to turn the beeper in at 0700 and be finished except for out-processing. Should I call them back? Maybe I should wait and have them call me again. If they really wanted me, they would call twice. Maybe by the second time, I would not have the beeper.

I looked at the number – the emergency room. There is no choice there. I called, and the story began as follows:

"We got this young airman here who is unresponsive."

My response was, "Sounds like a neurological problem to me."

"We called them twice with no response before we called you."

"How long has he been in the ER, and what do you think is going on?"

"He's been here about an hour and a half, and we think it's a probable overdose."

With resignation in my voice, "I'll be there in ten minutes."

When I entered the ER, almost everyone was around the nurses' station getting ready for staff shift change. I looked around for my young airman and found him on a table in the middle of a large trauma room. The only person in the room was a young specialist who was as far away from the patient as possible. I asked, "What's the story here?"

"I don't know, sir. I just got here."

176

There was a chart in the room, and the story went as follows. The airman had been seen in the Ramstein Air Force Base clinic at about 10:00 the night before. He complained of a bad headache and had a low-grade fever. He had no other complaints, so he was given some Tylenol and told to go to his quarters to see if the headache would ease. He was instructed to return if he worsened. His roommate had been out for the evening and returned at about 0300 to find our airman crawling around the room on his hands and knees. He was conscious but disoriented and complaining that his head hurt. His roommate took him back to the clinic, who decided to ship him to the LARMC ER. Upon his arrival, it was felt that he must be suffering from a drug overdose. He was given charcoal, and blood was sent for toxin screening; then, they called the neurologist. We later discovered that the neurology service had changed its call schedule without notifying anyone of the changes. That's a great idea. It must have significantly reduced the number of calls. When neurology did not respond, the ER called me, and here I was.

The young fellow was unresponsive to verbal stimuli but did respond to pain. He was pale and had black stuff running out of the corner of his mouth and onto his gown. He was hot to the touch. His neck was stiff, and his pupils were sluggishly reactive. This was not a drug overdose. I had seen this before. This was meningitis, and worse yet, it was meningococcemia.

I turned to the specialist. "Get me an IV set and some D5-half Normal saline. And get me some penicillin." As I put in the IV, I drew blood for a CBC, serum electrolytes, and one blood culture.

The specialist returned: "We don't have any penicillin."

"Get me the chief nurse."

"Yes, sir, what is the problem?"

"I think this airman has meningococcemia, and if he does not receive antibiotics in the next few minutes, he is going to die. He may

177

die anyway. Will you please get me some penicillin and bring it directly to me…and, on your way out, will you tell those people who are trying to leave that they will need to stay and be given prophylactic treatment for potential exposure to meningococcemia."

"Yes, Sir."

She returned with the penicillin within five minutes, and I pushed it. In the interim, I had continued my examination. Examination of his eyes revealed what I thought was papilledema. I had only seen it a few times, but I was pretty sure. This is a sign of increased intracranial pressure and makes a spinal tap risky. If the pressure is high inside the head and you put a hole in the sack around the spinal cord, spinal fluid under pressure will rapidly squirt out. The sudden decrease in the pressure around the spinal cord will cause the contents of the skull, which are still under high pressure, to try to "flow" out of the small hole at the base of the skull. This is called herniation. Of course, the brain is not liquid and cannot flow through the hole. It is solid and too big to fit through the hole. The brainstem is the part of the brain that is pushed into the hole. This structure regulates many critical, life-preserving functions, such as breathing. If there is pressure on the brain stem, breathing and multiple other critical activities stop. Brain herniation is thus a lethal event. Therefore, increased intracranial pressure is a contraindication to lumbar puncture.

This was a problem. I needed the spinal fluid to confirm the diagnosis and to isolate the organism. Perhaps a CT scan would help. I called radiology, and they said to roll the patient down for the scan. I called the ICU, where I had spent significant time caring for neurosurgery patients, and informed them that I was bringing a patient. As soon as the scan was done, we rolled to the ICU. By now, the labs were coming in and were not good. Sodium was low at 122, platelet count was less than one hundred thousand, PTT was prolonged by 15 seconds, and the white cell count was 23,000. Things did not look good. The patient's respirations were becoming more labored, so I decided to go ahead and place an endotracheal tube.

When we suctioned after tube placement, we got charcoal. Not only did the patient have meningitis, but he also probably had pneumonia secondary to aspiration of charcoal administered in the ER.

The neurologist, who had previously been unavailable, now appeared and stated that the call schedule had been changed without providing appropriate notification to all involved. Well, I guess someone got a good night's sleep. I showed him the CT scan, and he agreed there was probably evidence of increased pressure. He advised against an LP.

How was I going to confirm the diagnosis? I had only sent one blood culture before antibiotics. Pediatricians see this diagnosis more commonly than internists, so I called our "combat pediatrician" and asked about alternative ways of confirming the diagnosis. He suggested that we look for meningococcal antigens in the urine. The laboratory agreed to perform the test, but the result was negative.

By the next day, things began to look up. The fever fell, the white count started down, the DIC abated, and people began to question my diagnosis. "Patients with meningococcemia don't do this well; they die."

On day three, the one blood culture I had obtained grew meningococcus.

For Desert Storm, the military had gotten in the habit of flying 1st-degree relatives of severely injured or sick military personnel to Landstuhl to allow them to be close at a time when the patients were too critically ill to ship back to the States. The Air Force had called the airman's parents and helped arrange a rapid flight to Germany. They arrived on day three. The patient's father was a very bright engineer and had immediately gathered all the information he could find to read on the flight over. Based on his reading, he was sure that his son would be dead or dying by the time he got to his bedside. He was in for a surprise. His son was not dead. His son was not dying. His son was getting better.

When I met this gentleman for the first time, he said. "So, you are the one."

"Excuse me, the one what?"

"You're the guy in the ER who knew what was going on. You're the guy that saved my son's life."

"I saw your son and have been working with him, but many people have helped him get better."

"Well, I just want to get your name and address and let you know that his mother and I will always be grateful for what you have done."

A few days later, I was on a plane, heading home, still taking rifampin as prophylaxis for potential meningococcemia exposure. I had been given a "LARMC Commander's Coin" by the DCCS (Deputy Commander for Clinical Services – AKA Top Doc) at a final reserve briefing. It was very nice, but it did not compare to the letter I received from the airman's father a few months later, letting me know that his son was doing well and had just PCSed (permanent change of station – i.e., moved) to Japan.

Now, I had seen two cases of this relatively rare illness, and both had survived. In both cases, I was in places at times when I was not supposed to be there. If you think the reason I was held back in Germany, and the reason my call schedule was changed, and the reason the neurologist's call schedule was altered, was all just a series of fortunate unrelated events, then I would beg to differ. I don't believe it for a minute.

ISAIAH 55:8-9 For my thoughts are not your thoughts, neither are your ways my ways," declares the Lord. "As the heavens are higher than the earth, so are my ways higher than your ways and my thoughts than your thoughts.

1 CORINTHIANS 12:29 Are all apostles? Are all prophets? Are all teachers? Do all work miracles?

PSALMS 77:14 You are the God who performs miracles; you display your power among the peoples.

Head Trauma and Long-Distance MEDEVAC
(A Soldier, A Marine, and a missing ambulance)

Once the ground war was over, which occurred quickly after it started, it was apparent we would no longer need the burn unit. The downsizing began as we cleared the last few patients out, and the staff were reassigned to new duties. At that time, all the reservists were still at Landstuhl, so there was more than enough staff to staff the hospital, and it gradually returned to 300 beds from its peak of a thousand. My boss approached me one afternoon and said I would be temporarily assigned to the Baumholder clinic. I had been there once to cover the staff for a weekend. It was not a bad place, but it was certainly not a hub of activity and was not close to anything.

I asked how long "temporary" would be and was told a "few weeks...not more than a couple of months..." Well, that did not sit well with me. I did not want to spend two months by myself doing well-baby checks and pelvic exams far away from the rest of my unit. I was hoping to be home in a few months, and I was very concerned that the crew who served as our "full-time" support in the 56th Station Hospital would forget about me and leave me in Germany when the unit returned home. In the reserves, the term "no man left behind" does not always hold...

I did not mind working in the medicine clinic, inpatient ward, or intensive care units, but I did not want to be a family practice doctor. Many people loved that job and were, frankly, better at it than I was.

I attempted to make this point in a controlled manner the first time the "new job opportunity" was discussed, but I was unsuccessful in convincing him that he needed to make another choice.

He subsequently caught me in one of the long halls of Landstuhl Hospital to tell me I would be going to Baumholder. This time, I was much more animated in my protest and slapped the wall with my raised and open left hand. This made a rather loud noise that echoed down the hall. The commotion caught the attention of the Chief of Neurosurgery, who also served as the Surgery Department Chair, who happened to be walking past.

Several surgeons had served with me in the burn unit. One of them was in charge of surgery grand rounds and asked me if I would repeat a lecture that I had given to the Burn Unit staff for surgery grand rounds. That went well, and the Chief asked if I would provide a series of clotting lectures/updates to the weekly Surgery Breakfast meeting. As a result, I got several better-than-average breakfasts and got to know the Chief reasonably well.

About thirty minutes after the hallway explosion, the phone rang as I sat fuming in my office. It was the Neurosurgery Chief. He asked me what had been going on in the hallway. I told him they were sending me to the Baumholder clinic and that I did not want to go.

"Would you like to come work for me in the Neurosurgery ICU?" he asked.

"Why, yes, Sir, I would!" was my enthusiastic response.

"I'll take care of it," he said, his complete response ending the phone call.

Later that afternoon, my boss told me I would be temporarily assigned as the medical officer in the neurosurgery intensive care unit. I thanked him for this change of plans. Neither of us mentioned that the Chief of Surgery had played a role in the new assignment.

In the intensive care unit, I managed abnormal laboratory values, ventilator changes, antibiotic coverage, and other routine "medical" functions for the patients as they were stabilized, began their recovery from surgery, and were prepared for evacuation back to the US. Since I was the most "expendable" team member, I got to accompany multiple patients on the long flight home to the US.

This was my first experience with a long-distance evacuation, and I learned a great deal. First, you take a lot of stuff with you when you move an intensive care patient. Each patient must have a supply of seven days' worth of medication and medical supplies, including all necessary bandage changes and intravenous fluids. Second, at that time, at least, the Air Force would not fly a severely wounded soldier without an Army doctor on board to care for the patient during the flight. This sets the stage for this story.

Soon after I arrived in the neurosurgery intensive care unit, the chief approached me about moving two patients back to the States.

SGT Kevin J was a 29-year-old Marine with a completely smashed face. He was the assistant driver on a truck equipped with a spring-assisted load-lifting device on the back. The lifting device became partially buried in the sand. When triggered, it did not rise. The SGT went to check. The device released unexpectedly, striking Kevin full in the face. His left orbit, the bone around the left eye, was destroyed, and the left globe (eye) ruptured. His frontal sinuses were crushed and driven backward into the frontal lobes of his brain. His right eye was intact, but the floor of the orbit was destroyed, damaging the optic nerve. The cribriform plate (a bone located between the eyes) was destroyed. His palate (the roof of his mouth) was crushed, and most of his teeth were dislodged. The bony structure of his nose was destroyed. The maxillary sinuses (located on each side of his nose) and mandible (jawbone) were also destroyed. The injury occurred on

5 March, and therapy had consisted of wiring his lower face, tracheostomy to ease breathing, debridement (removal of dead tissue) from his frontal lobes, removal of his frontal sinuses, enucleation (removal) of the left globe with some bony stabilization. Packs were in place for the central face. Definitive repair of the bony central face would be performed at Bethesda Naval Hospital, and the packs would be left in place until transfer.

The other patient, John K, was an Army infantry soldier. He was also injured on 5 March with Shrapnel wounds to both sides of his brain. The wound on the right entered above his right eye and tracked across his brain from front to back. The wound on the left entered above his left eye, moved through his brain from front to back, struck the posterior skull, and tracked back into his left brain. He was initially treated with fragment removal, debridement of his brain, and removal of the frontal sinuses. His repair was revised at Landstuhl when a cerebrospinal fluid (CSF) leak was noted at the left frontal wound.

Kevin remained comatose with spontaneous movements (purposeful) of all limbs. He would feel his face, pull at lines, and scratch. John had dense paralysis of his right arm and minimal movement in response to pain in his right leg. He had spontaneous, random movements of his left leg and arm. Kevin was thought to be blind with a minimal pupil response to light.

As the day drew on, our departure time was steadily pushed backward. We finally departed Landstuhl via ambulance at 1955 hours for a planeside load at Ramstein Airbase. Kevin's wife and mother flew back on the plane with us. I had been working with them for two days before our departure, and we had a good rapport by the time we left. His mother told me on the plane, "We've been talking it over, and we're so glad that you are going with Kevin on the plane. I'd been dreading this trip, but your bedside manner, your human touch, gave me the confidence that we could make it."

The plane ride on the 141 was as bad as advertised – cold and loud, even with earplugs, and lasted 9 and 1/2 hours. The front part of the plane had a few rows of seats for patients who could sit up. The rear portion of the aircraft was for litter patients, who were stacked four high. This left only limited space to examine and work with each patient. There was also concern about controlling patient temperature. The heat was located at the top. Patients who were not closely monitored could "cook" in the top berth. In contrast, a patient on the bottom could become hypothermic. These are the things you learn by experience. The docs and family members sat on the sides of the plane facing the litter patients.

Both my patients lost their IVs within an hour of takeoff. Restarting an IV in flight is a real experience. I got a new one in Kevin's hand, which lasted 4 hours – long enough to administer his antibiotics, including chloramphenicol and oxacillin, his Dilantin, and his morphine sulfate. Since he was continuously moving, I had to hold his hand for most of the four hours that the IV functioned. I improvised an arm board from IV bags and cardboard, which worked while he slept. However, he tried to pull it off each time he began to awaken.

John lost his IV several times, and getting yet another angiocath in was not going to be easy. That's when a pediatrician stepped in to help. He was on board escorting an infant whom he had recently diagnosed with a brain tumor. He offered a 23-gauge butterfly catheter that I slipped into one of John's hand veins and nursed along for a couple of hours.

A third patient from Landstuhl, a Kuwaiti resistance leader injured in an assassination attempt, was cared for by an Air Force Doc. The Kuwaiti General was shot in the back with a pistol equipped with a silencer. He suffered thoracic and spinal injuries, and although he was medically stable, he was permanently paraplegic.

I had the two most severely injured patients on the plane, and the pilot made sure that the crew came to me on several occasions to assure me that my ambulances would be waiting for us at Andrews Air Force Base. I needed two ambulances: one to transport Kevin to the Naval Hospital and another to transport John to Walter Reed.

Upon arrival at Andrews, Kevin was loaded onto his ambulance and headed to Bethesda. The Navy had sent a doctor along so I could take John to Reed. John and I were loaded into the other waiting ambulance, headed (I thought) to Walter Reed. Instead, we were taken to a holding facility in a hangar. It was 0200 and cold, and we were assured on three separate occasions – the last at landing – that we had a direct ambulance to Walter Reed. I was disgusted and angry that my patient, taken directly from an intensive care unit, was now forced to lie openly in a "barn." Unfortunately, John's supplies had been loaded on another ambulance that had left for Reed.

The staff at Andrew's was not at fault and was clearly unprepared to care for sick/unstable patients in a hangar. All the other patients in the hangar were sitting up, talking, and eating donuts. John was comatose on a cot covered with a wool blanket. I asked the staff if any dividers were available that I could use to cut the draft and offer John a little privacy. The Air Force personnel jumped in to help once I started asking for things. Since John had lost his IV and had missed his midnight antibiotics, I started a new IV and ran in his chloramphenicol and ceftriaxone. He had spiked a temperature to 102

187

degrees, which I treated with a Tylenol suppository. I made a slurry of Dilantin (which does not dissolve readily in water), unclogged his NG tube, and administered Dilantin orally. By now, the Air Force Docs were impressed by John's acute problems. After about 20 minutes, an Air Force LTC walked in and asked why I was treating an acutely ill patient in his hangar. I told him someone had taken my patient's ambulance, and to this point, it had not returned or been replaced. He said he would solve my problem. Since Reed still had not dispatched an ambulance, the Air Force provided one. John grabbed my hand as we rode to Reed and would not let go. Before this time, his movements had continued to be almost entirely random. I wondered if the continuous one-on-one contact for > 24 hours had not established some link. The EMT in the ambulance certainly noticed the attachment and asked if I had been with John since Saudi Arabia. Perhaps John was beginning to wake up and recognized me as his advocate or friend. I certainly seemed to be the one on his side all day. Upon arrival at Walter Reed, the ER personnel knew nothing of John. A few calls later, we found he would be a direct admission to ward 58. We found our way up, put John to bed, and I checked out with the nurses.

I was later told, although I could never confirm, that there had been a phone call to the Air Force from someone very high in the Joint Chiefs of Staff that the Army ambulance sitting at Andrews was to be used to bring the Kuwaiti General to Reed. Unfortunately, the ambulance that was supposed to pick John up had mechanical problems. God bless the Air Force for addressing the issue.

I mentioned that Kevin's parents were in Germany and on the plane flying back to the States. This was possible because the ground war had been short, efficient, and relatively one-sided. The number of severely wounded personnel was much lower than anticipated. Given the situation, the military decided that they would fly family members of severely injured soldiers to Germany to allow them to be with their service members earlier in their recovery. Since there would also be room on the plane, some were allowed to accompany them back to the States when evacuated. This seemed like a good idea. I did notice, however, that it was challenging for some of the parents. The war had been an enormous success. We had won…and no one got hurt…well, that seemed to be the general opinion of most. Unfortunately, this was, of course, not true. Because relatively few were killed or severely wounded, it seemed somehow "unfair" to these parents that their child had been "singled out." It was like some terrible twist of fate had reached out and touched just their family…When looking into a mother's or father's eyes, a doctor's assurances that "we will do everything possible to improve your son's prospects for recovery" … seem to fall short…

I have often considered that flight to the States and the night we landed. While I cannot speak to why God might not have prevented his injury, I can say that God put his hand on John in that hangar to ensure that he got where he needed to be.

I got back on a plane and flew back to Germany, and I never saw John or Kevin again.

ECCLESIASTES 3:1 There is a time for everything, and a season for every activity under the heavens.

ROMANS 8:28 And we know that in all things God works for the good of those who love him, who have been called according to his purpose.

Cold Nights, Alcohol Lamps, and a Terrible Burn
(Why are poncho liners flammable?)

The war to liberate Kuwait (Operation Desert Storm) was supposed to be a tank war. The Iraqis had many tanks. However, we had better tanks and every intention of using them. Medical support had to consider the type of casualties encountered in an armored conflict.

There are two ways tankers die when their tank is hit. They either die from the force of the concussion or they die from burns. Tanks carry a lot of fuel. When a round hits, it is very hot, and a fire is almost always ignited. The situation was even more concerning for the Kuwaiti conflict because many tanks were being operated using aviation (jet) fuel supplied by coalition allies. Jet fuel is an excellent propellant, but it ignites easily and burns at a very high temperature. This being said, a blast injury is typically lethal, but you have a chance to save a burn patient.

The burn center in Landstuhl did not exist before the war. Before that time, all patients were transported to the military burn center at Fort Sam Houston in San Antonio, Texas. That burn center is probably the best in the world, but it is not big enough to acutely handle the large number of patients that might be seen in a significant armor battle. It was also far from the theater of operation, and many acute burn patients would require ICU-level care during transport. That type of capability is limited even for the Air Force. The concern was simply that there were more burn patients than could be handled by Fort Sam. The answer was to put a burn center at LARMC.

How could a burn center be constructed in four months? First, you relocate military dependents from the hospital to the German economy for their medical care. Once that is done, you close the labor and delivery section and the pediatric intensive care unit. Then, the Germans come in and install miles of new wiring, and you bring in additional intensive care and operating room equipment. Then, you activate medical reservists to staff the whole operation. The only things missing were the curtains to provide privacy and the tanks to debride the burns. The nurses who stitched white curtains from bed sheets handled the first situation. The second problem was addressed by arranging a movable chair where the patient would be seated while being brushed and sprayed with a hose to remove dead tissue. It is not the best solution, but it would work.

The first patient we received who needed our modified debridement technique was a young female soldier who was shipped to us from the Kuwaiti theater with a 40% body surface area burn. The story was an unfortunate one.

Although Kuwait and northern Saudi Arabia are virtually entirely desert, the temperature can drop dramatically in winter. While some tents were heated, all could be cold at night. This young soldier had wrapped herself in her poncho liner to keep warm. When this did not prove adequate, she apparently tried to heat her sleeping area with an alcohol lamp.

If a safety officer had been aware of this activity, it would have been immediately stopped due to the fire risk. An alcohol lamp provides light and limited heat by burning alcohol with an open flame as it is drawn up through a fabric wick. The lamp typically has a metal cap used to put out the flame and slow the evaporation of the alcohol between uses.

This particular evening, either the soldier bumped the lamp or someone coming in knocked it over (we were never clear on exactly what happened), but the result was alcohol saturating the poncho liner she had wrapped around her. It immediately ignited and burst into intense flames. All she had on under the poncho was her bra, which partially protected her. She immediately tried to throw the poncho liner on the ground. In an instant, she had sustained second and third-degree burns to her anterior (and partial posterior) chest, her arms, her face, and her neck. Parts of the poncho liner melted into the tissue, intensifying and concentrating the thermal damage and worsening the injury.

When the soldier arrived in Landstuhl, she began her debridement in the operatory suite, and it was continued during her stay using our improvised non-tank tanking procedures. I had witnessed tanking procedures during my plastic surgery rotation through the burn unit in medical school. It was not pleasant then, but our procedure seemed even more painful. Although premedicated with opiates, the scrubbing (rubbing) of raw tissue, followed by rinsing with water, was one of the more gruesome events I have ever witnessed. Most of the work was managed by the nurses. After three days, she was evacuated to Brooke Army Hospital Burn Center for additional treatment and grafting.

The memories of her treatment have stayed fresh in my memory. The poncho liner is a beautiful piece of equipment. It is warm, soft, almost weightless, and can be rolled into a ball so small that it fits anywhere. However, after helping to take care of this soldier, I could not help but wonder why poncho liners are not fire-retardant. Pajamas are fire-retardant...

LAMENTATIONS 3:56 You heard my plea: "Do not close your ears to my cry for relief."

1 SAMUEL 16:23 Whenever the spirit from God came on Saul, David would take up his lyre and play. Then relief would come to Saul; he would feel better, and the evil spirit would leave him.

REVELATION 21:4 'He will wipe every tear from their eyes. There will be no more death' or mourning or crying or pain, for the old order of things has passed away.

Operation Enduring Freedom –
(Darnell Army Community Hospital, Fort Hood, Texas)

The Two-Week Annual Training at USAISR that Turned into Four Months of Active Duty
(Don't sit in Tony's seat at Ft. Sam)

USAISR at Ft Sam Houston

Fort Hood – The Great Place

Darnell Army Community Hospital - DACH

Soldiers are typically in excellent physical condition and generally healthy. Therefore, when wounded, they have a better-than-average chance of surviving. Most mortal combat wounds are lethal from the moment of impact – gunshot wounds to the head or heart, devastating explosions, etc. Nothing a medic, nurse, or doctor can do in these cases will make a difference. Most soldiers who die of a potentially survivable injury do so from bleeding. Therefore, stopping bleeding has the highest potential for saving lives in combat trauma. The effort to stop bleeding begins with the first hands on the scene. These may be the hands of the wounded soldier. Therefore, the combat tourniquet is designed to be used by someone with only one hand. The hands may belong to a fellow soldier who applies pressure. They may be the hands of a medic applying a bandage made of materials designed to promote blood clotting. As the soldier passes from hand to hand, each receiving caregiver will continue increasing efforts to stop the blood flow. In the first medical facility with nurses and doctors, this effort will include administering blood products and considering surgery to close large vessels.

My work at the Medical College of Virginia, where I was developing methods to stop bleeding in trauma patients, introduced me to the remarkable individuals at the United States Army Institute of Surgical Research in San Antonio, Texas, and Fort Sam Houston. I received funding from the military to help develop a bandage that would expand to apply pressure in areas where external pressure could not be applied to the patient. This work, along with my continued participation in the US Army Reserve, allowed me to collaborate with COL John H's group at USAISR.

Dr. Tony P was involved in the request for application process for funding for Defense Department-related medical research. He was a great guy who was a civilian employee at USAISR. He had an ongoing interest in hemorrhage control and was also a member of the Army Reserves. He helped run the annual ATACCC (Advanced Technology Applications to Combat Casualty Care) conference and invited me to present some of our research at that meeting. He later invited me to USAISR to talk about platelet function, and I was introduced to several team members.

In the fall of 2002, Tony invited me to lunch at the best pizza place in San Antonio while visiting the facility. As we walked to his car, he carried a recently cleaned uniform. As he put it in the trunk of his car, he explained that he would be wearing that fresh set of BDUs in his upcoming change of command ceremony. He had recently taken command of a civil affairs unit.

I congratulated him and gently asked when he had become "homozygous stupid." He gave me a puzzled look, and then I explained that I thought he would probably be in Afghanistan within six months. It was post-9/11, and the two reserve units constantly pulled to active duty were transportation and civil affairs units. Medical personnel were also at high risk of activation, but the Army had stopped activating medical units and was "cherry-picking" the medical personnel they wanted out of those units.

Tony's response was, "You really think so...?"

This all set the stage for my next active-duty adventure. After not receiving a general command in 2000, I decided I had as much command time as I needed and stepped out of command to spend my last few years in the reserves as an ordinary Army doctor. I moved to the 7202nd, a small medical unit of about 50 people under the command of LTC Ken S. Ken was another great guy who had served on my staff as the training officer during one of my stents as Commander of the 4215th US Army Hospital. All was well until 9-11...

As one of the few physicians in the 7202nd, I was allowed to arrange my annual training if the unit did not need me for their training. In the winter of 2003, I was seeking a suitable opportunity. Combining my research work with my reserve commitment would be nice, and I sought opportunities at USAISR. COL H said he would be glad to have me for a few weeks, and we settled on the last two weeks in June.

When I arrived on Sunday, Tony's civil affairs unit had been activated, and he was in Afghanistan. Sometimes, I hate being a prophet.

COL H suggested: "Since Tony is not here, why don't you take his office?" Well, when one door closes, another opens!

My first task on Monday was to complete the mandatory information technology training and clearance, which allowed me to obtain my codes for the computer network and email systems. I worked my way through the testing and paperwork, and by lunch, I had my codes. I opened my emails to find one from SFC Hill, with whom I had worked at the 4215th. She was terrific. As a training NCO, she always had my back.

The email was somewhat cryptic. "Something coming your way."

"What kind of 'something'?" I responded.

"A set of orders."

"But I already have my orders for annual training…"

"This is a new set of orders, and it is not for training…"

"When might I expect such orders to arrive?"

"Later today."

This entire exchange took about 30 minutes, and by 1600 hrs., I had activation orders to report to Fort Hood, Texas. The army had transferred me from the 7202nd in Richmond, VA, to a reserve hospital in Seago, Texas, and then activated me from that unit. It was classic cherry-picking.

There were several problems. First, I was to report to Ft Hood the next Tuesday while I was still on orders to USAISR. That is technically not legal, but more importantly, I would have no time with my family before activation. In addition, I had only brought the equipment I would need at USAISR and would need to get home to pack.

I walked down the hall to the commander's office and showed COL H my new orders. He was very understanding. "Go get yourself a flight home. We will cancel the remaining orders here. I will also request that your activation be delayed for a week. Sorry to see you go."

All that was left was to call home and break the news. I had learned one lesson…don't sit in Tony's chair…if you do, you will end up on active duty.

Two weeks later, on July 4, I reported to Fort Hood. I was backfilling for a doctor who had been deployed to Iraq. The stories below come from the time I spent at Fort Hood— 'The Great Place'— at that time, home to 37,000 soldiers of the 4th Infantry Division and the "First Team" 1st Cavalry.

PROVERBS 16:9 In their hearts humans plan their course, but the Lord establishes their steps.

PROVERBS 19:21 Many are the plans in a person's heart, but it is the Lord's purpose that prevails.

JEREMIAH 29:11 "For I know the plans I have for you," declares the Lord, "plans to prosper you and not to harm you, plans to give you hope and a future."

Rapid Onset Alzheimer's
(He was OK until a few months ago...)

An 82-year-old male with a history of hypertension, diabetes, and hyperlipidemia was brought to the emergency room by his wife. She said that he was in his usual state of health until six months prior, when she began to note increasing confusion and memory loss. "He began to be forgetful like he was developing Alzheimer's." Her only other complaint was that his snoring kept her awake.

The patient spoke rather slowly but could respond reasonably to most questions. He stated he had been having trouble for six weeks with an increasing headache and weakness in his left arm and leg. He was concerned about his declining hand strength, which caused him to drop things.

He had been evaluated at another hospital, where a CT scan was performed. The scan reportedly revealed an area of edema in the anterior 1/2 of the right cerebral hemisphere that was significant enough to cause a leftward shift of the right side of the brain across 1.5 cm of the midline. The patient was sent to the Darnell Army Community Hospital emergency department for additional evaluation. A typed report of the CT came with the patient, but the films did not.

The past medical history confirmed diabetes, hypertension, and hyperlipidemia, and was also positive for Bell's palsy, benign prostatic hypertrophy treated by transurethral resection, and bilateral cataract removal with lens implants. His medications included insulin, Zocor, Norvasc, Zyrtec, Aciphex, and lisinopril. He had no known drug allergies but was intolerant of aspirin, which caused gastrointestinal bleeding. He neither smoked nor drank alcohol. He denied other complaints or symptoms, but his wife complained of his snoring.

Physical examination revealed mild hypertension (141/74) on multiple medications, bradycardia (pulse 52 beats per minute), a

198

respiratory rate of 18 per minute, and no fever. He tended to keep his right eye closed but could open it upon command. His lungs had crackles at both bases, and his cardiac exam revealed a loud fourth sound consistent with his long history of high blood pressure. His abdominal examination was normal, and his legs or feet had no swelling. He could transfer from the wheelchair to the bed, but struggled to stand, so I did not try to have him walk. A neurologic examination confirmed that his left-hand grip strength was decreased.

I admitted the gentleman to the hospital, started Decadron to relieve his increased intracranial pressure and cerebral edema, and scheduled him for an MRI the next morning. By the following day, his headache had improved, and his hand strength had returned to normal. The wife was very impressed by the improvement in his mental status.

A couple of images from his MRI are shown below.

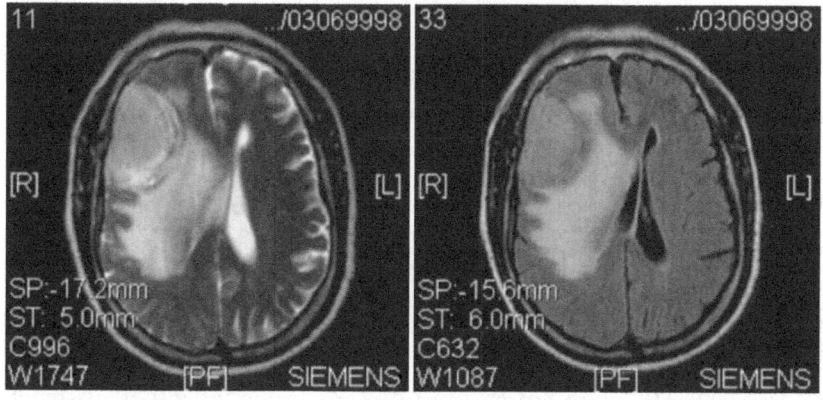

The top of the scan corresponds to the front of the skull, and the right and left sides are indicated by 'R' and 'L', respectively. In the right frontal aspect of the scan, a mass (the gray potato-shaped object) can be seen, which appears to be adherent to or originating from the meningeal lining that separates the brain from the skull. The larger, less well-defined, whitish object surrounding the mass is an area of associated edema. The right lateral ventricle (best seen in the right panel) is the dark area in the middle of the brain. The left and right ventricles should be about the same shape and size. The left ventricle appears relatively normal, although pushed to the left. The area of edema partially collapses the right ventricle. The differences in the colors of the two images are due to two ways of weighting the images (T1 and T2), where structures containing increased liquid appear darker in one and lighter in the other.

Based on location and appearance, the presumptive diagnosis was meningioma with associated vasogenic edema. The initial treatment with Decadron decreased the edema and reduced the symptoms. The definitive treatment was resection of the mass, which confirmed the diagnosis of meningioma and entirely resolved his symptoms of headache, diminished mental capacity, and weakness. Given the slow-growing nature of these tumors and the age of the patient, it is likely that this gentleman would succumb to one of his other maladies rather than recurrent meningioma.

Unfortunately, the wife reported that the surgery had not alleviated his snoring.

Lesson learned: Not all memory loss is Alzheimer's disease. Late-onset, rather rapidly progressing mental dysfunction is probably not dementia. Treatments for mental status changes rarely help snoring...

PSALMS 86:11 Teach me your way, Lord, that I may rely on your faithfulness; give me an undivided heart, that I may fear your name.

ISAIAH 50:4 The Sovereign Lord has given me a well-instructed tongue, to know the word that sustains the weary. He wakens me morning by morning, wakens my ear to listen like one being instructed.

Suddenly, the Warfarin Just Didn't Seem to Work
(No Noni for You!)

Although my primary role at Darnall Army Community Hospital was that of an internist, my secondary role as a hematologist was soon recognized by the hem/onc nurses who ran the oncology and "Coumadin" clinics. The Coumadin clinic was used to follow patients who were on anticoagulant medication for conditions that put them at risk for thrombosis. Typical patients had suffered from a previous deep venous thrombosis (a blood clot in the leg) and/or a pulmonary embolus (a clot that breaks free and travels to the lungs). Another common category of patients was people at increased risk for stroke due to an abnormal heart valve or the presence of atrial fibrillation. Such individuals can form clots on their abnormal valves or in their erratically beating heart chambers. Clots formed in the heart have a short and rather direct trip to the brain and can cause devastating strokes. Thus, both categories of patients significantly benefit from drugs that prevent clot formation.

These patients were followed in the Coumadin clinic to ensure that their dose of anticoagulant (commonly referred to as "blood thinners" by many) was correct and effective. This is important because if they do not take enough anticoagulants, their blood will still clot normally, and the risk of thrombosis will not be reduced. Conversely, if they are taking too much of a drug, their blood may take too long to clot, and they might be at risk for bleeding. The balance is maintained by testing how long it takes the patient's blood to clot and adjusting the drug dose to keep that time in a range where thrombotic risk is reduced, but the risk of bleeding is not excessively increased. Patients typically come in regularly to have their INR (International Normalization Ratio) checked. The INR needs to be above 1.5 to reduce the risk of thrombosis, and it should not go much above 2 to avoid increased bleeding.

One day, the head nurse asked if I could see a patient they had been following for a long time. She had been on a stable dose of the drug for years, but several months earlier, she began to require ever-increasing amounts of anticoagulant. Since I saw all the "hard to control" anticoagulant patients at the Medical College of Virginia, I thought this would be right down my alley.

The patient was a charming forty-one-year-old lady who had suffered from rheumatic fever at the age of ten. Consequently, her mitral valve was damaged and replaced in 1971 with a mechanical (Starr-Edwards) valve. She was placed on anticoagulation and had remained stable for the previous thirty years. When I saw her, her daily dose of Coumadin was a whopping 7 mgs, alternating with 6 mgs. Despite this high dose, her INR was only borderline therapeutic.

Coumadin, a form of warfarin, works by inhibiting the ability of Vitamin K to be recycled. Anytime a substance is critical to bodily function, the body finds a way to recycle it. This is true for Vitamin K, which must be consumed in one's diet and is necessary for the normal function of many proteins, including several clotting factors. When Vitamin K is absent or cannot be recycled, the proteins that rely on Vitamin K are abnormal and do not function properly. Vitamin K levels drop when one consumes Coumadin; consequently, clotting protein activities also drop.

When thinking about what could have caused this patient's Coumadin to stop working, the causes were relatively limited and obvious. First, she might have stopped taking her Coumadin, but I believed she was taking it. Second, she might have stopped absorbing the medication due to changes in her liver or bowel function, but she had no signs, symptoms, or complaints consistent with that scenario. Third, she might be breaking down the Coumadin more rapidly due to a drug-drug interaction, but she was not taking any new drugs. Finally, perhaps her diet had changed, and she was consuming more vitamin K, meaning she did not have to recycle as much, and therefore, Coumadin would be less effective.

A review of her laboratory record revealed that her INR first deviated from therapeutic values in May 2003. Since May, her

Coumadin dose had steadily increased with minimal change in her INR. Her INR when I saw her was barely therapeutic at 1.5.

After asking what dose of Coumadin she was currently taking and obtaining the correct response, I asked if she had altered her diet. She confirmed that she had not. I then asked if she was taking medicines other than those in her chart. Once again, the answer was no.

Well, this was getting a little tougher than I thought. So, I asked about vitamins, diet control substances, or supplements.

She paused for a moment and then said, "Nothing but NONI. My husband started taking it, and he felt so good he thought it would be good for me."

No one in the clinic had ever heard of or seen this material. The patient started taking NONI in May and had recently doubled her intake. An internet website revealed that the NONI juice she took was a brown liquid containing extracts and derivatives from more than 115 substances. Many of the plants and other components contained Vitamin K; her brand was fortified with vitamin K.

The mystery was solved, and the timeline fit perfectly. I admitted the patient and treated her with heparin (an intravenous anticoagulant that does not work by inhibiting vitamin K) to bring her into a therapeutic range. I also temporarily increased her Coumadin to 10 mg per day. I also told her to stop the NONI and not to take any supplement or home remedy without checking with the clinic. The next day, her INR was 2.1, and she was discharged on her previous dose of Coumadin.

The case was so unusual that I researched whether Coumadin resistance secondary to Noni juice had ever been reported. It had not. We submitted the case report as a letter, and it was published in the American Journal of Hematology.

I ended the note with the following conclusion: Bottom line upfront—if you are on warfarin or coumadin, NO NONI FOR YOU!!

To my surprise, within a week of its publication, I began getting nasty letters from Noni product manufacturers implying that I was attacking a worthwhile and "safe" product. I responded that it might be safe for most folks, but if you were taking Coumadin or warfarin, Noni was a bad idea.

The citation of this published case is as follows:

M.E. Carr, J. Klotz, M. Bergeron. Coumadin resistance and the vitamin supplement "Noni." Am J Hematol. 2004;77:103-4

PROVERBS 3:5 Trust in the Lord with all your heart and lean not on your own understanding.

JEREMIAH 29:11 "For I know the plans I have for you," declares the Lord, "plans to prosper you and not to harm you, plans to give you hope and a future."

1 CORINTHIANS 3:19 For the wisdom of this world is foolishness in God's sight. As it is written: "He catches the wise in their craftiness;"

JAMES 1:5 If any of you lacks wisdom, you should ask God, who gives generously to all without finding fault, and it will be given to you.

A Fishing Trip, Fire Ants, and Red Hands and Feet
(Hand-foot syndrome without chemotherapy)

Occasionally, you uncover unexpected findings in what, at first glance, should be a routine medical visit. This is the case of a very pleasant 77-year-old gentleman who came a week early for his routine sixth-month visit. He was being followed for multiple medical conditions, including heart disease (atherosclerotic coronary vascular disease), chronic obstructive pulmonary disease from years of smoking (he had quit about ten years earlier), high blood pressure, hypothyroidism, and gastroesophageal reflux disease (GERD). He had also survived cancer of the prostate and bladder. He came in early to the clinic because of a new complaint – pain in his feet.

The previous weekend, he had gone fishing with his grandson. He had a grand time but had gotten into some fire ants along the pond's edge. Fire ants are common in many parts of the Southeastern United States (see map below), and they are particularly prevalent in many areas of Texas. On flat grassy areas, the ant hills are easy to see (photo after the map), but in higher grass typically found around ponds, you can be amid an ant nest before you know what is happening.

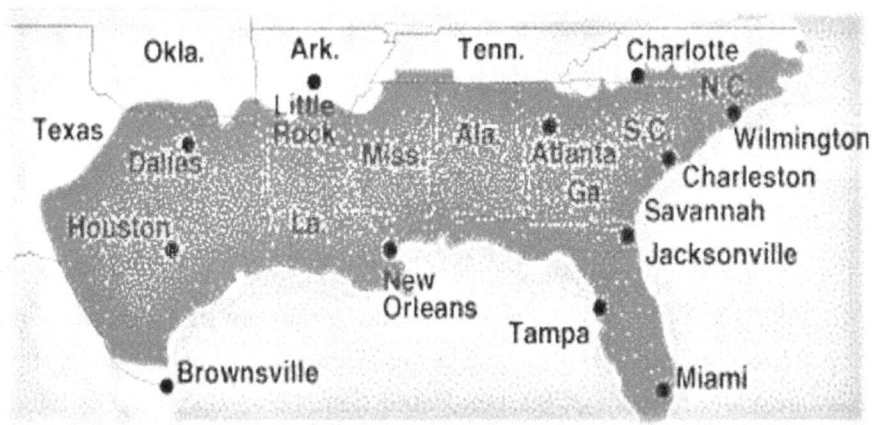

If you disturb these aggressive creatures, they will quickly retaliate. People often ask if the ants bite or sting. The answer is - they do both. They bite to establish a grip, then sting via their abdomen (photo below to the left). It is the sting that gives these invasive creatures their fame and name. Although initially painful, skin lesions caused by the sting are typically self-limiting and resolve without scarring within seven to ten days (see photo to the right). However, the situation can become much more complex and severe in individuals who have allergic reactions to the sting, a person with diabetes, or anyone at increased risk of infection.

My patient, who had been stung several times, was familiar with fire ants. On this occasion, he was stung about ten times on his right leg. One day later, despite not being stung on either, he developed swelling and redness of the hands and feet. The redness of his hands was primarily on the fingers and the webbing of the hand between the fingers. The redness of his feet was on the plantar aspect (bottom) and extended onto the lateral surfaces. By day three, his hands improved, but his feet remained red and somewhat painful.

When he came to the clinic, it had been five days since the stings occurred, and his only complaint was continued pain in his feet upon standing. He was on no new medications, but continued to take his routine medications, including Allegra, Auralgan, ammonium lactate, naproxen, Hytrin, Zocor, Synthroid, Ecotrin, Lopid, Aciphex, Tiazac, and Nitrostat.

On physical examination, his blood pressure was normal (131/63 mmHg), and he was afebrile (98.1° F). He had ten circular lesions, each approximately 1 cm in diameter, on his right lower leg. His hands appeared to be normal. Examination of his feet revealed redness and some swelling of the plantar surface that extended upward onto the medial aspect of the ankles. Both feet were minimally tender, with no apparent puncture wounds or sores.

I had seen similar presentations in the oncology clinic where a variety of chemotherapy agents can cause what is termed "hand-foot syndrome." The syndrome was initially described in patients with sickle β-thalassemia and sickle cell acute crisis; however, the etiology or pathogenesis of the syndrome had not been defined in the context of chemotherapy or hemoglobinopathy. Since, in most cases, the problem was self-limited and responded to the resolution of the acute event or removal of the drug, therapy was typically supportive pain relief. My patient did not have sickle cell disease (or any other hemoglobinopathy) and had not been given chemotherapy in the last year. As mentioned, he was also not on any new medications.

So, what did he have, and what should I do about it? It resembled hand-foot syndrome and did not appear to be worsening. The skin lesions also appeared to be resolving. I called dermatology, who recommended applying fluocinonide to the affected areas. Since the gentleman already had an appointment scheduled for next week, I advised him to contact me if his condition did not continue to improve and to reschedule his appointment for the following week.

When he returned the following Friday, the skin lesions had completely healed, and the swelling and pain in his feet had dissipated with the resolution of the skin lesions.

Well, that was interesting. The hand-foot syndrome was temporally related to the fire ant stings, resolved with the healing of the stings, and I could find no other reason for its occurrence.

The citation for this published case is as follows:

M.E. Carr. Hand-foot syndrome in a patient with multiple fire ant stings. South Med J. 2004, Jul; 97(7): 707-09.

PSALMS 78:45 He sent swarms of flies that devoured them, and frogs that devastated them.

EXODUS 8:17 They did this, and when Aaron stretched out his hand with the staff and struck the dust of the ground, gnats came on the people.

25-Year-Old Pale Captain Preparing to Deploy to Iraq
(*Worried - he could no longer keep up with his men when running*)

The 26-year-old male infantry Captain walked into my office on a warm Monday afternoon. He was tall and lean and as white as the paint on the wall.

"What can I help you with today?"

"Well, Sir, I am getting ready to take my company to Iraq, and I can no longer keep up on our company runs. My energy level is also down, and I find myself gasping for air after exercise that would not have had any effect on me a few months ago."

Those complaints, combined with his pale skin and eyes, gave me a pretty good diagnosis before I had even begun my examination. Of course, I had to rule out cardiac or pulmonary problems, but this guy was profoundly anemic.

As I examined his crystal-clear lungs and his heart, which sounded normal except for a relatively rapid rate for someone in as good a shape as this young Captain, I began the questions that would lead me to the cause of the anemia.

Anemia is not a diagnosis. It is an indicator of an underlying disease process. Red blood cells have a lifespan of about 120 days. Therefore, a normal person's bone marrow will produce and replace about 1% of their red cells daily. The process is amazingly exact, so the percentage of red cells in a person's blood (hematocrit) remains virtually constant. When one is anemic, they have less than the normal percentage of red blood cells. This can only occur by destroying red blood cells, losing red blood cells, or not producing enough. Brisk destruction of red blood cells (hemolysis) is unusual and has a characteristic laboratory profile, which allows for rapid diagnosis. Decreased production of red cells is typically caused by either a deficiency of a required component (iron, vitamin B12, etc.) or a primary problem with the bone marrow. Blood loss is bleeding.

As I asked about his medical history and recent symptoms, the captain told me that he had undergone an appendectomy for acute appendicitis in March 2003. In April, he started bloating, which was treated with Aciphex. In June, he was noted to be anemic and was started on oral iron. He continued to have crampy abdominal pain, which he attributed to the oral iron therapy. Despite the continued symptoms, he continued to take the medication. More recently, he had noted transient dizziness upon standing (typically due to a transient drop in blood pressure termed orthostatic hypotension). His appetite was poor, and his weight had dropped from 190 to 170 pounds over the last three months. His stools were dark, which he had attributed to his iron therapy. The more he spoke, the more concerned I became.

The remainder of his past medical history was benign, and he had been on no medications before the start of his abdominal symptoms in March. He did not smoke, used very little alcohol, and had no known drug allergies. His family history was positive for endometrial cancer in his mother, and his social history was significant for an engagement to his long-term girlfriend.

In addition to his normal heart and lungs, physical examination confirmed the pale skin and mucus membranes, a healed right lower quadrant appendectomy scar with some underlying tenderness, and the reported weight loss.

Laboratory evaluation revealed a normal white count (5,300 per microliter), an elevated platelet count (444,000 per microliter), and a remarkably low hemoglobin of 8.0 grams per deciliter (about half of what his hemoglobin should have been). Laboratory markers of hemolysis were normal. He was producing red blood cells, but his percentage of young red blood cells (reticulocytes) was not as high as it should have been for his severe anemia. The white blood cell and platelet counts argued against a primary bone marrow problem, and the iron studies confirmed that the reduced reticulocyte count was likely due to a profound iron deficiency. His ferritin level (a protein marker of iron stores) was deficient at 2 (normal 24 to 336), and his serum iron was 11 (normal 45 to 182). Both values were profoundly abnormal despite several months of oral iron supplements. I was convinced this Captain had taken his iron supplements.

My assessment was iron deficiency, almost certainly secondary to GI blood loss. Other than the symptoms of his anemia, all his signs and symptoms were abdominal. He needed a gastrointestinal evaluation as soon as possible. Although very young, the loss of appetite and weight was concerning for an underlying malignancy.

I walked next door to my GI colleague (an excellent physician and a West Point Graduate) and gave him a thumbnail history and my impression. He immediately came to my office, introduced himself to the Captain, described the bowel clearance prep, and told him he would see him the following morning for a colonoscopy. Now that's service!

I told the Captain I would like to speed up his iron replacement by infusing him with an iron preparation (1000 mg) in the oncology clinic. He agreed, and we infused him with iron before he left to begin his bowel prep.

I had started utilizing the chemotherapy nurses for the iron infusion procedure soon after my arrival at DACH. Many patients are intolerant of oral iron or do not take it. Therefore, if you cannot absorb iron through the gut, you can administer it directly into the bloodstream, and it will be delivered to all iron-deficient tissues. The procedure was not new or novel, but many places did not use it because of a history of severe allergic reactions to some of the early intravenous iron preparations. It turned out that low-level contaminants were causing the reactions. The new preparations appeared to be free of these contaminants, and I had been able to administer intravenous infusions without any reactions. Out of an abundance of caution, we administered a test dose before beginning the routine infusion to ensure there would be no problem. The nurses enjoyed giving the infusions (they were more pleasant than administering chemotherapy), the patients appreciated receiving the therapy (which was completed in an hour rather than weeks to months), and I appreciated knowing the iron was being administered to the patient (there was no question of non-compliance here!). We were infusing iron so often, and with such good results, that the local newspaper came, interviewed the nurses, and wrote a nice article, including photos of the chief chemotherapy nurse. I'll tell you, I scored some points there!

The following day, the captain stopped by my office on the way to his colonoscopy to tell me how much better he felt after his iron infusion. This was not an uncommon occurrence. Many other patients reported feeling better the day after their infusion, even though it would take several weeks for their hemoglobin levels to increase significantly. They were still profoundly anemic, but they felt better "with more energy." At first, I thought this was a placebo effect, but eventually, I decided that there are many proteins that bind iron, and that many of these are essential for muscle and mitochondrial function (small energy-producing organelles within cells). Perhaps the replenishment of iron in these areas was the cause of the perceived increased well-being.

The captain had his colonoscopy that morning, and in the early afternoon, my West Point Doc came by to give me a report and show me some photos (see below). It was not good. A large, fungating mass in the cecum (near the area where the appendectomy had been performed). He had taken several biopsies. The early report was consistent with adenocarcinoma. The appearance was at least stage II or III, and the tumor might have extended through the bowel wall. He told the captain that an abnormal area was the source of the blood loss and instructed him to return the next day when the pathology results were available. I said that I would like to know as soon as possible and that I could squeeze the patient into my morning schedule the next day.

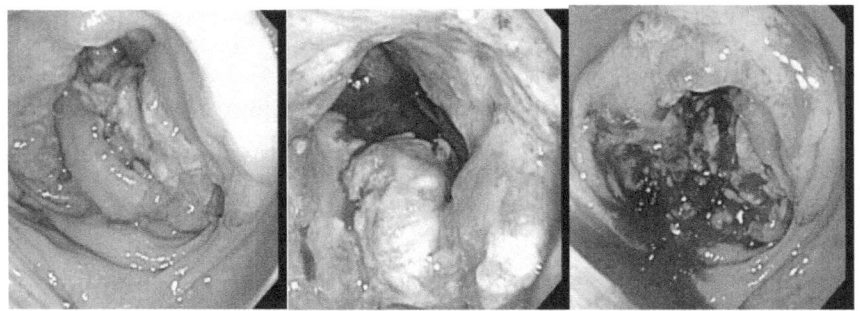

I called the captain to confirm that he could be available in the morning, and he asked if it would be OK if he brought his fiancée. The Captain appropriately interpreted my communication with my GI colleague after the colonoscopy. I said that it would be fine for her to come.

The next morning, the final readings were in, and the diagnosis was adenocarcinoma of the colon. The captain and his fiancée arrived and sat beside each other on the other side of my desk. Once again, the Captain complimented the nurses and the response to the IV iron. I told him I was also pleased, but that the next step was addressing the underlying problem found at the colonoscopy. I reviewed the photos supplied by the gastroenterologist and spoke the words "malignant tumor" of the colon.

There was a moment of silence, and then the fiancée asked, "Does that mean cancer?"

I replied that it did.

"How could a healthy, young soldier have cancer?" she asked.

I told her that, unfortunately, sometimes these things happen. I did not have a better answer.

I went on to say that we needed to move quickly to remove the tumor and evaluate the extent of the problem.

"How quickly?" the Captain asked.

I told him that we had contacted the Medical Center at Fort Sam Houston in San Antonio, and they would admit him the next day and perform surgery the following morning if he would be able to come immediately.

I could see the wheels turning as the Captain processed what I was saying. I could also see the tears begin to flow down his fiancée's face. She had been preparing to send him off to war, but she was not prepared for this.

The Captain asked, "Does this mean I will not be going to Iraq with my troops?" I told him that if they were leaving any time soon, he would probably not be with them.

"I will need to talk to my chain of command, and I need to let my soldiers know that I will try to join them as soon as I get this problem handled…"

I assured him that we would provide his commander's information and make all necessary arrangements for transport and transfer to get him to Fort Sam.

It was clear that this couple would have many questions over the next few weeks, and I told them that if they did not understand what they were being told, they should call me, and I would do my best to clarify things for them. At that moment, the most important thing was to move quickly.

The next morning, the Captain was at Fort Sam, and on Friday morning, surgery was performed to remove the right half of his colon. A preliminary report was an extension of the tumor through the wall to involve the pericolonic fascia. I did not receive a report about associated node involvement.

Unfortunately, I never saw the captain again. One unpleasant reality of military medicine is that both the patients and doctors are prone to movement. I still occasionally think of him and pray that he did well. It all seemed so unfair.

LAMENTATIONS 3:36 to deprive them of justice – would not the Lord see such things?

MICAH 6:8 He has shown you, O mortal, what is good. And what does the Lord require of you? To act justly and to love mercy and to walk humbly with your God.

ISAIAH 40:31 but those who hope in the Lord will renew their strength. They will soar on wings like eagles; they will run and not grow weary, they will walk and not be faint.

Operation Medical Falcon -
(Camp Bondsteel, Kosovo)

Mount Duke from Bondsteel Hospital.

Camp Bondsteel from the air.

Air transportation was by helicopter.   Primary mode of ground Transportation: HUMVEE

Avoiding Being Trapped by Seatbelts
(...but there were four of us, and I only see three...where is PVT...)

While not particularly known for mountains, Kosovo (formerly part of Yugoslavia) is amazingly mountainous. It seemed to me to be a series of valleys and mountains. Camp Bondsteel was situated in a beautiful valley overlooked by Mount Duke. While I am sure the US was taking care of some of the mountains, the other NATO forces (Germany, Sweden, France, Greece, Britain, etc.) also monitored their respective shares of the mountains. What brings this all to mind is one of the strange episodes during my time at Bondsteel.

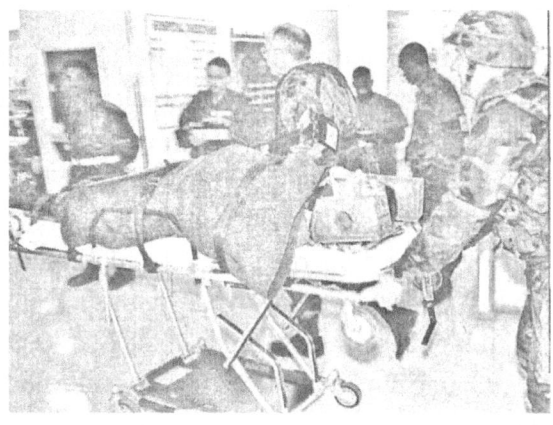

It was early evening when we got word of a potential mass casualty event involving British personnel and an overturned vehicle. There were reportedly three injured soldiers and one fatality. A Swedish Medical Team brought them in. After a quick triage of the three survivors, my team attended to each one while I spoke with the Swedish Officer in Charge. She was young, attractive, blond, and spoke perfect English. She told me the vehicle had rolled over on a curvy mountain road. The fatality occurred when one of the soldiers was thrown from the vehicle. They were not wearing seat belts. Someone in their command chain had instructed them not to wear seatbelts on the mountainous roads out of concern that they might

217

become trapped inside the vehicle by their seatbelts if the vehicle should roll over. I was dumbfounded. I was also sure the soldier would have probably survived if he had not been crushed by the vehicle as it rolled over him after he was thrown out. Of course, the information I was given was hearsay. However, if it were true, what was that commander thinking?

I was glad that the Swedish physician shared this information with me early in her report, because as she continued to speak, I suddenly realized that I was staring into her blue eyes and not hearing a word she said. At that moment, I became acutely aware that I had been away from home way too long. However, no problem. The patients were all talking (and not nearly so attractive), so I could get any information I needed from them.

In the process of gathering information, I spoke to the driver. Since the event was technically a motor vehicle accident involving a fatality, the whole thing was handled as a potential criminal investigation. Therefore, they had not informed the driver about the fatality. The first thing he said when I spoke to him was, "Where is Private....?" "There were four of us, but I only see three." At that point, I told him that one had not survived. He became understandably emotional. I could not help but think that if a crime had been committed here, it had been committed by whoever told these soldiers not to wear their seatbelts.

MATTHEW 8:9 For I myself am a man under authority, with soldiers under me. I tell this one, 'GO,' and he goes; and that one, 'Come,' and he comes. I say to my servant, 'Do this,' and he does it."

PROVERBS 12:15 The way of fools seems right to them, but the wise listen to advice.

MARK 14:38 Watch and pray so that you will not fall into temptation. The spirit is willing, but the flesh is weak.

CPR for a Lethal PE
(He was the luckiest, unlucky guy in the world.)

One of the more exciting and gratifying cases I was involved with while at Camp Bondsteel involved a Czech Soldier who was transferred to us, having suffered sudden death in the morning chow line. That might sound like a bad joke about the poor quality of the food, but it was no laughing matter.

The 29-year-old male soldier was in his usual state of excellent health until nine days before admission, when he complained of leg pain after an 18-hour bus ride. He was seen at the medical aid station and treated for muscle strain. Eight days later, while waiting in line for breakfast, he suddenly collapsed. Luckily for him, the fellow standing two people behind him was a medic. He immediately felt for a pulse, and when he did not find one, he initiated CPR. After a few minutes, the soldier began to revive, and the pulse was rapid but stable. At this point, the soldier complained of severe chest pain and was profoundly short of breath. He was immediately given 10,000 units of unfractionated heparin (a medicine to slow blood clotting) for a suspected pulmonary embolism (blood clot in the lungs). He was transferred to Task Force Medical Falcon at Camp Bondsteel.

Upon arrival, he was breathing 26 times per minute (about twice as fast as he should have been). Breathing at this rate with four liters of oxygen being blown into his nose via nasal prongs, he maintained a pulse oximetry reading of 98% saturation (normal). His past medical history was negative for any significant medical problems. He was not taking any medications, and he was not known to be allergic to any drugs. His family history was negative for deep venous thrombosis (blood clots in the veins of the legs), pulmonary embolism, stroke (clot to the brain), myocardial infarction (heart attack – clot to heart arteries), or sudden death (was fine and then dropped dead – as the patient had done earlier in the day).

Physical examination revealed a well-developed, normal-appearing white male who was mildly agitated and short of breath. Listening to his lungs revealed diffuse wheezing in all areas. Examination of his heart was normal except for a rapid heart rate. His left calf was tender, and the pain increased when his calf muscle was stretched by pushing his toes toward his shin. This finding is a positive "Homans' sign" and can be caused by a blood clot in the leg. Everything else was normal.

The diagnostic evaluation included a normal electrocardiogram, except for a rapid heart rate and an inversion (flipping) of part of the normal heartbeat tracing in some leads. The chest X-ray was normal except for increased prominence of the blood vessels on the right side. An ultrasound (use of sound waves to "listen" to blood flow in vessels) of the right upper leg was negative for clots, but it was impossible to image the lower part of the leg.

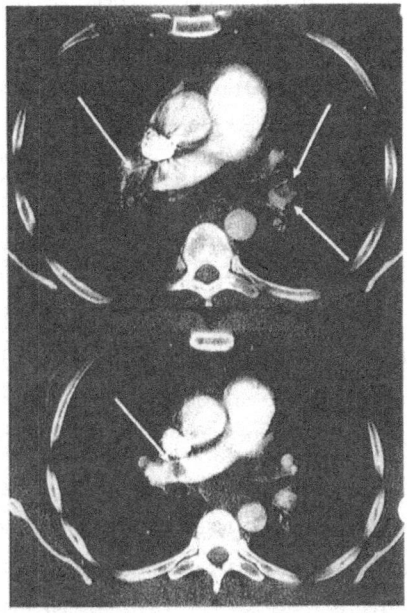

A CT scan of his chest revealed a large thrombus virtually occluding the right pulmonary artery. Several large clots were also present in the first two branches of the left pulmonary artery (see upper panel of figure at right). The pressure needed to pump blood through these clogged vessels was causing the right side of the heart to increase in diameter.

All findings were consistent with a clot forming in the soldier's leg during that long bus ride. This caused his initial pain. For whatever reason, some (maybe all) of the clot had broken loose and moved up the veins of the leg into the vena cava (the largest vein in the abdomen) and on to and through the right side of the heart, which pumped the clot into the large blood vessels going into the lungs. At the critical point, the vessel emerging from the right side of the heart divides, with one branch supplying the right lung and the other the left. Looking at the vessel at that point, one can imagine a saddle with one leg going down each branch. For that reason, this area is called the "saddle" of the pulmonary tree. If a large clot makes it through the heart and to the saddle but cannot go any further, flow can be blocked to both lungs. This is called a saddle embolus. No blood flow to the lungs means no new oxygen in the blood and dramatically diminished blood flow out of the heart on both sides. This is a rapidly lethal event – sudden death. The person just drops, as did our soldier.

So why was he still alive? The medic could not have known that the soldier had just suffered a pulmonary embolus, but he did know that the patient did not have a palpable pulse. This could mean that the heart had stopped beating/pumping. The acute treatment for that problem is cardiopulmonary resuscitation (CPR). One pushes blood through the heart by squeezing it between the sternum (the bone in the middle of the front of the rib cage) and the spine (the backbone). This is less effective than a normal heartbeat, but it can temporarily move enough blood to keep someone alive. CPR requires repetitive pushing on the chest area just above the "saddle." Although it cannot be said with absolute confidence, it seems a good bet that the medic's chest compressions mechanically fractured the clot, causing it to break into smaller pieces, which then moved further into the right and left pulmonary arteries. This allowed enough blood to pass for the patient to revive and temporarily stabilize. This could have only been possible in someone with an underlying excellent pulmonary status, precisely what this otherwise healthy 29-year-old had. This scenario is consistent with the acute presentation and the CT scan findings.

All was not well, however. Questions remained. How long would he stay stable with the clots still present? Would his right heart tire under the stress? Was there more clot in the legs? Should we consider using drugs to dissolve the clots? All critical and pertinent questions. We could not answer the first question because there is no good data on the acute outcomes of folks who survive saddle emboli (there are not enough survivors). However, the patient appeared to be stable (with good oxygenation on 4L of supplemental oxygen and a stable, albeit rapid, heart rate) at the time, and he was young and otherwise in excellent health. How would his heart do? There is no way to know, but he was young. The possibility of more clots in the legs was problematic. If there were more clots, would there be more emboli? If we used clot-dissolving agents, would the risk of clots breaking off and entering the lungs increase? We could not be sure. If we had been able to place a filter in the vena cava to catch and stop clots, the risk could have been reduced, but we did not have access to a filter. We also had no additional diagnostic tests to confirm whether an additional clot was present. Given the unknowns, our inability to better evaluate the legs, and the patient's relative stability, it was decided to continue the blood thinner (heparin) and monitor the patient's condition over the next 24 hours.

Although the patient did not deteriorate, his vital signs and symptoms remained unchanged after 24 hours. A repeat CT scan revealed little to no improvement.

At this point, I decided that it was worth a trial of a fibrinolytic agent. Fibrinolytic agents are enzymes that can be given intravenously to trigger the dissolution of the clots. Such enzymes are given to people with heart attacks and strokes, and can be given to patients with extensive pulmonary emboli. The best results with fibrinolytic agents occur when they are given as soon as possible. In this case, we had delayed their use for the reasons outlined above. We did not know how old the clots were, but I did know my patient was not improving, and I had a fibrinolytic agent available. It was worth a try.

We administered a 10 mg bolus of Alteplase, followed by an additional 90 mg infusion over 2 hours. Within 12 hours, his rapid heart rate, rapid breathing, shortness of breath, and chest pain all resolved. A repeat CT scan revealed a significant reduction in clots in the lungs. It had worked (lower panel of previous figure).

We drew blood to see if the soldier had an underlying condition, a hypercoagulable state, that was putting him at risk for clot formation. This would be important for his family members and for determining how long the patient should remain on anticoagulants (blood thinners). He had a significant deficiency of Protein C. Protein C is a protein inhibitor of clotting that is present in all normal individuals. A low level indicates that the person is at an increased risk for spontaneous clot formation, such as deep vein thrombosis and pulmonary embolism. We had our story.

We later learned this was the first documented use of a fibrinolytic agent for treating pulmonary embolus in Kosovo.

What a lucky, unfortunate man this soldier was. He was unfortunate to have a Protein C deficiency and dropped dead in the chow line. He was lucky enough to have a medic in the line with him, who saved his life by fracturing the clot during CPR. He was lucky enough to be brought to a US Army hospital in the middle of Kosovo with the ability to dissolve his clots. He would walk away with an incredible story to tell.

We documented the case in a publication. Unfortunately, we could never identify the medic who saved the soldier's life and really should have all the credit.

The citation for this published case is as follows:

M.E. Carr, C. Muller. Treatment of Massive Pulmonary Embolism in a Soldier in Kosovo: The Potential Value of Cardiopulmonary Resuscitation and Fibrinolytic Therapy. Military Medicine 2011;176: 1453-6.

LUKE 10:33-34 But a Samaritan, as he traveled, came where the man was; and when he saw him, he took pity on him. He went to him and bandaged his wounds, pouring on oil and wine.

2 TIMOTHY 3:17 so that the servant of God may be thoroughly equipped for every good work.

Taking Care of a Spook
(HIPPA is not a problem if you have no name...)

Combat and imminent danger zones are fascinating, complex, and challenging environments. I am usually able to recognize the "good guys," and most of the time, I have a good idea about who may be a "bad guy." However, there have been occasions when individuals move through who seem to have successfully concealed their true identity. The following story is based on such a case.

At Camp Bondsteel, we took care of all US Military personnel, all US civilian government personnel, all NATO forces as required, and Kosovo civilians on a restricted basis for emergencies. Therefore, it was not surprising when we got Mr. Smith, a contractor with the US State Department, who had developed intermittent lower abdominal pain.

The pain had started the evening before, and he had initially gone to the Pristina hospital. They had sent him on to us at Bondsteel. On x-ray, he had no gas in the right colon, which potentially indicated a bowel obstruction. A CT scan confirmed a complete bowel obstruction and provided evidence of a volvulus, which is a twisting of the bowel upon itself. The possibility of a tumor was also raised. Either way, his condition required surgical intervention.

There was a problem. My general surgeon was in Sofia, Bulgaria, for three days of well-deserved rest and relaxation. My only available surgeon was a young orthopedic surgeon who had independently come to me to express his discomfort with the general surgeon being away. He specifically stated that he "would not open a belly" due to a bad experience in the past. Of course, we had seen only one hot belly, an appendicitis, in the past two months, so we had anticipated that "the odds would be low..." Well, the odds were not zero or nearly low enough, in the young Major's opinion.

Luckily, a potential solution to my problem presented itself. Several German physicians were in the hospital due to their impending rotation home the following Thursday. Their commander and an anesthesiologist came to see the patient. They called their surgeon, who was willing to take the patient. They felt that the patient should go to the German camp by helicopter as soon as possible. They did not want to try to move him across the snowy mountain via ambulance.

Unfortunately, the low ceiling (the height at which you enter the clouds) of less than 500 feet would not allow a trip by helicopter across the mountain.

OK, what now? If he had already been to Pristina Hospital, they would have been aware of his condition and could have taken him back. It would have been best to send him by helicopter. Our ceiling was a little higher in the valley, and no mountains were between us and Pristina. Even though the pilots were hot to fly, our commander blocked the flight out of concern that the ceiling might drop and ground the helicopter in Pristina.

Fortunately, I was able to get the patient accepted at the Pristina hospital, and we sent him via ambulance.

Once I got the patient in the ambulance, I stepped out of the hospital for the first time that day to try to get a bite to eat. Before I got to the DFAC, my beeper went off. It had been 15 minutes since the ambulance departed, and I had gotten a call from a State Department doctor. He wanted to discuss sending Mr. Smith to Pristina with me. I could not reach him via the "non-secure" phones available in the MWR, so I returned to the hospital to make the call.

He began the conversation by saying, "Mr. Smith should not go to Pristina."

"May I ask why?" I responded.

"Well...it's a poor hospital...and the complication rates would be...10 times higher than...anywhere else."

I carefully explained that we did not have a surgeon at the moment, that we had tried to utilize the German hospital, and that the patient had an emergent condition that required surgery to avoid the possibility of bowel infarction. He understood our situation, but he was still uncomfortable. It was also apparent that he was concerned about Mr. Smith undergoing anesthesia and being placed on a hefty dose of narcotics.

He wanted us to check on the patient first thing in the morning and try to move him back to our facility for post-operative care as soon as possible. I had no problem with that plan and agreed that we would do so and keep him informed of "Mr. Smith's" status.

The following day, we got Mr. Smith back from Pristina status post an appendectomy and an appendicostomy. I had never heard of such a procedure. He had a midline incision and two large drains. One drain was the appendicostomy. At surgery, he had a cecal torsion (twisting) that had been relieved. He looked pretty good, so I wrote his admission orders and waited for my surgeon to return to assist with the removal of drains. Mr. Smith was a model patient who required very little pain relief. He was also a quiet fellow who did not offer details about his work for the State Department.

As soon as the drains were out, Mr. Smith left for the US. Every piece of paper regarding his care went with him. Having been exposed to several members of various intelligence organizations within my family, it was clear that "Mr. Smith" worked for the State Department only tangentially. There were just too many people concerned about him being dosed with mind-altering drugs outside the purview of US hands, and when he left our hands, it was like he had never been there. There is a reason we called these guys "Spooks."

PSALMS 144:4 They are like a breath; their days are like a fleeting shadow.

ECCLESIASTES 6:12 For who knows what is good for a person in life, during the few and meaningless days they pass through like a shadow?

Bilateral Retinoblastoma
(Our Falcon Angel)

The following is excerpted from a journal I kept during my time in Kosovo.

December 4, 2004 - A two-year-old girl presented at the Camp Bondsteel gate with her family, having been referred by Pristina Hospital. COL M, our ophthalmologist, met the family at the gate. The child had obvious left-sided leukocoria (whiteness seen through the pupil). He immediately made the presumptive diagnosis of retinoblastoma. Retinoblastoma is a malignant tumor that originates in the eye. COL M was keenly aware of this rare tumor since he had previously diagnosed one in a little boy at a MEDCAP. A MEDCAP is a mobile medical exercise where a medical, dental, or veterinary team is deployed to a village for a day. We arranged further care for that patient at a hospital in Germany.

The little girl met the "Life, Limb, or Eyesight rule" for treatment at Bondsteel. The criteria for admission and treatment of non-supported (NATO military) personnel at Bondsteel Hospital were that they had to have an acute life, limb, or eyesight-threatening condition. Retinoblastoma met the criteria for both life and eyesight.

When we got the child to the hospital, it was clear that she had a large retinoblastoma in her left eye. Ophthalmoscopic evaluation of the right eye revealed a second contralateral focus (both eyes had tumors). She also had frontal bossing (very prominent forehead), which I was sure was caused by metastatic disease to the bone or brain. I mobilized everyone to prepare for a CT scan – including the CNAs (certified nurse anesthetists), the radiologist, the x-ray technician, the optometrist, and the pharmacist. By the time this was accomplished, someone had given the child something to eat, and we would have to wait another five hours to do the study. Since it was already late, I told them to return the following Tuesday and hold any food until after the X-ray test. It was depressing to watch the family leave. I told them that the situation was dire, but I didn't reveal the full extent of my concern. I thought the child had no chance for salvageable vision and that even survival would probably be short-term. The parents were already dealing with enough. They had seven children, and their home was destroyed by shelling during the 1999 conflict.

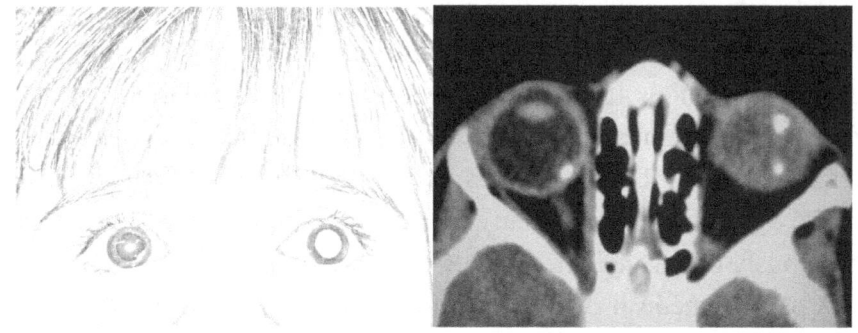

Falcon Angel Eyes
Bilateral Retinoblastoma

CT Scan Confirming

When the family returned, COL M performed dilated retinal exams on the 4-year-old sister and 7-year-old brother to exclude occult autosomal dominant disease (one inherited form of retinoblastoma can be found in multiple siblings in the same family). With the assistance of anesthesia, a sedated, non-contrast (no dye was given) CT examination of the brain and orbits was performed with thin cuts (3mm thick) to evaluate the extent of the disease. Amazingly, the CT revealed no evidence of bony metastasis, optic nerve enlargement, or extension beyond the globes of the eyes. We performed an enhanced scan (with dye), and still, there was no evidence of metastatic disease. COL M performed a dilated exam on the less affected eye and believed the lesion was peripheral to the optic nerve, potentially allowing for treatment via cold laser therapy. Suddenly, there appeared to be a slight chance that the child might survive and even have vision in one eye.

We needed an MRI to evaluate the optic nerve, and we eventually got consent to have it done in Skopje, Macedonia. The physicians there might also be able to perform the left enucleation (removal of the left eye containing the large tumor). However, the MRI would cost 400 Euros (€), which the family could not afford, and we would not be allowed to pay for the procedure from our budget.

I thought I could get the doctors at Bondsteel to contribute enough to cover the charge. I emailed the physicians to explain the situation and request a contribution of 40 €. While waiting for their response, I contacted the French for possible assistance. Unfortunately, their initial reaction was negative. I contacted the Italians, knowing we could probably count on the Germans since they had helped with the previous retinoblastoma patient.

The response from the Bondsteel physicians was rapid, and most wanted to contribute more than 40 Euros. Somehow, word of the fundraising effort got out to the nursing staff, who became upset that they had not been asked to contribute. A similar response from other hospital personnel followed this. COL M and I decided to establish a "Falcon Angel Fund" to cover the cost of medical procedures outside Kosovo and contribute to the family's travel expenses.

I sent a second email to hospital personnel, using the term "Falcon Angel" and including a picture of the little girl. The response was overwhelming. By the end of the day, I had taken in almost 1500 €, with commitments for several hundred more. We could put together at least 2,000 €, which was about $3,000 then.

The MRI was attempted in Skopje, Macedonia, but was canceled when the child developed an upper respiratory infection and could not be sedated.

Dec 10th - Money continued to pour in for the Falcon Angel Fund. Hospital personnel had shared the email with some Bondsteel soldiers, who wanted to contribute. Others had shared the email with family and friends at home, and I began to get emails from people all over the United States who wanted to help. I got an email that all the "Santa fund" proceeds would go to the angel fund, and the general had heard about the effort and was making a personal contribution.

The chaplain came to my office to inform me about the rules regarding establishing "Funds" in the army. There are strict regulations in place to prevent requests for money that are diverted into "slush" funds, which might be used for activities unrelated to the Army's mission. He offered to help me ensure all the correct requests and paperwork were done. Given the way the fund grew, I was concerned that excess funds might accumulate. I suggested that an appropriate place for such funds would be the Chapel Fund, and I thought the "Falcon Angel Fund" should be merged into the Chapel Fund after my departure. The chaplain agreed to the plan.

On Dec 14th, COL M and CSM K took the mother and child to Macedonia for the MRI. Several hospitals are starting to compete for the child, including the University of Cincinnati Medical Center, an eye hospital in Germany, a large hospital in Greece, a Shriners hospital in Pennsylvania, and, most recently, a French hospital.

After their initial hesitation, the French have stepped up. COL F of the French Camp stated that the Ministry of Medicine had agreed to cover the cost, and he was raising funds at the French Camp and in his village in France. I sent him more information; hopefully, one of these possibilities will come through. The first hospital to commit is going to get this child.

Dec. 15th - The French now appear to be on the verge of taking the little girl. The Falcon Angel fund continues to grow, and we may have the child in Paris before Christmas. The desire to contribute to the Falcon Angel Fund continues to grow, and we may receive significant funding from companies and service organizations. I just hope we get the little girl treated soon.

Dec 20th—The angel child's family was in, and she will fly to Paris tomorrow. COL Bruno F was instrumental in procuring treatment at a children's hospital in Paris, France.

This was indeed a Christmas miracle. So many people from all walks of life and from all over the world could not bear the thought of not trying to help this small child from a battered family in a battered country. You might think it's because people are inherently good, but I know God is great. If you look, there are Angels among us.

PSALMS 91:11 For he will command his angels concerning you to guard you in all your ways;

MATTHEW 18:10 "See that you do not despise one of these little ones. For I tell you that their angels in heaven always see the face of my Father.

A Father, A Son, and an Ambulance at the Gate
(*Pseudomonas and the smell of grapes*)

Bondsteel Hospital was the best medical facility in Kosovo. It did not take long for people to find out, so it became a daily occurrence for locals to show up at the gate, hoping to receive medical help. Although we were allowed and did treat civilian Kosovo citizens, we had limited resources and were primarily tasked to care for the NATO forces comprising KFOR (Kosovo Force). I have previously mentioned that for a local citizen to qualify for treatment, they needed to have a condition representing an imminent threat to "life, limb, or sight."

On a daily (and nightly) basis, we had people showing up at the Bondsteel gates hoping to gain access to the hospital for medical assistance. When this occurred, the gate would contact the hospital, and a medic would be dispatched to evaluate the patient's eligibility for treatment. The medics would call back to report their findings and assessment, which would be endorsed or overruled by one of the medical staff members. Over time, the medics became increasingly skillful and made the right call. The following was an example of a case that offered a teaching moment for a medic and, for me, an illustration of a father's love.

It was the twenty-third of December, and although Christmas was just hours away, the hospital hummed along like any other day. As late afternoon approached, it was already dark, so I decided to get a little exercise. I arrived at the gym, changed, and climbed onto my stationary bike. I was beginning to pedal when my phone rang. It was a call from the Tactical Operations Center (TOC) about a burn patient from Ferzei who had arrived at the gate via ambulance.

Usually, a transfer from another hospital would have at least triggered a phone call, but I had heard nothing. I was aware that a two-year-old boy had suffered burns to both hands a few days earlier, and I initially assumed that his condition must have worsened and he was

234

being sent for additional evaluation. If this were the case, I thought the medic was wrestling with whether this represented an imminent danger of losing the patient's hands. The TOC did not have additional information but did say the medic was asking if I could come to the gate. I told them I would be there as soon as possible and asked them to arrange an ambulance to take me there. If the patient comes to the hospital, we must transport him in one of our vehicles.

When I got to the gate, I found that all my musings and suppositions were utterly wrong. The medic was standing outside the ambulance with a middle-aged gentleman who turned out to be the patient's father. The patient was in the back of the ambulance and was a young man who had been burned several months earlier. The medic who had initially gone to the gate to evaluate the patient had been "overwhelmed." He was overwhelmed by the sight of a young man with extensive, poorly healing burns that covered much of his back and legs. He had not been able to get into the ambulance to examine the patient because, with each attempt, he had been overwhelmed by an intense, pungent odor of "rotting grapes."

I spoke to the father with the aid of an interpreter. What an unfortunate story he told. His son was working in a factory, where one of the processing steps involved the use of boiling water. Something had gone wrong, resulting in the patient being scaled on his back and legs. He was immediately stripped of his clothing, but the damage was done, and he had about a 30-40% body surface area, primarily third-degree burns. A third-degree burn involves the full thickness of the skin. There is no skin left to heal the area. The only options are to cover the area with "new" grafted skin or to let the area cover with scar tissue. This had all occurred about four months prior. The young man had been taken to a local hospital, where he had remained since the accident. The father was concerned that his son was not getting better, so he hired an ambulance, went to the hospital, picked up his son, and brought him to Bondsteel. He was not a wealthy man, and I could only imagine what portion of his annual income he had invested in this effort to save his son. It was an unfortunate story.

Enough talk; it's time to see the patient. When I opened the door, the vehicle reeked of Pseudomonas, the overwhelming grape smell the medic initially encountered. The young man was a culture medium. Great greenish heaps of Pseudomonas covered the wounds on his back and legs. Despite the extent of his injury, he was amazingly alert and afebrile. Although the wounds looked amazingly painful, the patient did not complain.

I used the moment to instruct the medic about the origin and significance of the smell. I also told him that this was common in burn patients.

I considered for a few minutes what I might be able to do for the patient and how I was going to tell the father that we could not admit his son to our hospital. Although he had suffered a terrible injury, he was not at imminent risk of dying. He had already survived for months. He did not have eye involvement, and although the wounds to his legs were significant, he did not appear to be in imminent danger of losing a limb.

In addition, we were not a burn center. If we had seen him acutely, we would have admitted him, but would have transferred him to a local facility once he was stabilized. I had worked in a burn center during Desert Storm, and I knew that this type of patient would overwhelm our staff and drain our logistical capabilities. He would be at Bondsteel for months, growing Pseudomonas and contaminating the entire hospital.

I told his father that, although he was healing slowly, he had obviously had reasonable care given his present condition. I explained that we did not have a burn center and that his son needed these wounds cleaned and dressed daily. I told him I would write a treatment plan to outline the steps we would take if the patient were being treated at our center. I also requested that two days' worth of supplies be sent back with the patient to ensure that the instructions could at least be started. I also agreed to speak with his doctor the next day regarding the plan and medications. I ended by explaining our "life, limb, sight" admission policy and the fact that we could not admit his son to our hospital.

This was all accomplished through the interpreter. After each sentence, the father stoically nodded. There was no outburst, no flood of questions, no protest. In the end, he simply thanked me.

I knew this man would now climb into that ambulance and return to Ferzei. He would breathe the smell of rotting grapes, which I am sure he would interpret as the rotting flesh of his son, for a couple of hours. He would wonder if his son would survive and whether this had all been worthwhile.

Things would have been different if we had been in the States. Unfortunately, we were not, and I was left to make excuses. The world is not an equal playing field, and life is often unfair.

What did shine through in this bleak case was a father's love for his son. Sometimes, it is good to remember what a powerful force love can be.

PSALMS 103:13 As a father has compassion on his children, so the Lord has compassion on those who fear him;

LUKE 15:20 So he got up and went to his father. "But while he was still a long way off, his father saw him and was filled with compassion for him; he ran to his son, threw his arms around him and kissed him.

Operation Iraqi Freedom –
(28th Combat Support Hospital
Forward Operating Base Diamondback – North of Mosul)

Introduction
("They're not here yet...welcome to FOB Diamondback...")

When I opened my emails on December 26th, 2006, I got a belated Christmas present from the US Army. I was on the latest activation list for Southeast Asia (AKA Iraq). It was nice of them to wait until after Christmas, but it certainly impacted my New Year's resolutions. I had to resolve to see the world because I would be going on a trip within the next 90 days.

On this occasion, I was transferred from my unit in Richmond to the 865th Army Hospital, which required a doctor to be deployed to Operation Iraqi Freedom. I must say that I never saw or worked with the 865th, but my paperwork must have been processed (at least electronically) through them for a few months, as I was now headed to Camp Arifjan, Kuwait.

When I arrived in Kuwait in early March 2007, I was informed that I would be the new Division Surgeon for the commander in Arifjan. Wow, that is a nice job! As such, I would be on the staff of the 3rd Transportation Command. Unfortunately, there was a problem. The 3rd Transportation Command had not yet deployed to Kuwait; they were still back in the States.

"When will they get here?" I asked.

"They are expected by the middle of June," was the response.

"Well, what do I do until they arrive?"

"You could go home and come back…or we can find you a new job."

I could not go home. I was not going to put my family through the trauma of leaving a second time within three months. Also, I had made work arrangements to cover my absence.

"What kind of jobs do you have?"

"Well, there is a Navy Hospital on base…maybe you can work there."

So, the next day, I went to the Navy hospital. It was a typical DEPMEDS tent city facility. The folks were friendly, but I could tell I made the new Hospital commander uneasy since I outranked him. I am sure he wondered what an Army COL was doing nosing around his hospital. However, the big problem was that they had no patients. Lots of nice doctors and nurses, but only two patients. I knew that would not work for me. I do not do well sitting on my hands. Time would crawl by…I need to be busy.

When I returned to the operations shop, I told them I needed to be somewhere I would be busy.

"Do you really mean that? If so, we have just the job for you."

The primary medical facility in Iraq – the 28th Combat Support Hospital based out of Fort Bragg, North Carolina – was busy running "Baghdad ER" while supporting operations in Northern Iraq through a Forward Operating Base (FOB) Diamondback facility. I knew the name Diamondback well because 22 soldiers from my former command (the 99th Regional Support Command) had been killed when an Iraqi Civilian had blown himself up in the Diamondback mess hall earlier in the conflict. The "surge" was starting, and the soldiers and marines working in that area were having a tough time. Therefore, the 28th sent about 100 personnel to run a hospital on the FOB.

"You want to be busy – well, they are busy."

Two days later, I was somewhere near Mosul at what was formerly the Mosul airport, but now it was FOB Diamondback. It would be an experience that would forever change my life.

JEREMIAH 29:11 "For I know the plans I have for you," declares the Lord, "plans to prosper you and not to harm you, plans to give you hope and a future."

PROVERBS 3:5-6 Trust in the Lord with all your heart and lean not on your own understanding; in all your ways submit to him, and he will make your paths straight.

ISAIAH 41:10 So do not fear, for I am with you; do not be dismayed, for I am your God. I will strengthen you and help you; I will uphold you with my righteous right hand.

ROMANS 8:28 And we know that in all things God works for the good of those who love him, who have been called according to his purpose.

EPHESIANS 2:10 For we are God's handiwork, created in Christ Jesus to do good works, which God prepared in advance for us to do.

First Night in Iraq
(Into the darkness, Scorpions, and "more good news...")

In early 2007, the landing strip in Mosul was considered "hot." This meant that the C-130 I and several other (much younger) soldiers made an "assault" landing at Mosul. The plane seemed to drop out of the sky—it was much like a roller coaster ride. When we landed, the plane's rear door opened, and the pallet with our gear was rapidly pulled out. We followed, and the plane was gone. The props never stopped turning.

I could not believe it. It was the middle of the night, and it had been raining! Remember, I had just spent several days in a real desert. There was standing water in what was a very Spartan reception area. Some of the troops were replacements, and some were returning from leave. I was brand new and somewhat unexpected (all the orders had been arranged and cut within the last 48 hours). The other guys grabbed their bags and scattered. Mine were on the bottom of the pallet – three duffel bags, each weighing between 50 and 75 pounds.

I asked the fellow standing near the bags where the 28th Combat Support Hospital might be.

"Not too far," he responded, pointing into the darkness. "You need to go that way about 100 meters. You will come to a wall. A guard will show you how to get through the wall. The hospital will be about 50 meters on the other side of the wall."

Well, that seemed simple enough. "How do I find the guard?"

"Oh, Sir. He will find you."

So, at about 0200 hours, with one duffel bag on my back and one in each hand, I walked off into the darkness in the indicated direction. Sure enough, a guard with night vision goggles showed me where to get through the wall and pointed me toward the hospital.

The walls/barriers separating various activities are made of individual slabs of concrete, each about ten to twelve feet tall, three feet wide, and 10 inches thick. Each slab has a base, and when placed side by side, they provide an excellent barrier. At strategic points along the length of the wall, a couple of slabs will be brought forward, parallel to the remainder of the wall, and two more slabs will be placed parallel to but on the other side of the wall. If one is running for cover, you can slip behind the offset slabs and through the wall in either direction. When one looks directly at the wall, it appears solid. It is ingenious and necessary in an environment where explosives drop unexpectedly out of the sky.

Once through the wall, I moved in the indicated direction until I found a building and what I assumed was the front door. I pushed my way in and did not see a soul. To my left was what I thought might be a reception window (no one there). To my right was a small area I took to be a waiting room. Directly in front of me stretched a hallway with doors on either side. The hallway appeared to end at a wall, which I considered to be a perpendicular hallway. It is late, I am tired (I had not slept for the last 36 hours), and I did not see anyone. I dropped the two duffel bags I was carrying.

Their sound must have appropriately announced my presence because a head popped out of one of the side doors. Good. Signs of life! The person looked me up and down and asked, "Are you a doctor?"

Oh, rarely is that a good question at 0200 hrs...

"Why yes, I am a doctor," I replied.

"Good, we have a patient." (Well, welcome to Iraq, Doctor Carr…)

I removed my remaining duffel bag and moved down the hall to find that the medic had been looking out the emergency department door.

"What do we have here?" I inquired.

What we had was an Iraqi civilian with a scorpion sting. Oh great, I've seen a lot of those. I was soon to find that the 28th CSH took care of everybody who needed acute care – US Soldiers and Marines, US Contractors, Iraqi soldiers, Iraqi civilians, and even bad guys.

Since I did not (and still do not) speak Arabic (or Kurdish), I was glad to see the interpreter already engaged with the patient. I asked the medic if we had anything for scorpion stings. He excitedly said, "Yes, we have antivenom!" I asked if he would bring me the package insert for the antivenom while I spoke to the patient.

I examined the area of the sting on the patient's forearm. There appeared to be multiple puncture wounds. I asked the interpreter to ask the patient how many times he had been stung. A rather animated conversation ensued between the interpreter and the patient, after which the interpreter turned to me and said, "Once." I wondered what had been said, but not having a clue, I asked why there appeared to be so many puncture wounds. After another exchange with the patient, the interpreter said that the patient had used a needle to repeatedly puncture the area to get the venom out. I had already noted that Iraq was one of the dirtiest places I had ever been. Multiple puncture wounds were not a particularly good idea (see photo on left).

I realized at this point that I needed a thorough education on scorpions, so I turned to the computer on an adjacent desk and quickly searched for information on scorpions. What came up on the first three pages were references to a rock band. When I finally encountered eight-legged scorpions, I found that they had a worldwide distribution, with some species being harmless, some being dangerous, and some being potentially deadly. Their sting was similar to that of a pit viper in that antivenom was not typically required unless progressive swelling, neuropathy, or coagulopathy developed.

At this point, the medic returned with a stack of papers. I informed him that I needed the package insert. He said that there was not one because the antivenom was not FDA-approved. I responded that we could not use anything that was not FDA-approved in patients. He said that since the allied forces did not have an FDA-approved antivenom, the FDA had granted a waiver to use an equine polyvalent

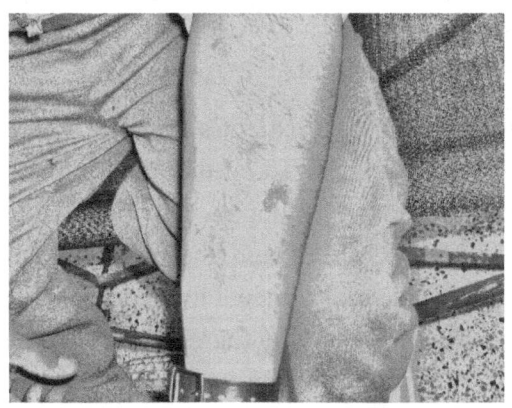

antivenom from Saudi Arabia. The packet of paper he had brought was what would need to be filled out for any patient who received the antivenom.

I responded, "How many times have you used the antivenom?"

"This is our first scorpion sting."

Great. I read the first page of the instructions. It was a polyvalent antivenom effective in treating the stings of 37 scorpions in the region. It could only be given if the patient had a running large-bore (preferably 16-gauge) IV and an Ambu bag and epinephrine available. This was required because the anaphylaxis rate with antivenom administration approached 30% (i.e., about one-third of your treated patients would be at risk for a potentially lethal reaction…). Well, that's not good news.

I needed more information. "Do we have any additional information about scorpions?"

"Well, we have the scorpion chart." At this point, the medic opened a door to reveal a chart of "scorpions of Northern Iraq." The scorpions were neatly categorized into three groups: minimally dangerous, dangerous, and potentially lethal. I quickly scanned the chart for anything that might be helpful and noted various colors and sizes (see the photo to the left).

I asked the interpreter to ask what the scorpion looked like. The patient responded that it was "black." Unfortunately, there were black scorpions in each category. I re-examined the patient, who did not appear to be worsening. After asking again when the sting had occurred (it had been more than an hour), I made the "strategic decision" to treat the patient as a puncture wound (clean and disinfect the skin, topical antibiotics, gauze dressing, and tetanus shot). I instructed the medic to hold the patient in the ER for another two hours. He was to call me if the patient worsened, but discharge him if he remained stable. I was not going to give an antivenom that might

stop the guy's breathing. He looked pretty good to me.

It is always bad to walk through the door and proceed to kill your first patient. People tend to lose confidence in your abilities.

It was about 0300 as I finished my treatment note on the patient. I was dead tired and beginning to wonder what I would do next when I heard a booming voice behind me say, "Col Carr, is that you?"

I turned around to see SGT Briggs, with whom I had worked in Kosovo several years earlier. He was a dental assistant at that time. He was larger (about 6' 4" tall) than life and a great guy.

I asked, "Sgt Briggs, are you cleaning teeth in Iraq?"

"No, sir. I'm in logistics now. I saw your name on the manifest and thought it had to be you. I have your billet."

My response was, "Sgt, you must be an angel."

Briggs grabbed two of my duffel bags as if they were nothing and asked me to follow him out the other side of the hospital. He talked as we went.

"Sir, I made sure I got you a good billet. The bad news is that it is not right here at the hospital. It's about 100 meters on the other side of the street behind the hospital."

"That's no problem, Sgt. I appreciate your looking after me."

"Well, the only bad thing about the billets across the street is that they do not have the sandbags on top. But the good news is you have a great bunker outside your door."

My Bunker – Outside   My Bunker - Inside

"Well, I guess that is good news, Sgt…"

Sgt Briggs continued, "And there is more good news. Do you remember those bunker drills we had to do in Kosovo? We don't have to do those here."

"Sgt, that is good news. I hated those drills," I replied. (Those drills were a complete waste of time and interrupted busy work schedules.)

"Yes, Sir, we get mortared so much, we never have to drill."

"Well, Sgt, I'm not sure that is good news."

"Oh, Sir, don't worry about it. It is all automatic."

"What do you mean, automatic?' I asked.

"Well, sir, there are detectors that pick up incoming rounds. They are on poles; you will see them when it gets light. The detectors are connected to speakers, and when rounds are detected, the speakers will say either 'Incoming, Incoming' or 'bunkers, bunkers, bunkers.' If they say "bunkers, bunkers, bunkers," you have 8 to 9 seconds to get in the bunker. If they say "incoming, incoming," the rounds are close and will hit soon, so you lie down, wait for the first few booms, and then get up and run to the bunker."

Detectors for incoming rounds   Speakers to issue warning – Also beautiful billets!

Well, for a tired man, the Sgt certainly managed to get my attention. "Is there any particular time they like to mortar the Americans?"

"Not really, sir. It's all pretty random, and they're terrible shots. I have noticed that they tend to lob a few in on us right after the first call to morning prayer."

The call to morning prayer is a haunting song chant from each mosque's minaret.

"Well, Sgt, do you have any more advice for an old soldier?" I asked.

"Well, sir, I would just say stay low and move fast."

"Sgt, I can't do both of those at the same time..." I replied.

His response was, "Well then, move fast."

The Sgt opened my billet, put my two duffel bags on my bed, shook my hand, gave a sharp salute, and disappeared into the night.

I was dog-tired. I pulled off my boots, removed my uniform, and collapsed across the mattress.

The next thing I heard was "bunkers, bunkers, bunkers." I tore out the door and into the bunker. A couple more folks came in after me. The bunker is about five feet high, so you are bent over as you wait. The bottom is composed of gravel and earth, and it is open to the outside. A few seconds later, we heard boom, boom, boom, and then silence.

I had been reading about scorpions. They are nocturnal and active at night. I was barefoot and wondered what might be crawling on (or at least near) my toes. I gently asked the guy beside me, "How long before the all-clear?"

"Oh, not long, sir. Usually not longer than 15 minutes," was the response.

"15 minutes...I don't think I can stay here for that long," I offered.

"You're not barefooted, are you? Don't ever come in here barefooted."

My feeble excuse was, "Well, I'm sure that is good advice, but unfortunately, I did not have time to get my shoes."

"This is what you should do. Tomorrow, get yourself a chair and put it beside the door of your houch. Put a light, a T-shirt, and something for your feet on that chair. When you hear the alert, grab whatever is on that chair as you run out."

I thanked the young soldier for his advice and followed it as soon as it got light.

Welcome to FOB Diamondback, Doctor Carr...

JEREMIAH 29:11 "For I know the plans I have for you," declares the Lord, "plans to prosper you and not to harm you, plans to give you hope and a future."

PROVERBS 16:9 In their hearts humans plan their course, but the Lord establishes their steps.

ISAIAH 55:8 "For my thoughts are not your thoughts, neither are your ways my ways," declares the Lord.

ROMANS 8:28 And we know that in all things God works for the good of those who love him, who have been called according to his to his purpose.

Life or limb in the setting of limited blood products
(*"I think I can save that arm"*)

I think I mentioned earlier that mass casualty events were a regular occurrence at 28th CSH (North). A mass casualty means that you have multiple injured or sick patients arriving at your facility in a short period of time. While I was with the 28th, the maximum number of patients in one event was 34 (a massive explosion caused by a VBID – Vehicular Born Improvised Device – a bomb hidden in a truck). Still, it was not uncommon to get three to five severely wounded patients at a time. Responding to such events requires an efficient, coordinated effort. The 28th was excellent in this regard. The Navy uses a phrase when everyone needs to react simultaneously – "all hands on deck." The Marines have a phrase to describe the philosophy underlying their purpose: "Every Marine is a rifleman." At the 28th, during a mass casualty, it was "every soldier present and every soldier is a medic."

This was not as difficult as it might sound, because all our personnel were well-trained, and we essentially lived in the hospital. When notification of an impending mass casualty was received, people automatically appeared in the emergency room. It was what we were there for. It was actually what we lived for.

Because we were far forward and a "step-child" of the 28th CSH, housed primarily in the "Green Zone" of Baghdad, we did have to deal with a few limitations. Our CT scanner was outdated and prone to overheating. You could get about six cuts, and then you would have to stop. If the CT overheated, it would be down for several hours. So, if you had a soldier with multiple wounds, you would need to decide what was the most concerning for short-term survival. If the patient were wounded in the chest and abdomen, you would be able to get a few cuts of the chest or the abdomen, but not both – dealer's choice.

We also had an X-ray machine and developer. Unfortunately, the automated developer had died. Our radiologist and radiology tech had rigged up an old-fashioned developing technique. This was slower but worked reasonably well. It did have the side effect of causing the hallway in which radiology resided to smell of vinegar (acetic acid) continuously. At one point, one of the radiologists in Baghdad rotated out, and it was decided that our radiologist should fill his spot. This "temporary" situation went on for weeks. Since we had a marginal CT and an old-fashioned X-ray developer, the "powers-that-be" felt we did not need a "real" radiologist. We managed.

Perhaps the most significant limitation we regularly encountered was a limited blood supply. We would typically have 30 units of blood on hand at the beginning of any day. Multiple simultaneous bleeding patients or one severely bleeding patient could quickly deplete 30 units. This would immediately impact our ability to render acute care in our casualty-rich environment. Our only possibility for quick replacement was the people walking around the hospital. All our personnel had their blood types recorded on their dog tags, but the most valuable ones were those with an O blood type. Such folks are known as "universal donors." Their blood can be given to patients of virtually any blood type. Guess who has O-negative blood...

One problem with the walking blood bank is the loss of a worker if they have to lie down to donate. Another problem is the potential for going to the same "well" too often and ending up with an anemic staff member.

The best thing to do for any bleeding patient (and the most effective way to avoid a blood shortage) is to stop the bleeding as soon as possible. The army is good at this. The effort to stop the bleeding begins at the moment of wounding by the application of direct pressure by the wounded soldier or a buddy. Direct pressure will be supplemented by applying a "hemostatic" bandage containing materials that speed clotting. If bleeding is brisk, a tourniquet will be applied by the soldier (the combat tourniquet is designed to be used with one hand), his buddy, or a medic. When the soldier is passed from the medic to a nurse or doctor, the efforts to stop the bleeding are continued and intensified. Blood will be transfused, and bleeding vessels will be clamped and surgically repaired or bypassed.

The following is the case of a patient who presented during a mass casualty situation and was bleeding so severely from an arm wound that amputation of a potentially salvageable arm was considered due to the rapid utilization of our limited blood supply.

The patient was a 27-year-old male Iraqi civilian who had suffered multiple gunshot wounds. He had been shot through the liver, through the right chest, and the left upper arm (left panel in photos below – note the combat tourniquet present near the left shoulder). Significant injuries included a hepatic laceration, fractured sternum, and an open grade III-C humeral fracture of the left arm (middle panel x-ray below). The injuries occurred at 1345 hours local time, and the patient arrived in the emergency department on the 28th at 1450 hours. Initial vital signs were recorded as a respiratory rate (RR) of 30 breaths per minute, a Temperature (Temp) of 98.1°F, a heart rate (HR) of 141 beats per minute, and a blood pressure (BP) of 129/105 mmHg. The admitting physician "doubted" the accuracy of the blood pressure and indicated in his note that the patient was "very cold upon arrival." Initial laboratory evaluation revealed a hemoglobin of 10.1 gms (indicating significant blood loss – at least a third of his blood volume), an INR (International Normalization Ratio) of 1.3 (indicating early development of a coagulopathy – decreased ability of the blood to clot), and a normal platelet count (299K/μL). The patient was felt to be unstable with a Class III hemorrhage. At 1503 in the operating room (thirteen minutes after arrival on the 28th), the HR was 157, BP was 64/35 (that one we could believe), Temp was 35.4 °C, and the patient was felt to be in Class III shock.

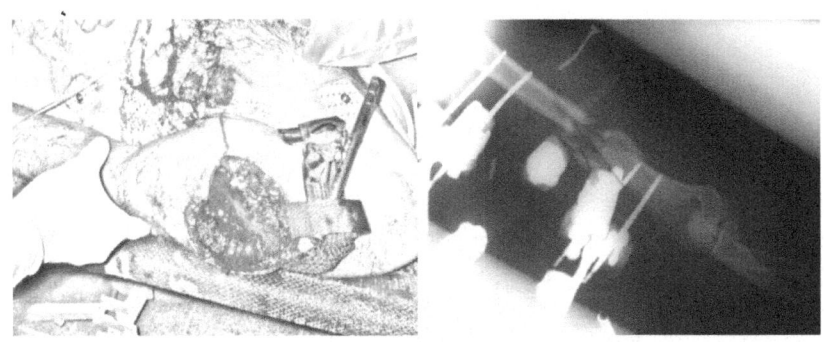

During the first twenty minutes in the OR, the systolic BP remained less than 90 mm Hg despite the rapid transfusion of 7 units of packed red blood cells (with an additional two units infusing) and two units of fresh frozen plasma. Intraoperatively, the team was notified that only two more units of packed red cells were available for transfusion in this patient. He continued to have rapid blood loss and a non-revascularized extremity (absent pulses below the elbow).

The orthopedic surgeon was convinced he could save the arm. Still, the continuing rapid blood loss and the dwindling blood supply raised the possibility that the arm might have to be amputated to control bleeding as a life-sparing move.

We had available recombinant FVIIa (a potent activated clotting factor that could be given rapidly as an intravenous hemostatic agent). Still, we tended not to use it because it was expensive, we had a limited supply, it took time to get it from the blood bank to the ER, and it did not have FDA approval for hemorrhage secondary to trauma. The extreme nature of this case led to the decision to use rFVIIa.

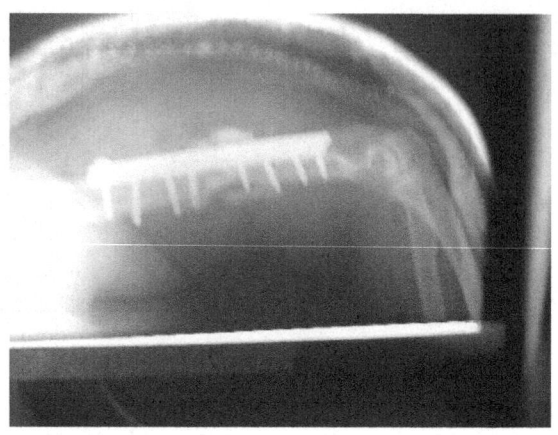

While 7.2 mgs of rFVIIa were being administered intravenously, initiation of a whole blood drive versus amputation of the extremity was considered. Within a few minutes of rFVIIa administration, the bleeding slowed dramatically. An exploratory laparotomy (abdominal surgery) with surgical repair of the liver laceration, revascularization of the left arm via left brachial artery shunt, vascular repair of the brachial artery, and left humerus alignment and debridement with external fixation were achieved (x-ray in right panel above). Two additional units of packed red cells and six units of FFP were administered during and after the procedure. Subsequent internal stabilization was completed, and a successful humeral repair was performed (second x-ray seen above). The patient recovered completely from all his wounds and survived with a functional arm.

In advanced trauma centers, amputation for hemorrhage control is, fortunately, a rare event. Still, amputation in the setting of massive bleeding due to vascular compromise continues to be a significant problem. The situation may differ significantly in a mass casualty setting with limited blood product supplies. Such conditions are encountered in forward treatment facilities supporting combat operations or populations exposed to terrorist violence. In these settings, blood components are available in limited amounts, and casualties can be severe, multiple, and episodic in nature. A single patient can exhaust the entire blood supply, compromising the facility's treatment capability.

Although improvements in topical therapies, tourniquets, and hemostatic bandages have improved the situation, hemorrhage may remain uncontrolled in trauma patients. The Chitosan bandage is available in US Army-issued first aid kits, and, at the time of this case, Quikclot (zeolite) topical powder was available for first aid use by the Marines. The new version of the combat tourniquet (CAT) was frequently used in Iraq, and this patient (see photo of arm). Despite these advances, hemorrhage remains a principal cause of morbidity and the primary reversible cause of mortality in military trauma.

Additional advances in hemorrhage treatment have included the introduction of damage control resuscitation. This treatment protocol/regimen is based on studies of trauma patients and recent military conflicts, where there is increasing evidence of the early development of trauma and treatment-related coagulopathy. Clotting factor deficiencies may rapidly develop due to utilization and dilution by resuscitation fluids. This situation led to recommendations to increase the use of fresh frozen plasma and decrease the use of electrolyte solutions and plasma expanders. The recommended ratio of fresh frozen plasma units to packed red cell units transfused was increased from 1-to-5 to 1-to-1. The infusion of solutions such as Ringer's Lactate was recommended to be severely restricted and avoided whenever possible. This recommendation was consistent with the shift toward relative hypotensive resuscitation, where a systolic blood pressure target of 90 mmHg is considered acceptable.

Early detection of coagulopathy has been and continues to be a problem. The availability of prothrombin time and INR measurements at forward treatment locations, along with the relative sensitivity of these measures to factor VII levels, led to their early evaluation in hemorrhaging trauma patients. An INR greater than 1.5 develops rapidly in some trauma patients and is associated with an increased risk of massive blood loss. This association between early abnormal

INR and bleeding risk in trauma patients prompted the recommendation for early use of intravenous hemostatic agents in such patients with active bleeding.

This case illustrates the influences of tactical environment and blood supply constraints on clinical decision-making. In this patient, bleeding from a potentially salvageable injured extremity was poorly controlled by tourniquet use. Continued bleeding rapidly exhausted available blood for the patient and markedly degraded the capability of the hospital to accept and treat other trauma patients. Control of bleeding coincident with the use of rFVIIa allowed salvage of the arm and avoided amputation as a mode of hemorrhage control. It can be argued that other factors may have contributed to the stoppage of bleeding in this patient. Indeed, continued tourniquet use and hypotensive systolic blood pressure may have played significant roles. However, both were already in use or present at the time of rFVIIa administration, and bleeding was not controlled until the infusion of rFVIIa. The question arises as to whether the earlier use of this agent might have been preferred for both the patient's care and the conservation of blood products for the hospital. This topic was reviewed and discussed by the hospital medical staff. The necessity of ordering rFVIIa from the pharmacy was identified as an impediment to its early use. After consultation with the pharmacy, a procedure was developed to allow the storage of a limited supply of rFVIIa in the emergency department. Administration would only be done under the direction of the treating physician, but could be accomplished rapidly once the decision to use the agent had been made. Novel modes of administration and off-label use of therapeutic agents may be reasonable approaches under certain conditions. In every case, the decisions should be made after considering the potential risks and benefits. The implications of patient population and medical supply constraints should also be considered where appropriate.

The citation for this published case is as follows:

M.E. Carr, B. Vickaryous. Life, Limb or Off-Label Recombinant

VIIa Use in the Setting of Limited Blood Assets: A Case Study. Blood Coagulation and Fibrinolysis 2013;24:436-438.

2 Corinthians 9:8 And God is able to bless you abundantly, so that in all things at all times, having all that you need, you will abound in every good work.

What Do You Do When Your Commander Walks in from LaLa Land?
("Don't answer that banana, it may be the commander...")

Humphrey Bogart is one of my favorite actors, and his performance as the unstable Commander Queeg in "The Caine Mutiny" is a classic. Watching him roll the steel balls in his hand as his testimony became increasingly animated during the trial became all too real for me during my time in Mosul.

When I first arrived in Mosul, the DCCS (Deputy Commander for Clinical Services), an orthopedic surgeon, served as acting commander while the commander was traveling. When the commander returned during my second week, I got an introductory one-on-one with him. He was a former enlisted Marine who had joined the Army after completing medical school, and was an anesthesiologist, as well as a colonel with more than twenty years of active-duty service. During our conversation, he expressed concern about the number of awards being handed out. He expressed that he would be looking for "exceptional performance" from "anyone—enlisted or officer" if they were expecting to get a service award. I explained that I completely agreed and understood. He went on to say that he was interested in developing relationships with Iraqi civilian physicians, which was what he had been trying to do during his recent travels. I responded that I had been involved in educational programs with civilian physicians in Kosovo, where we would provide continuing education seminars along with certificates of participation and appreciation. The commander became very interested in this approach and said it was "just the kind of activity" he would look for when considering awards. He suggested I develop a plan for starting a local medical cooperative society in Mosul. I assured him I would give it some thought. Otherwise, he seemed a reasonable guy and someone I could work with.

The next several weeks were very hectic, and time flew by. The commander typically came to early morning rounds in the ER to hear about acute treatments, admissions, and the progress/status of patients in the hospital. I noticed he had been absent for several days and was told he was again "traveling." Then, one morning, he reappeared. He walked in and stood at the back of the group as various staff members reviewed their patients. Finally, he blurted out – "Are you through? If so, I have a few things to say."

He launched into a tirade about the inappropriate conduct of staff and officers. He was particularly concerned about the lack of appropriate "military courtesy." He felt that soldiers were lax in how they saluted and addressed one another. He made it clear that he would not let this "civilian environment" continue. Starting tonight, we will have a mandatory "officer call" from 1900 to 2100, and this will be a "daily" event until conditions improve.

That evening, we dutifully assembled in the largest meeting room in the hospital. As we sat outside a rectangle formed by tables, the commander sat on one side by himself and opened a small book. From that book, which appeared to be a diary or journal, he read sections relating to his childhood, including his very strict father, his role in helping raise his younger brother, and his early enlistment in the Marines. We sat around and wondered where this was all going. No one said a word.

The commander explained the readings as he closed the journal. He was concerned that we were not grasping his concept of command. We did not seem to know what he wanted unless he told us. He felt we could anticipate his expectations if we understood him better. Thus, he would explain what motivated him by giving us a glimpse into his development...

Well, this seemed more than a little strange.

After a second night of journal reading and a growing restlessness in the staff, I made an appointment to speak with the commander. As we spoke, I could see the commander's increasing agitation (and even anger), and I tried to convey to him, in a non-confrontational way, that I had been very impressed with his unit. The medical care was exceptional in less-than-optimal circumstances. I told him the officers worked very collegially, with everyone pulling their weight and covering any gaps due to the limited number of physicians. I told him that he could take pride in the performance of his command. I also suggested that his officers would work to meet his expectations and correct specific deficiencies he had identified. Finally, I suggested that the nightly commander briefings were becoming a burden to an overworked staff, and I hoped this might soon come to an end. He listened but made no promises.

It was clear to me that some of the staff, while concerned about the commander's behavior, had also decided that they had had it with the "briefings." A significant component of the hospital medical staff had come from an FST (Forward Surgical Team). This group was housed together (on my side of the road) and had their own LTC commander, orthopedic surgeon, who also had "had it" with the nightly briefings. "I'm not coming tonight, and I'm telling my folks they don't have to show up."

Things were not going well. The day continued to be busy, and I missed lunch again. In the afternoon, I walked three-quarters of a mile to the DFAC (Dining Facility, formerly called the mess hall), where I sat down to have a very late lunch, the main component of which was a large yellow banana. As I sat by myself, I was joined by the Chief Nurse, the DCCS, and the FST team commander.

I explained that I had spoken with the commander and hoped the briefings would end soon. When they asked, "What the hell is wrong with the commander?" I explained that I was not a psychiatrist. This was met with rather blank expressions.

I then picked up the banana lying by my plate, held it to my ear, and said, "Hello...yes, he is here." I then handed the banana across the table to the FST commander. I said, "It's the commander, and it's for you."

Suddenly, for the first time in a week, everyone was laughing.

I was unsure if I had made an impact on the commander, but the mandatory commander briefings ceased, and the commander departed for Baghdad to attend a meeting with the 28th CSH commander. When he returned, he was much more reserved for a few days. Unfortunately, when he reappeared at morning rounds, he was again fuming about the lack of military courtesy. He demonstrated how we should properly salute. He said that the salute should be so crisp and solid that the end of the hand should vibrate slightly as it ended just to the right of the right eyebrow. He demonstrated this several times for us, and sure enough, his hand shook at the end of the salute.

I was standing near the back of the group as this was occurring, and I felt that someone had walked in behind me. I cut my eyes to the right, and the commander of the 28th CSH stood there. He was carefully observing the whole episode.

When our local commander saw the 28th commander, he welcomed him to "rounds," which immediately came to an end. The 28th commander indicated to our commander that he would like to speak with him in private, and everyone immediately vacated the area.

We soon learned that the 28th commander had relieved our commander and would be making arrangements for his imminent departure for home. The 28th Commander announced that he would be at our site for a few days and would like to speak one-on-one with as many soldiers as possible. He needed to talk to all officers and NCOs (Non-Commissioned Officers).

I had my interview, and the 28th commander asked if there was any way he could persuade me to stay on as commander of the 28th CSH (North). I explained that I thought this was an excellent unit, but that I had already been away from work and home long enough for a

261

reservist, so I'd better call it quits at the end of my rotation. I did offer that he might call my wife to discuss it with her. He smiled and declined.

The DCCS took over as acting commander, and a couple of weeks later, our new commander arrived from Baghdad. She was a COL nurse and slipped into command with minimal fanfare. Once out of command, our former commander seemed to settle down, and he was close to his old self at the going-away party we gave before his departure. He told me he had had enough and was going home to retire.

The army handled this one well, but I never understood why a long-term veteran of multiple conflicts should suddenly have a problem.

My two key takeaways were that humor can be a godsend in difficult situations and that even seasoned veterans are at risk for stress-induced mental health difficulties. Sitting there listening to the commander read from his journal, I could almost see the steel marbles rolling in his hand...

PROVERBS 17:22 A cheerful heart is good medicine, but a crushed spirit dries up the bones.

ECCLESIASTES 2:12 Then I turned my thoughts to consider wisdom, and also madness and folly.

1 SAMUEL 16:23 Whenever the spirit from God came on Saul, David would take up his lyre and play. Then relief would come to Saul; he would feel better, and the evil spirit would leave him.

VII. FAMILY STORIES

This effort appears to be continually evolving. I had initially intended to compile stories that I have frequently (perhaps too often) shared with my family and friends. These stories typically involve situations at work or war. Recently, however, I spent a week at the beach with Sherri, one son, a nephew, and two good friends. After a few drinks, somehow, when asked about my sisters, I began to tell the story about how my sister Jane had passed away. As I told it, I felt both rage and an overwhelming sadness. I thought I had failed her when she needed me most, and the story caught in my throat the way some other stories (that cut too close to the bone) do. I am trying to record some of these family events. I am sure these stories will be special to some, but given my understanding of family dynamics, I believe they will be relevant to most.

Abdominal Pain and Coagulopathy
in the Emergency Room
(*What are they missing...*)

My sister Jane was one of my favorite people on the planet. She was pretty, funny, and a great cook! Also, at times, she bore a striking resemblance to my mother. My mother told me that when I was a little boy, and Jane was planning to get married, I told her, "If Tommy does not marry you, I will marry you." Well, I guess it was good that Tommy married her because he was a nice guy and brought new things into the family like pizza, French onion dip, and Wise potato chips! All of which I still love.

Tom Crowder had just gotten out of the Navy and was starting a job with Western Electric. He did not have a formal degree in electrical engineering, but he was one of the best engineers I've ever known. Due to his exceptional work ethic and obvious talent, he quickly advanced within the company and subsequently took an opportunity with Bell Labs. Unfortunately, that meant a move to Whippany, New Jersey. Suddenly, Jane was gone, and she was only intermittently back in our lives for most of her life. Tom was later hired by one of the earliest computer companies, and they moved to Gaithersburg, Maryland. Jane became so homesick that Tom quit his job and moved the family back to Greensboro. That did not last long. The fellow who had hired Tom in Maryland left and started his own company, Scientific Data Systems (SDS), in Huntsville, Alabama. Tom was one of his first hires, and the Crowders moved to Huntsville. Eventually, Xerox bought SDS, and Jane found herself in Fountain Valley, California, near Los Angeles, Anaheim, and Huntington Beach. They stayed there until Tom retired, and then they moved back to Greensboro.

By that time, I had been away from Greensboro for several decades.

When Jane moved back to Greensboro, all my sisters lived in one place, so I could visit them all in a few days. It also meant that the whole family could be together again during holidays. By that time, my parents were in their late eighties, and my mother was in relatively fragile health due to congestive heart failure and atrial fibrillation. Before I knew it, my eldest sister, Igenia, was also diagnosed with atrial fibrillation. Then, within a few months, Jane was also found to suffer from the same abnormal heart rhythm.

Atrial fibrillation occurs when the right atrium (the heart's upper right chamber) begins to spontaneously fire electrical signals from all regions of the chamber wall. Usually, the signal comes from one "pacemaker" part of the atrium. The signal fires on a rhythmic basis, causing the atrium to contract, and then it travels down a conduction pathway to the lower part of the heart, causing the ventricle to contract. The atrial contraction pushes blood down into the ventricle, and the ventricle pushes the blood out of the heart either into the lungs (the job of the right ventricle) or under high pressure out through the aorta to the rest of the body (the job of the left ventricle). When atrial fibrillation occurs, the random firing of the atria leads to variable intervals between ventricular beats. Sometimes beats are close together, and sometimes further apart. This type of rhythm is not as efficient as a normal rhythm, but if it does not become too rapid, the symptoms that result are simply a mild decrease in exercise tolerance and "energy" level. The treatment is typically an initial effort to shock the heart into a normal rhythm. If this does not work, medications are used to keep the heart rate within the normal range.

The primary concern with atrial fibrillation is the tendency to spontaneously go back and forth between a regular rhythm and atrial fibrillation. The reason this is a concern is that when someone has atrial fibrillation, they are at increased risk of forming blood clots within their heart. If a clot forms while a patient is in atrial fibrillation, it can be thrown out of the heart when/if the ventricle starts beating normally again. If this happens, the blood clot will travel out through the aorta and will go down a major artery until it reaches a point where the artery diameter decreases to less than the diameter of the clot. The clot cannot advance further, and blood flow beyond that point ceases. Any tissue being supplied by that vessel will soon become oxygen-starved and will be at risk of dying. The most common scenario is for a clot to go from the aorta to the carotid artery and into the brain. The result is a stroke. However, the clot can go anywhere, depending on which arterial branch it takes. Because of the risk of arterial embolism and its potentially dire consequences, patients are typically put on drugs called anticoagulants to reduce the risk of clot formation. Anticoagulants are sometimes referred to as "blood thinners." This is not the case. They do not make the blood "thinner;" they slow down how fast the blood makes a clot.

So, I had a mother and two sisters on warfarin, the most common anticoagulant drug at the time, to avoid this complication.

One night, about midnight, the phone rang. Sherri dutifully answered, and Tommy called from an emergency room in Greensboro. Jane had developed abdominal pain in the afternoon that did not respond to the usual antacids and gradually worsened to the point that Tommy had taken her to the hospital. He called "just to let me know" that she was not feeling well, but that it looked like she would be alright.

I asked what the doctors had told him, and he replied, "Well, not much." They had said to him that Jane's bowel sounds had decreased and that her stomach was tender on physical examination. Lab work reportedly showed that her white count was slightly up and that her clotting tests were abnormal. They were concerned that perhaps she had bled into her abdomen, and they were going to get a CT scan. The only other abnormal lab result was an elevated lactate level.

Still coming out of sleep, I tried to make sense of this report. First, the clotting tests should have been prolonged because she was supposedly on warfarin. Second, to spontaneously bleed into the abdomen would be very unusual and typically "catastrophic." That diagnosis did not fit with a story that now stretched for hours, from the afternoon into the evening. The tender abdomen and absence of bowel sounds were concerning for an "acute abdomen" (meaning a significant, rapidly evolving problem) that might require surgery.

I asked Tom if a surgeon had seen Jane, and he replied, "Not yet." He quickly followed that with, "Why would she need to if the problem is a clotting problem?" I told him that everything we initially knew did not seem to fit with a clotting problem, but if she were stable, we could wait to see what the CT scan revealed. I asked him to call me when he heard the CT scan results.

I hung up the phone and rolled over, still ruminating over the report Tom had given me. What was that elevated lactate all about…?

Suddenly, it hit me. I sat bolt upright in bed and said – "Oh my God, Jane has dead bowel."

I immediately called Tom back. I had one question: "Has Jane been taking her warfarin?"

He responded, "I don't think she always takes it. I'm not sure when she took it last."

That response was supportive of what I feared most.

"Tom, I must speak to the physician caring for Jane as soon as possible. Tell him I am Jane's brother and a doctor."

Within a few minutes, I had the doctor on the line. I wanted him to share his thoughts with me before I expressed my concerns. He said that he felt she had bled into her abdomen due to her anticoagulant medication. I asked how abnormal the tests were, and he told me the test that is commonly used to follow warfarin therapy was prolonged by six seconds.

My mind was now entirely in doctor mode. Six-second prolongation would have barely been therapeutic, certainly not abnormal enough to put her at risk for abdominal bleeding.

My next question was about what he thought elevated lactate was about. "Well, I don't have an explanation for that at the moment."

Now, I was convinced that I was correct. Jane had not taken her warfarin. She had formed a clot in her heart while in atrial fibrillation. She must have slipped into a normal heart rhythm for some time and pushed all or part of that clot out of her heart sometime in the afternoon. Instead of moving upward through the carotid artery and causing a stroke, the clot traveled down into the abdominal aorta and out into one of the mesenteric arteries, which supplies the bowel. It went as far as it could go and then lodged. The blood could no longer flow to that part of the gut, and it became oxygen-deprived, causing the onset of pain. Time had passed, and ischemia, lack of oxygen, had caused the bowel to begin to die. This is what was causing the elevated lactic acid and lactate.

I began to lay this out for the physician and told him this was a surgical emergency. When he started to push back a little, I told him that I was a professor of Medicine and Pathology at the Medical College of Virginia and used warfarin daily as the director of the clotting center. This convinced him I probably (or at least may) know what I was talking about.

Jane was still in the CT scan, but a surgeon was called and responded immediately. He examined Jane and agreed that this was a surgical emergency and he would be taking her directly to the operating room.

I got Tom back on the phone and told him what I thought was going on and that I agreed with the sudden change in plans to take her to surgery. I also told him I would be leaving home and would be there as soon as I could.

It was typically a five-hour drive from our house in Midlothian, Virginia, to Greensboro, North Carolina, but I managed to make it in four hours, in the middle of the night.

Unfortunately, when I got there, things were not going well. She was out of surgery and in the intensive care unit. As expected, she had a dead bowel, which the surgeon removed, but by this point, bacteria from the bowel had entered her bloodstream, and she was septic. She had required massive amounts of fluids and intravenous medications to support her low blood pressure. These measures had resulted in massive swelling to the point that her abdomen could not be closed, and she was so swollen as to be non-recognizable.

To make matters worse, she had developed a complication known as disseminated intravascular coagulation, where the clotting proteins and blood platelets that typically control bleeding are consumed, and the patient begins to bleed diffusely. I had seen this in many patients I had consulted in intensive care units, and I knew that the only proper treatment was to treat the underlying disease. That had been done in this case, but it had been too late, and the consequences would be dire.

I spoke to the surgeon, who stated that there was nothing else he could do and that he had already relayed that information to Tom. Tom, of course, was completely taken aback and was unwilling to listen to any talk about any treatment other than the most aggressive that could be offered.

It was challenging to be placed in the middle as soon as I arrived. I knew the surgeon was correct. I also knew Tom was unprepared for this decision, and I would not have been either.

I spoke to the surgeon and recommended that Tom spend time at Jane's side. He would need to see for himself that the situation had moved far beyond the suggestion that her pain could be handled by giving an antidote to a blood thinner. The surgeon agreed.

While Tom was with Jane, I spoke to the rest of the family and tried to explain the dire situation.

When Tom reappeared, his attitude had changed. Jane showed no responsiveness and was only being kept alive by ventilators and fluids running in as quickly as they were pouring out. He looked at me with those engineer eyes, and I knew he understood. His life was so intertwined with hers that he knew she was gone. He asked if we could allow each family member to have their moment to say goodbye. I assured him that it would be possible.

After everyone had an opportunity for a private moment, the staff allowed the group to go in together for one final goodbye. Then Tom told the surgeon that the fluids could be cut back. She was gone in an hour.

I never saw the emergency room physician.

I went home and brought back my family for the funeral. It was all beautiful. Tom had arranged for doves to be released at the site. Jane had always loved doves and kept a pair in her kitchen window for years in California and again after she moved back to Greensboro. When the doves were released, three immediately turned South and banked together as they flew. One flew directly west but then turned to join the others. It was so poetic of Jane's life, and I was sure that this last flight indicated that she had joined the angels in heaven.

Tom lasted a couple of years before he joined his forever love.

JOHN 11:3 So the sisters sent word to Jesus, "Lord, the one you love is sick."

SONG OF SONGS 1:2 Let him kiss me with the kisses of his mouth – for your love is more delightful than wine.

1 JOHN 4:12 No one has ever seen God; but if we love one another, God lives in us and his love is made complete in us.

1 CORINTHIANS 13:4-8 Love is patient, love is kind. It does not envy, it does not boast, it is not proud. It does not dishonor others, it is not self-seeking, it is not easily angered, it keeps no record of wrongs. Love does not delight in evil but rejoices with the truth. It always protects, always trusts, always hopes, always perseveres. Love never fails.

Christmas and a Sister I Had Not Seen in a While
(*What's going on with you...you look terrible...*)

At the age of 18, I left home to go to college. My mother and father drove me to Davidson College in Davidson, North Carolina, and they dropped me off behind what I would learn was the student union. I had never been to Davidson, so I had no idea where anything was. I had all I would bring to college in a single trunk, and my father helped me remove it from the car trunk and set it on the sidewalk. My mother hugged me, my father shook my hand, and they drove away. I would attend orientation with the rest of the freshmen, and then, in a couple of days, I would begin college in earnest.

I was 18 years old, and at that time, at that age, you were supposed to be a man. Although I would spend a couple of months at home during the summer breaks, I never lived at home again. All my siblings, four wonderful sisters, would marry soon after high school graduation and start their families. Three of them would live their entire lives in the town where they were born. I, however, never lived in Greensboro again.

I spent so much time in school that I didn't get a house until I was on the attending staff at NC Memorial Hospital. Although I lived only an hour from Greensboro in Chapel Hill, North Carolina, it was like the road ran only one way. Typically, I would see Mom and Dad (Mamaw and Pawpaw) at their house, and either see the sisters there or try to drop by to see them at their homes. None of them had ever been to see me in Chapel Hill.

In the fall of 1984, I finally had a house, and it was the first opportunity I had to have my sisters come to my home for a meal. I had been working in Chapel Hill or Siler City nonstop, so I had not seen any of them for several months. My parents, three sisters, their husbands, and some of my nieces and nephews made it to my house for an afternoon holiday meal. I was so excited.

272

They all arrived at once in a family caravan (I guess that way, no one would get lost!), and I welcomed and ushered each one into my home. When Nancy, my twin sister, came in, I was struck by her appearance. She did not look well.

When I spoke with her, I asked, "What is going on with you?"

"Well, I have been tired a lot. I'm always hungry and thirsty, but I've lost weight. And I can't seem to stay out of the bathroom. I'm peeing all the time."

"How long has this been going on?" I asked.

"Oh, several months," she responded.

"Nancy, you need to see a doctor. You have diabetes." The diagnosis could not have been more apparent.

"Do you really think so?" she replied.

"You need to go tomorrow."

Nancy was 35 years old at the time and should have been past the high-risk period for juvenile-onset diabetes. However, when she went to her physician the following Monday, her fasting blood sugar was greater than 400 mg per 100 ml of blood. It should have been less than 100. She was admitted to the hospital and immediately started on insulin to bring her blood sugar down into the normal range.

Unfortunately, when I spoke to her the next day, her vision was so blurred that she could not recognize people. Her blood sugar had been so high for so long that she had deposited large amounts of sugar into the soft tissues of her retinas. When the insulin lowered her blood sugar into the normal range, an osmotic gradient formed due to the high sugar levels in the retinal tissue, causing water to flow from the blood vessels into the tissues. This caused retinal edema (swelling), and her vision was markedly impaired.

I felt terrible that she had to endure that, but it was only temporary. The edema resolved as the sugar re-equilibrated and

273

returned to the bloodstream, and her vision returned to normal. She behaved as a juvenile diabetic requiring insulin from day one and later suffered from the side effects of impaired renal and hepatic function. The good thing is that she is a tough old bird and has weathered many medical storms. I was just glad she came to my house that day, and I'm so happy that I didn't hesitate to tell her she looked terrible. Sometimes, the truth is needed to get things back on track.

GALATIANS 4:16 Have I now become your enemy by telling you the truth?

2 CORINTHIANS 6:7 in truthful speech and in the power of God; with weapons of righteousness in the right hand and in the left;

PROVERBS 12:18 The words of the reckless pierce like swords, but the tongue of the wise brings healing.

Daddy's in the Hospital
(*Moaning from a man with high pain tolerance...*)

I lived in Richmond, Virginia, for twenty years while I served on the medical faculty of the Medical College of Virginia. During this time, I would intermittently travel to Greensboro to visit my parents and sisters. It was a five-hour trip, but it became more manageable when I discovered a backroad route that avoided I-95 and I-85, routing me down US-29 through Danville. That way, I could cut 30 to 45 minutes off the trip.

One summer day, I drove down because I had heard my father was in the hospital. It was unclear what the problem was, so I thought it would be a good idea to investigate for myself. After dropping by home to see Momma, I headed to Moses Cone Memorial Hospital to check on Daddy.

I asked at the nursing station which room Mr. Carr was in and then headed down the hallway. As I approached the two-bed patient room, I heard moaning. I went in to find that my father was the only patient in the room, but the curtain had been drawn around his bed. When I pulled it back, I found my father sitting with the head of his bed raised. He was bent at the waist, and his legs were drawn up at a 90-degree angle. His hair was uncombed, his mouth was held open, and he was groaning with every breath. There was an untouched tray of food on the bedside table.

It took several attempts to get him to acknowledge that I was there. He eventually turned his head enough to try to focus on me without his glasses. After a moment, he tried to mouth my name.

When he clearly knew who I was, I asked why he was moaning and what was hurting.

He motioned that his legs were hurting. I uncovered them to find that both knees had large effusions. They were warm and tender to the touch. I went out to the nurse's station to check on why my father had been admitted and what was going on with his knees.

I was told that he had been admitted for confusion and mental status changes. I asked about the diagnosis and was told, "presumed TIA." OK, what had been done to work this up, and what was the treatment plan?

"We are not at liberty to discuss this information with you. You will need to speak with his physician," came the canned response.

"I'll be more than happy to speak with his physician. When will he be in to see my father?"

"He has already rounded today," came the same flat response.

"Well, you tell his physician or whoever is covering for him that Dr. Carr from the Medical College of Virginia is down to see his father and would like an update on his status." I had been down this road before and did not have time to play this game with a passive-aggressive staff member.

Within a few minutes, I was handed the phone to speak with the covering physician. He told me it was his impression that Mr. Carr had suffered a TIA or minor stroke.

I asked what the evidence was for a stroke and what the treatment plan was. The response was that the CT scan did not show a bleed or a definitive infarct, so the plan was to monitor for improvement and rehab as appropriate.

So, there was no evidence of a stroke. How do you rehab from a TIA? I did not ask that question. Instead, I asked what was going on with my father's knees and whether he was being given anything for pain.

"I was not aware that he had a problem with his knees or that he was in pain," was the response.

"Well, I just saw him, and he is moaning with pain, and he has huge effusions on both knees. May I tap those and have pathology rule out gout? I would also like to have him started on anti-inflammatories for osteoarthritis."

"Sure, that would be fine with me. I will instruct the nurse to make supplies available for the arthrocentesis, and I will write for bupropion," came (thankfully) the very cooperative response.

Within 30 minutes, I had tapped more than 50 mLs of clear, slightly yellow fluid off both knees. The decreased pressure in the knees offered some initial pain relief. The lab confirmed the absence of urate crystals, ruling out gout.

Dad was starting to wake up a little and began to get additional pain relief from his ibuprofen. As I wrote a brief procedure note in the chart, I took the opportunity to glance at my father's progress and nursing notes. Whatever the plan was for him, the interpretation by the staff caring for him was that he was a 'gorked-out' little old man who had suffered a stroke. He was left in his room with notes stating that he was not eating. Well, he was not eating because he was unable to feed himself.

When the covering physician came by, I told him that I would prefer to have my father discharged and taken home. He looked at me for a moment and then said he would contact his primary physician and make the necessary arrangements.

After he left, a member of the nutrition team came by to pick up the tray. I asked if he could leave it for a little longer so I could try to get my father to eat a little. The response was, "Sure, no problem."

I spoke with my father, and he took some sips of liquid and even a few bites of food. I told him I would take him home and thought he would recover more quickly there. He seemed surprised at this possibility and became even more awake. I asked if he could move his legs, and he said he could, but it was difficult and painful.

I told him his joints would "freeze up" if he did not move them. He immediately showed me that he could partially straighten his legs. I said, "Good job. Now, let's get you out of here."

I had to take him by wheelchair out to the car and lift him into the seat. I knew he was hurting, but he did not complain. I had called home to have one of my sisters prepare the guest bedroom for Daddy. When I got him home, I put him in that bed and called my home to let them know that I would need to stay in Greensboro for a couple of extra days. As I turned to leave his room, Daddy motioned for me to come back to his bedside. As I bent down to see what he wanted, he looked at me and said, "I'm not going to die, am I?"

I looked at him and smiled, and I could confidently say, " Well, not anytime soon!"

During my time in Greensboro, we added a bedside commode as it rapidly became apparent that he had not had a bowel movement while in the hospital. By the second day at home, much of the constipation problem had been solved, and Dad was now eating at a pretty good clip. On the third day, I left him in the excellent care of my sisters and headed back to Richmond. As he ate, his energy returned. As his energy returned, he worked to stand and take a few steps. As he moved more, his strength returned.

He completely recovered from whatever problem caused him to be taken to the hospital, and he planted and cared for several extensive vegetable gardens over the next 14 years. He also survived colon cancer, several major operations, and two broken hips before going on to glory at the age of 89.

I was never sure how the episode had unfolded in the hospital, but it was clear that the staff had given up on him, and he was close to giving up on himself. I don't know what would have happened if I hadn't stopped by. When I heard my father moaning, I knew that something was terribly wrong. He was one of the toughest guys I have ever known, and he had a very high pain threshold. If he was moaning, something was hurting.

I may have been the only person who would have walked down that hall and realized the import of his moans. So, God got me up, put me in the car, got me to Greensboro, and had me walk down the hall. He was obviously not ready to take that wonderful old man home.

2 CORINTHIANS 1:3 Praise be to the God and Father of our Lord Jesus Christ, the Father of compassion and the God of all comfort.

GALATIANS 6:2 Carry each other's burdens, and in this way you will fulfill the law of Christ.

1 PETER 3:8 Finally, all of you, be like-minded, be sympathetic, love one another, be compassionate and humble.

EXODUS 20:12 "Honor your father and mother, so that you may live long in the land the Lord your God is giving you.

Gone within Thirty Days
(*After sixty-plus years,*
there is a connection that cannot be broken...)

As I think I mentioned, my mother suffered from atrial fibrillation. Because of the increased risk of clot formation in her heart and the secondary risk of stroke, she (like two of my sisters) was on anticoagulants to slow clotting. The main side effect of anticoagulant therapy is an increased risk of bleeding. In the last year of her life, my mother was hospitalized on several occasions for GI bleeding. On these occasions, she would be admitted, transfused, and discharged within a few days without additional evaluation. The cardiologist was unwilling to reverse the anticoagulation for any reason, so further assessment was neither possible nor indicated. I knew this, and I think the rest of the family also understood.

When my mother was admitted to the hospital, I would receive a call from one of the sisters, and I would make every effort to get down to see her. One Thursday evening in late spring, I received such a call, and I took the next day off work to get an early start driving to Greensboro. When I arrived mid-morning, Mom looked alert, and we had a pleasant several-hour visit. As other visitors arrived, I thought I would take the opportunity to slip away and visit my father, who was in a rehabilitation/nursing home after his second hip fracture. He had recovered well from his first hip fracture, but he had never gotten out of his wheelchair after this one. It was clear to me that not a lot of rehabilitation was going on and that Daddy had given up ever being back home again.

I was shocked at his appearance when I arrived and entered his room. He was fragile, and his eyes were sunken into their sockets. He would look at me, but he could not speak. When I asked him what was happening, he mouthed, "Marc, I'm dying." His lips were chapped, and his tongue was so dry that it looked like a prune.

I have been in enough tough situations to know you must take that statement seriously, especially when it is coming from a very tough but bedridden 89-year-old man. I pulled back the sheet to find a very emaciated man whose legs were cold, and his feet had the unmistakable stigmata of purpura fulminans. Purpura fulminans looks like a purple bruise, but it is not a bruise; rather, it is dead tissue due to blood clots blocking small blood vessels in a process known as disseminated intravascular coagulation (DIC). Disseminated (everywhere) intravascular (inside the blood vessels) coagulation (clotting) is a very severe condition and has been called a "harbinger of death."

My father was very malnourished, extremely dehydrated, and was correct in his pronounced prognosis – he was dying.

I went to the nursing station and asked to speak with the on-call physician. I also asked when Mr. Carr had eaten or drunk anything. I was told that he had quit eating for the last two weeks and drinking for the previous five days. I asked if the family had been informed of these changes, and was assured that they had.

When the physician called in, I wasted no time with small talk. I informed him that my father was very dehydrated, had signs of DIC, and would probably not last the rest of the day. I asked if he would write the order for D5-normal saline at 100 cc per hour. I would place the IV and get it running. I explained that I thought this might lengthen the time I would have to call the family in. He agreed.

I put the IV in, started the drip, and began to call my sisters. They were all shocked at the news, but I told them in no uncertain terms that Daddy was dying, and if they wanted to see him alive to say goodbye, they needed to come right away.

"What do we tell Momma?" came the response from my sisters in visiting with my mother.

"Tell her that Daddy is not doing well and that we will inform her how he is doing. Tell her to remember him in her prayers." That is all I could come up with.

The sisters and their children soon began to stream in to see my father. The fluids were having a positive effect, and he had become more alert, able to respond to each as they spoke to him. They all stayed until late evening, and then I sat with Dad through the night. As the sisters began to reappear the following day, I took the opportunity to run home and gather a few clothes, then let my family know how things were going. I then turned around and headed back to Greensboro.

When I arrived, he was gone. Mom was still in the hospital, so we met to tell her that Daddy was gone.

My sisters spoke to Mom, and the arrangements were made for the funeral. I stayed in Greensboro, and the next day, my mother was discharged, and I took her home. When we got home, she told me she wanted to go to the funeral. She was too weak to walk, stand, or even get out of a car. We spoke to her physicians, and they said we might be able to arrange a private ambulance to take her to the graveside. I talked to Mom, and she said she would like that. The sisters made the arrangements.

My father's funeral was to be on Saturday, and Sherri was driving our family down. I was staying with Momma. About 1:00 in the morning, she called to me. I got up to find that she was having rectal bleeding. I called 911, and she was taken back to the hospital. I was there most of the night as more transfusions were initiated.

As it was getting light, I left for Mom's house to meet my family, get dressed, and go to the funeral. I do not remember a lot about the funeral, but I do remember that, for some reason, all the children had written poems about our father. I do not know if Dad was a poet or even that he enjoyed poetry, but the fact that we all had written poems could not have been a coincidence.

After the funeral, we all went to see Mom. She was doing better, but was sorry that she had missed the funeral. I told her it was okay and that I was sure Dad knew she wanted to be there.

Later that day, my crew departed to return to Richmond. I was dead tired and concerned that Mom's health was so tenuous. I was sure that, although my mother and father had been living apart for months due to my father being in the rehab facility, my father's passing would have a negative impact on her condition.

I was right to be concerned. In less than a month, Mom was readmitted to the hospital for the last time. She was gone in a couple of days, but I knew she was again with the man she had loved and tolerated for over sixty years. They had done the "to death do us part," and now they could continue in the warmth of God's perfect love.

MARK 10:6-9 "But at the beginning of creation God 'made them male and female.' For this reason, a man will leave his father and mother and be united to his wife, and the two will become one flesh.' So they are no longer two, but one flesh. Therefore what God has joined together, let no one separate."

EPHESIANS 5:33 However, each one of you also must love his wife as he loves himself, and the wife must respect her husband.

EPHESIANS 5:21 Submit to one another out of reverence for Christ.

EPHESIANS 5:25 Husbands, love your wives, just as Christ loved the church and gave himself up for her.

ECCLESIASTES 4:9-10 Two are better than one, because they have a good return for their labor: If either of them falls down, one can help the other up. But pity anyone who falls and has no one to help them up.

Liver Failure in the Wrong Hospital
(Liver transplants…we don't do those here…)

Communication in families is variable. I have one sister who never misses sending birthday and Christmas cards to everyone in the family. I have other sisters whom I never hear from unless there is family news (usually bad) of some kind that needs to be disseminated – uncle or aunt X died or is sick, etc. Usually, I would get a call if a sibling was in the hospital, but not always. That was the case with this episode.

I had called to catch up on news with one of my sisters, and after a pleasant conversation, she casually mentioned, "By the way, Nancy is in the hospital." Nancy was my twin sister and had long suffered from diabetes.

"Where, why, and for how long has she been in the hospital? Is her diabetes out of control?" I asked.

"Oh, she has been in Cone Hospital for two days. I do not think it is her diabetes…I think it has something to do with her liver…" came the response.

Her liver? Nancy had renal insufficiency from years of diabetes, but I had never heard her mention any liver problems.

I asked how she was doing and was told she was a little yellow and swollen. Well, that's not good. I needed to get down to Greensboro to see what was happening.

I had obligations in the morning, but left after lunch and arrived in Nancy's room just after dinner. I could not believe my eyes. She was *yellow*, both her skin and eyes. Her abdomen was more prominent than when she was pregnant, and her ankles and feet were also swollen. By pushing on her foot, you could indent the flesh, and the pit formed would remain for a couple of minutes after you released the pressure. Such "pitting" edema is graded from trace to 3+. Trace is a little, and 3+ is a lot. She had 3+ pitting edema.

I asked the nurse if I could speak to the physician caring for my sister, and she said she thought he was still in the hospital and would call him. While I waited, I spoke with Nancy and asked how it all had started. She said that she had been told for years that she had "fatty liver" secondary to her diabetes and that, more recently, her "albumin" had been falling because she had "cirrhosis."

Doctor mode kicked in, and I began to connect the dots. Fatty liver is a complication of diabetes. In olden times (when dinosaurs roamed the land and I was in medical school), we were taught that this was a relatively benign condition. It was felt to differ from the "fatty liver" of alcohol abuse, which led to cirrhosis with continued drinking. Over time, this proved to be incorrect. Non-alcoholic Steatorrheic Hepatitis (NASH) was now thought to be the primary cause of cirrhosis. Diabetes causes fatty liver – fatty liver is associated with NASH – NASH leads to cirrhosis – cirrhosis leads to liver failure. Diabetes was now the second most common cause of cirrhosis, behind alcohol abuse.

The physician arrived, introduced himself, and confirmed my thoughts. My sister had liver failure secondary to cirrhosis caused by NASH secondary to diabetes. Wow, this was not on my radar and was bad.

My next question is, "So what are we going to do about this?"

This was met with a relatively blank response and then a repetition of her diagnosis with the addendum that this was irreversible, end-stage liver disease.

I pointed out that if a liver is not working and there is no hope of improvement, then the liver needs to be replaced. The plan should be a liver transplant.

The response was, "We don't do those here."

It suddenly hit me that there was no treatment plan because, in this hospital, this was a "hopeless case." The course was crystal clear

– we needed a new hospital where her case would not be so "hopeless."

"Have you considered transferring to one of the academic centers in the area where they perform liver transplantation?"

"Not to this point, but we certainly could inquire if you think your sister would like to go that route," was the response.

"I will speak to her, but I am sure that she would like to pursue that course of action. After all, she is in her fifties and is not an alcoholic."

When I spoke to Nancy, she was a little taken aback by her prognosis. "Of course, I want a transplant if that is the only option. I'm not ready to die," came the straightforward response, which I considered appropriate.

In a couple of days, arrangements had been made to transfer Nancy to the Duke University Medical Center in Durham, less than an hour from the hospital. There, they did "do transplants…"

The initial evaluation at Duke went well, and within 36 hours, Nancy was on the transplant list. At that point, someone questioned on rounds whether Nancy might have underlying heart failure as the cause of her lower extremity edema. If I had been on rounds, I would have offered the opinion that the edema was entirely consistent with her low albumin and pressure on the blood vessels in her abdomen (due to her ascites), limiting venous flow out of her legs. However, I was not there, and when I arrived to visit, I found that Nancy had been taken for a stress MUGA scan to see how well her heart was pumping.

A stress MUGA test is typically performed to assess the heart's response to exercise. A scan is performed at rest, during, and after exercise. Since Nancy had been bedridden for almost two weeks, she was too weak even to walk. Therefore, the team decided to do a chemically induced stress MUGA. This is achieved by administering a cardiac stimulant that speeds up the heart in a manner equivalent to

286

exercise. She was taken to the cardiology suite, and the resting phase went reasonably well. Then the cardiac stimulant was given, and Nancy's heart rate went to more than 200 and stayed there for more than 20 minutes. It seems that the fact that her liver was not able to rapidly metabolize and clear the stimulant had not been considered. It was a good thing that her heart was in reasonable shape, or she could have slipped into heart failure or an unstable heart rhythm. The cardiology team concluded that she was too "unstable" to undergo a transplant, and they took her off the transplant list. Unfortunately, the entire episode, including the radionucleotide administered during the test, tipped Nancy into complete renal failure. A complication that would require renal dialysis for several years.

I was a little confused by the events at Duke, but I was later told that the transplant teams at Duke were being very conservative in their approach due to a recent disaster in which a patient died after receiving a mismatched transplant. They were not taking any chances…

OK…now what? Nancy's situation was not improving, and now she was in renal failure. How was I going to get her back on the transplant list?

I could think of only two places that might take Nancy – the University of Pittsburgh Medical Center or the Medical College of Virginia in Richmond. Both had excellent surgical departments and performed numerous transplants. I had spent twenty years on the faculty of Richmond's Medical College of Virginia, but I had left several years earlier. I had several close professional relationships with folks in the GI division. They had helped me on multiple occasions with my hemophilia patients, many of whom suffered from liver abnormalities. I decided to ask if they would evaluate Nancy. I told them I knew there were no promises, and I would understand if they thought she was not a suitable candidate for transplant. They asked that we arrange a transfer to Richmond.

Two days later, my sister arrived in Richmond just before a massive snowstorm. Within 24 hours, she was back on the transplant list, and on day seven, we heard that they had a potential donor. Unfortunately, when the first liver arrived, the surgeon was not satisfied with the quality of the organ, and the transplant did not occur. Two days later, another potential donor did not pan out, but a few days after that, Nancy got her new liver.

She did amazingly well, and within a couple of weeks, she was back home in Greensboro. There were numerous trips to Richmond for follow-up, but the intervals continued to lengthen, and eventually, she was only there every six months.

Her kidneys never recovered enough function to keep her off dialysis, which she continued to have routinely for several years. However, her improved health allowed her to go on the renal transplant list, and she eventually underwent a renal transplant at Bowman Gray Medical Center of Wake Forest University in Winston-Salem, North Carolina. This ended her need for dialysis, and she returned to her chronic care for diabetes.

That was more than ten years ago. Not bad for a lady given up for dead from liver failure. It is always important to consider all your options, and if someone tells you that you have no options, perhaps it is time to seek a second opinion.

It is also important not to underestimate the importance of past personal and professional relationships. Someday, they might make all the difference.

JOB 14:5 A person's days are determined; you have decreed the number of his months and have set limits he cannot exceed.

PSALMS 39:4 Show me, Lord, my life's end and the number of my days; let me know how fleeting my life is.

ECCLESIASTES 3:2 a time to be born and a time to die, a time to plant and a time to uproot,

ISAIAH 41:10 So do not fear, for I am with you; do not be dismayed, for I am your God. I will strengthen you and help you; I will uphold you with my righteous right hand.

PSALMS 18:2 The Lord is my rock, my fortress and my deliverer; my God is my rock, in whom I take refuge, my shield and the horn of my salvation, my stronghold.

JOB 24:17 "Have pity on me, my friends, have pity, for the hand of God has struck me.

VII. POINTS IN TIME
(DO YOU REMEMBER WHAT YOU WERE DOING WHEN...?)

These are stories I tell when I am asked if I remember when Kennedy was shot, when Elvis died, or when the planes hit the Twin Towers on 9/11. These are the "where were you" and "what were you doing when" questions that bring history to life (or perhaps more accurately, bring life to history). I sometimes wish I had asked my mother and father more questions about what happened to them when the stock market crashed, or what the great depression was like, or how they heard about Pearl Harbor...Perhaps I did ask, but I have forgotten what they said. I think it is important for folks to know how such events affected normal, "everyday" people, especially those they knew who were alive and "there" when events that changed the course of history occurred.

The Day John F. Kennedy Was Shot
(It was a Friday afternoon, and I was in 9th Grade Industrial Arts Class)

Anyone over the age of six in 1963 can probably tell you where they were when they heard that President Kennedy had been shot. I was in the ninth grade and was in industrial arts (shop) class at Bessemer Junior High School in Greensboro, North Carolina. It was a nice late fall Indian Summer afternoon on a Friday. We had almost made it to the weekend...

At that time, the school's public address (PA) system was operated from the principal's office and was rarely used, except for morning announcements. We were all intently working on our "drafting" projects using our sharpened pencils and our "straight edge" (otherwise known as a ruler). Then the speaker crackled, and the principal's office was heard to say, "We have received word that the President has been shot while riding in a parade in Dallas..." We were all stunned. The teacher stopped his pacing and looking over student's shoulders at their work. We sat silently for a few minutes, and then some of us jumped when the bell rang to move us to our last class of the day.

When I arrived at Mr. Latta's civics class (a class about American Government), we all took our seats without talking. It was hushed.

The speaker clicked again, and we all looked up at the top of the wall where it was mounted. This time, the voice was not that of the principal. It was Walter Cronkite. The folks in the office had moved either a television or a radio to the PA microphone and were putting the CBS broadcast live over the PA system.

Before we were able to listen, Cronkite had reported first that shots had been fired at the president's motorcade and then, a few minutes later, that both the president and the governor of Texas had been struck.

There was a pause, and then the unmistakable voice of Cronkite said, "From Dallas, Texas, the flash apparently official: President Kennedy died at 1 p.m. Central Standard Time - 2 o'clock Eastern Standard Time - some 38 minutes ago." Mr. Latta, a tall, thin fellow with a strong jaw, was not an openly emotional person. He moved to the center of the class and said we would not have our regular class due to ongoing events. We would be allowed to listen to the broadcast for the rest of the hour and be dismissed when the buses arrived.

When the buses came, I walked home (about three-fourths of a mile) and found my mother sitting in front of the television. It would be where we would spend most of our time for the next several days. We would learn that Governor Connelly of Texas was struck but was expected to survive, that vice-president Lyndon Johnson had taken the oath of office on the plane and was now president of the United States, that the first lady (Jackie) had flown back to Washington to be with her children and arrangements for lying in state in the Capitol and the funeral were underway. We also learned that a local police officer, J.D. Tippet, had been shot soon after the assassination and that a man, Lee Harvey Oswald, had been arrested.

If you went outside the home, it was the only thing people talked about. It did not matter whether you were pro-Kennedy or not; the fact that an American President could be shot and killed in our country was just more than most folks could get their head around. The government had lived through two world wars, the Korean conflict, the Roaring Twenties, prohibition, and the great depression since McKinley was assassinated in 1901. It was simply unthinkable.

On Sunday morning, I was watching TV before we left for church. It was not something I was typically allowed to do, but this was a different time, and I suppose my mother knew I was watching history unfold. I had heard the name Lee Harvey Oswald, but I had not seen him. They were going to transfer him from one jail to another, and a live broadcast showed the transfer from one building to another in an armored vehicle. As I watched the black and white image, a skinny, rather unkempt young man came around the corner of a packed hallway, a Sheriff's Deputy holding him by the right arm. Suddenly, a man with a hat stepped out directly in front of Oswald, and there was a quick bang. There were shouts and commotion as a crowd of officers and reporters jumped the man. It was all so fast. At first, I did not know what had happened. Then, it was clear that the man had shot Oswald in front of the whole nation. I called out to my parents, but by now, there would be "no more TV until after church. We must attend church and pray for the president, his family, and the country."

When we got home, the man in the hat had been identified as Jack Ruby, a local Dallas bar owner, and Oswald was dead. The questions of how many shots were fired in Dallas and whether more people were involved in the assassination were now joined by how Jack Ruby got into jail and why he shot Oswald. I was particularly interested in why Oswald had died when he was immediately taken to the hospital and was shot in the abdomen.

While the answer to most of these questions was answered (and subsequently forever debated) by the Warren Commission, the answer to why Oswald died was announced after I got home from church. Oswald had been taken to Parkland Memorial Hospital, the same hospital that had taken care of Kennedy and Connally just two days before. The surgeon explained that the bullet entered Oswald's abdomen and traveled right to left, just below the diaphragm. In so doing, it hit the liver, pancreas, spleen, aorta, and vena cava. Despite heroic efforts, he was dead by the time he reached the hospital.

The remainder of the following week was spent watching continuous coverage of the investigation in Dallas and the events in Washington. I will never forget the funeral with the President's brothers, Bobbie and Teddy. However, the most touching moment occurred as the caisson moved along the streets of Washington. As the riderless horse and the flag-draped casket passed in front of the First Lady and her children, the president's son, John-John (who must have been two or three years old), saluted his father. It was a moment I will never forget.

MATTHEW 5:4 Blessed are those who mourn, for they will be comforted.

PSALMS 34:18 The Lord is close to the brokenhearted and saves those who are crushed in spirit.

ROMANS 12:15 Rejoice with those who rejoice; mourn with those who mourn.

2 CORINTHIANS 1:3-4 Praise be to the God and Father of our Lord Jesus Christ, the Father of compassion and the God of all comfort, who comforts us in all our troubles, so that we can comfort those in any trouble with the comfort we ourselves receive.

Where Were You on 11 September 2001
(Giving a lecture at ATACCC)

The world changed for everyone on September 11, 2001. Everyone alive and above the age of three that day must remember what they were doing. I know I do.

With multiple colleagues from the School of Engineering and the School of Medicine at Virginia Commonwealth University, I had been working on a device to treat "non-compressible" hemorrhage. Non-compressible hemorrhage is bleeding that does not respond to direct pressure. When a hole in the skin and blood is oozing or running out, it can usually be stopped by applying direct pressure. If blood is squirting out, it implies that an artery has been involved, and the bleeding is now being pumped out at a higher pressure. There is a new squirt with each new heartbeat. This type of bleeding is so dramatic that most folks will automatically do the right thing, put something in the hole, and push to keep the blood from squirting out – i.e., *direct* pressure. If the bleeding continues to be brisk despite these efforts, pressure must be put on the artery closer to the heart to decrease blood flow to the area of injury. This is usually done by applying pressure to the artery at a point close to the skin or where it runs over a bony surface (a pressure point), or by using a tourniquet above the bleeding area. There are places where it is impossible to apply adequate direct pressure or a tourniquet to stop bleeding. An example would be bleeding into the abdomen.

The abdomen has many large vessels that can bleed dramatically when the abdomen is wounded. In combat, a soldier may suffer an otherwise survivable abdominal wound only to die because the bleeding cannot be stopped or adequately slowed to allow more definitive care after evacuation. Therefore, developing an acute treatment that can be used by medics to adequately control bleeding during evacuation is a high priority for the military. We were working on such a treatment. Being a "clotter" by trade and a "colonel" in the

US Army Medical Corps by choice, I had multiple reasons to make this effort.

We proposed putting hydrophilic polymer gels within a flexible, porous membrane. The device would be pushed into the wound and held in place by the hand or an ace wrap (or both). Blood would go into the bandage, causing the gel to swell. The pressure would develop as the bandage swelled within the wound, and the bleeding should be slowed. It was a simple idea.

We wrote a grant that the Defense Department approved, and went to work. An appropriate hydrophilic polymer gel was identified, and the outer membrane was electrospun from materials that allowed for the encasement of the polymer while permitting the entrance of blood. Early experiments revealed the rapid entrance of fluid, rapid swelling of the bandage, and significant pressure development. The early prototype worked!

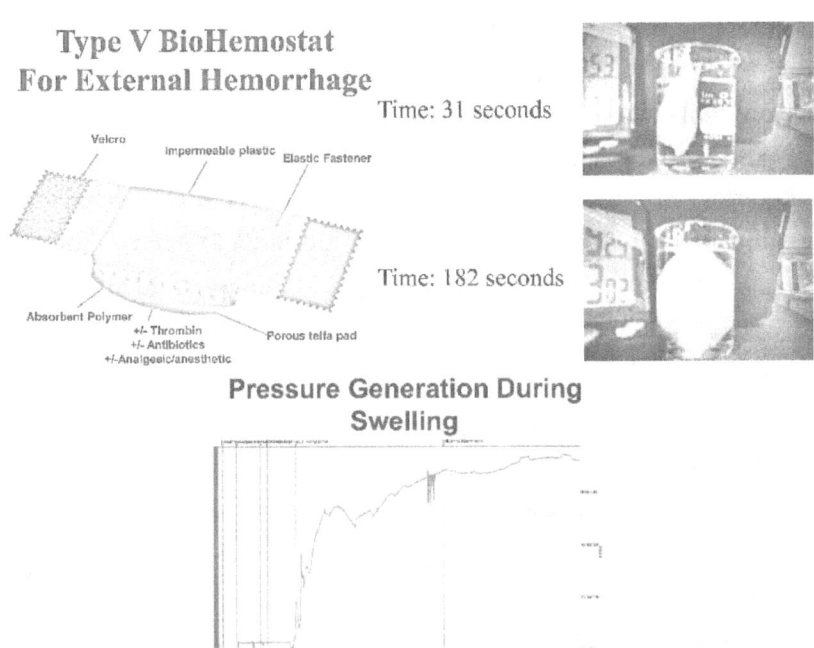

Type V BioHemostat For External Hemorrhage

Time: 31 seconds

Time: 182 seconds

Velcro

Impermeable plastic

Elastic Fastener

Absorbent Polymer
+/- Thrombin
+/- Antibiotics
+/-Analgesic/anesthetic

Porous telfa pad

Pressure Generation During Swelling

I was asked to attend the Advanced Technologies and Combat Casualty Care (ATACCC) annual meeting in Fort Walton Beach,

Florida, to give an early update on this new potential treatment. This exciting meeting involves academics, people from the defense department, members of all armed services, and a range of people from industry (large companies to biotech start-ups).

When you land at Fort Walton Beach, you quickly realize this is a military town. The airport is shared by civilian and military aircraft. The civilian terminal is located on the opposite side of the runway from the Air Force terminal, and it is smaller. Being an underpaid academic, I took the cheapest airline available (ValuJet) from Richmond to Fort Walton Beach. It required changing planes in Atlanta, but I did not mind; it got me there.

I was scheduled to speak in the first session on blood products on the morning of September 11, 2001. The chair for the meeting was an Air Force Colonel who got the meeting going precisely on time and introduced the first speaker. The fellow gave an excellent talk about fibrin glue and its potential to stop bleeding in trauma. Fibrin glue is made by mixing two proteins (thrombin and fibrinogen) and applying the material to the bleeding area. The patient does not need to form the clot themselves; the treater forms a clot "right on the spot." It is pretty cool stuff, but not too effective in high-pressure bleeding because the gushing blood tends to wash it away.

When the first speaker finished, the Colonel got up to introduce the second speaker; he paused for a moment and then stated that he had some bad news. A plane seemed to have struck one of the Trade Towers in New York. We sat around and looked at each other for a moment—that's really odd...

Then, the Colonel went on to introduce the next speaker, who was a young physician with the public health service. He was giving an update on the development of "fibrin foam" for treating abdominal bleeding. Fibrin foam is similar to fibrin glue in that it is a material that forms a normal clot; however, in this case, it is sprayed on and contains bubbles, allowing it to fill an open space. The idea was that you could spray a foam of fibrin into the wound, which would serve initially to seal the wound and promote additional clotting. Unfortunately, the report was basically negative (i.e., it did not work), and unlike fibrin glue, which went on to be used, fibrin foam faded away into the ether of good ideas that don't work.

I was slated to be the third speaker, and I presented our report on the "Biohemostat," which looked very promising, although it was still in its early stages. I got a couple of questions and a couple of compliments, and then I sat down.

The Colonel got up to introduce the fourth speaker. This time, his tone had changed. He simply said, "It seems I have a little more bad news...a plane has hit the other trade tower." At this point, Air Force personnel began to get up and leave. Everyone knew this was bad. This was not a terrible accident. It was done intentionally by someone hoping to cause us great harm.

Initially, I just sat there. The Colonel introduced the next speaker, but I do not remember the topic. Before that speaker completed his talk, you could hear Air Force fighter jets taking off from the nearby base. When that talk was completed, a lady came into the back of the room and said, "Is there a professor, colonel, Doctor Marc Carr in the room?" Oh, this had just gone from bad to worse.

Since I was that man and had just given my talk, all eyes quickly turned to me, and I stood up and walked to the back of the room.

"Colonel Carr, we have an urgent call from your Reserve Unit. They would like to speak with you ASAP. We have a phone outside in the lobby that you can use."

At that time, I was the commander of the 4215th USAH (US Army Hospital), located in Richmond, Virginia, and occupying the Monteith US Army Reserve Center. As the senior member of the largest unit in the facility, I was also designated as the "Facility Commander." Now I was being called by one of the "full-timers" (civilian federal employees, some of whom were also members of the reserve units) who staffed and worked at the center daily. I called the indicated number.

"Is this Colonel Carr?"

"Yes, this is Colonel Carr."

"Sir, we are at DEFCON Delta. We need the codes for the arms room to issue weapons and ammunition to folks at the center…"

At that time, DEFCON Delta was the highest category of defense condition alert, requiring the commander's authorization of actions to ensure the defense of their command.

A brief pause for reflection. I had no idea how big the ongoing event was. However, I could think of many targets that were a higher priority than the Monteith Reserve Center. I also knew that some full-timers had a flair for the dramatic.

"I will authorize the issuing of weapons to guards at the gate. I also order that all access to the facility be either through the entrance adjacent to the parking lot or through the vehicular entrance, and that guards man both these entrances. Opening the vehicular entrance would be restricted to vehicular access and should be authorized by an on-site officer. I do not authorize the issuing of ammunition. The guards should be given ammo clips that do not contain live rounds. Is that clear?"

"But sir, DEFCON Delta requires armed guards on the gate."

I responded, "They will be armed, but the weapons will not contain rounds. I may alter this guidance as additional information becomes available to me. At this point, this telephone call is the only information I have. Please do your best to update me as the situation evolves. Also, please decline requests for interviews from the press. Tell them that they should consult with 'higher authorities.' I will be back in Richmond as soon as possible."

I could not imagine someone crashing a plane into the Monteith Reserve Center; however, I could have nightmares of someone with limited experience as an armed guard shooting someone by mistake. I was not going to let anyone get shot on my watch...

As I finished my phone call, I noticed that the people in the small area outside our presentation room had set up a television on a rolling cart and had it tuned to NBC News. On the screen, the Twin Towers of the Trade Center were smoking away. It was surreal. I heard someone say that all civilian air traffic had been grounded. There were reports of a plane crashing into the Pentagon and one going down in a field in Pennsylvania. All were hijacked.

I couldn't foresee the future, but I did know that the conference I was attending was scheduled to last a couple more days, and I had a ticket on ValuJet to fly back to Richmond on Thursday. Well, that was not going to happen.

I slipped back into the room, got my notes, and then went directly to my hotel room. I turned on the TV and began to call rental car agencies. I tried Alamo, National, Enterprise, Avis, and Budget. I tried everything listed. There was not a car left. I had not attempted Hertz because they tended to be a little more expensive (and I am frugal), and with all the business folks being "gold" Hertz club members, I thought there would be no car left. Well, I had no options left; I called Hertz. They were located at the airport and had one car (a small compact) left. I said I would take it and gave them my credit card number. I said I would pick it up in the morning. They said the airport was closed, but they would be open just inside the main doors.

Having secured a way home, I packed everything but the clothes I would wear and returned to the meeting. When I arrived, a friend of mine from VCU was already sitting at a table near the back. I joined him and told him I had a car if he wanted to drive back with me the next day. He said no, that he would be flying back on Thursday. I told him that no one would be flying except the military for the next few days. He gave me a strange look and said, "No, I think I'll keep my plans."

I told him that was fine, but the car was small, and I could not take more than one rider if someone else asked for one.

After the session finished, I got a cup of coffee and noticed how much the crowd had thinned. As I sat down for the next session, my friend came running up with a somewhat frantic look on his face.

"Is that offer of a ride to Richmond still open?" He asked.

"Sure," I responded.

"Then I'll take it," he replied with a smile of relief. "I found out my flight was canceled, and I could not find a bus or train that was going north and had a seat. I also found no more rental cars available this week."

I just smiled. "Glad I could help. I could use the company, and we can split the gas and driving."

The next day, after attending the first morning session, I took a cab to the airport. When I arrived, police tape surrounded the terminal. I asked the driver to wait while I checked to see if I could get in. I crossed the Police tape and found the terminal door open with someone sitting at the Hertz desk. After paying for the cab, I was relieved to get the last car out of Fort Walton Beach!

I drove back to the hotel, checked out, loaded the car, and found my friend. By 2:30 in the afternoon, we were on the road to Richmond. Fort Walton Beach is located so far out on the Florida Panhandle that we drove east to get to Birmingham, Alabama. We then headed due East to Atlanta. We listened to local radio stations all day long. It was mainly news and talk shows. It was interesting to hear what folks said about the attacks and how they made them feel. There was anger, confusion, and a deep sense of loss. Folks in Alabama and Georgia, many of whom had probably never been to New York City, were profoundly touched by the towers' collapse. Many struggled to express their feelings. It was unlike anything any of us had experienced, and I think it must have been something like what people experienced after the attack on Pearl Harbor.

We drove into the night, turning North on I-85 up through North Georgia, South Carolina, and Charlotte. The traffic was light, and we took turns driving until about 2:00 a.m., when we stopped in Greensboro, NC, at my friend's grandmother's house.

We got up early, thanked his grandmother, and were in Richmond before noon. I dropped my friend off and drove home. Later in the day, Sherri followed me to the airport to drop off the rental car. I did not want to keep it because I knew how many people would need one.

We spent the time with family and neighbors, thankful to be home and watching television. Everyone had a unique story to tell. Underlying it all was the question of how this could have happened and why someone would want to do such a thing.

GALATIANS 6:2 Carry each other's burdens, and in this way you will fulfill the law of Christ.

1 PETER 4:10 Each of you should use whatever gift you have received to serve others, as faithful stewards of God's grace in its various forms.

PROVERBS 24:10 If you falter in a time of trouble, how small is your strength!

PSALMS 9:9 The Lord is a refuge for the oppressed, a stronghold in times of trouble.

PROVERBS 17:17 A friend loves at all times, and a brother is born for a time of adversity.

PSALMS 41:1 Blessed are those who have regard for the weak; the Lord delivers them in times of trouble.

IX. OTHER STORIES

1970 ROTC Summer Camp – Ft. Bragg
(*It was a million-dollar wound...*)

When I went to Davidson College in 1967, it was a different place at a different time. It was an all-male school with approximately 1,000 students, divided into classes of 250 students each. As a freshman, you had to wear a beanie—a little red hat with a black bill. Freshmen were not allowed to talk outside a building until after the homecoming football game. Freshmen were also supposed to carry an upperclassman's books if asked. It was initially characterized by the rat-and-cat mentality prevalent in many military schools.

Most strikingly, virtually the entire student body was in the Reserve Officer Training Corps (ROTC). The first two years were mandatory (and unpaid), and then you could sign a contract for the last two years, for which you got $50 per month and a commission as a Second Lieutenant upon graduation. Vietnam was very "hot" then, with the "Tet Offensive" being an excellent example. So, most folks signed the contract with that conflict at the forefront of their minds. Thus, the entire student body was in uniform and marching when we had drill for three hours on Tuesday and Thursday afternoons.

I did not have much of a choice in the matter. I was on a national merit scholarship at the time, and one of the requirements for keeping the scholarship was to complete my education in four years. The war was unpopular and was met with nationwide protests. Remember the March on Washington and President Johnson's decision not to run for re-election. An unfortunate consequence of these protests was a growing resentment of the military. Veterans returning home from the conflict were not treated well, and even being seen in a uniform made you a target for some radicals. Most of those in the military were either

304

drafted into the Army or entered another branch of service as an alternative. Why and for what were they being blamed…? Not one of them started the war in Vietnam, but 55,000 would die fighting it.

I signed the contract, and in the summer of 1970, I found myself in beautiful Fort Bragg, North Carolina, at ROTC summer camp. My platoon and company got "front-ended" regarding the training schedule. We completed all the challenging tasks in the first two weeks. Initially, we did all the tower jumps for the airborne orientation and then spent much of the second week at the John F. Kennedy Special Forces Center – Home of the Green Berets. We did the slide for life, repelling (thirty- and sixty-foot tower and helicopter repel), and other exciting events there.

Kennedy Special Forces Center was about a 45-60-minute ride in a large diesel truck ("cattle car") from our housing area in Fort Bragg. These trucks had open-air tops, with bench seats down both sides and a double bench seat down the middle. You would be crammed into the truck, shoulder to shoulder, with the outer seats facing inward and the folks in the middle situated back-to-back, facing out. You had your duffel and rifle between your knees and bounced along.

We had been issued all kinds of fantastic personal items before our ride. One was a green can of insect repellent, which I thought might be useful. On the way out to the Center, I had the can in the side leg pocket of my fatigues. For some reason (probably because I had put Little Debbie cakes in my side leg pocket), I had moved the can to my right rear pocket for the Friday afternoon ride back to Bragg. As I sat on the bench, I grew increasingly uncomfortable. I was sitting on that can, but there was no way to "re-adjust" my position, and I certainly could not stand up. I just sat on that can all the way back to the base.

When we got back to base, we cleaned weapons because we had fired while at the JFK center. My butt felt better after standing up, but it continued to hurt and "burn." There was no chance to check if there was a problem because when we went to turn in our cleaned weapons, they were all turned down for being "filthy." That, of course, was not the case. They did not inspect them; they just returned them, and we all returned to clean them further. After another hour of cleaning, we returned our weapons, and they took them all without looking at them. It was all a game, and since it was getting late on a Friday afternoon, they didn't want to play anymore.

I couldn't wait to get out of that uniform and take a shower. I noticed an oily spot on the right rear pocket when I took off my fatigue pants. I quickly made my way to the shower, an open bay that would soon be full. I got a shower head and stood to the side to see if the water would be cold or scalding hot (rarely was there something in between).

Jay Mackintosh followed me in, and as I prepared to step into the water, he said, 'What the hell happened to you?'

I did not fully appreciate the gravity of his question until the water hit my back and ran down across my backside. It set me on fire, and I quickly stepped out of the shower.

I told Jay that whatever was back there hurt. He told me it looked like I had a hole in my right buttocks that went all the way to the muscle.

"You dry off; I will get the Sarge to look at this. I think you need a doctor," Jay said over his shoulder as he headed out of the shower.

As I was drying off, the next guy came in and said, "Wow, what happened?"

I had heard enough. I wrapped my towel around my waist and moved out to my bunk. Soon, Jay appeared with our Platoon Sergeant.

"OK, Carr, Mackintosh says you have a problem. Let's see it." I turned my back and dropped the towel.

"Damn, boy. What did you do?" came the sergeant's response. This had an impact on me because our sergeant had done multiple tours in Vietnam, had been wounded on several occasions, and was one of the toughest individuals I had ever met.

"I had a can of insect repellent in my back pocket, and it must have leaked," I responded.

"Well, you need a doctor. I'm sending you to the dispensary. I'll get you a ride."

It was getting late and dark, and the medic was reading a magazine when I walked in.

"What's your problem?" he asked as he looked up.

"I had a can of GI insect repellent in my back pocket; it leaked, and I must have had some kind of reaction," I explained.

"Well, let's take a look. God Damn! Does it hurt?"

By this point, the use of profanity and vocal acrobatics being induced by my rear end had me wondering what it must look like.

"I can't take care of this. I'm sending you to Womack. I'll get you an ambulance." Womack Army Medical Center is the primary medical treatment center on Fort Bragg.

I was in the emergency room at Womack in about half an hour. I was checked in by the medic and then seen by a nurse. Both continued to contribute to the ever-growing list of profanity being provoked by my butt.

"You have a bad burn. I'm calling our plastics guy," explained the nurse.

About twenty minutes later, the plastic surgeon arrived and looked at my "wound." At least he did not start with profanity. His questions were simple: " How and when did you do this?"

I explained that it had started in the afternoon while riding back from the special forces center and had continued for a couple of hours during weapons cleaning.

"You have a chemical burn. The most superficial part is about six inches in diameter and combines first- and second-degree burns. A four-inch central area extends into the subcutaneous fat, and a two-inch diameter area extends to the muscle."

Well, that did not sound good.

"We could graft the area, but the better approach is to let it heal by secondary intent. That means a scar for the two-inch diameter area, but I don't think that is a problem, given its location. I can send you home, and you can get dressing changes with a private doc, or you can stay here, and we will have a medic do your dressing changes twice daily."

I was one-third of the way through summer camp, and I had already done all the "hard" stuff, so I was not about to go home and come back the following year to do six more weeks. I'm staying.

So, I received orders for early morning and evening dressing changes, along with an imposing physical profile.

A physical profile outlines temporary restrictions on activity put in place by a physician to allow recovery from a condition or injury. My profile read: no prolonged standing, no prolonged sitting, no prolonged walking, no running, etc. I could have used it to escape many things, but I didn't because I didn't want to look like a wimp or have to return.

Dressing changes were handled in the dispensary when in camp and by the medic beside an ambulance if we were in the field. I would get up early and go to the ambulance. The same medic cared for me for the last four weeks of summer camp. The bandage was a little tricky because the worst part of the wound was in the lower fold of my right buttocks. The medic kept the bandage in place by anchoring it on the top around my hip and the bottom with tape that went almost, but not entirely, around my right upper leg. The tape he used did a fine job of removing all the hair. After a while, it also did a reasonable job of eliminating superficial skin. We always started by removing the previous bandage, and the medic always said the same thing: "Sorry about this…"

On one occasion, when we were in the field, the medic was at the latrine when I got to the ambulance, which was parked at the end of an open field. When he returned, I stood beside the ambulance, and we began the process. My rifle was propped up against the ambulance, I had both hands over my head and leaned against it, and the medic was kneeling behind me, doing the dressing change.

For some reason, the Lieutenant Colonel (LTC) company commander had a bee in his bonnet and decided to have formation early. It began to form in the open field beside the ambulance. Each day, the company would have a new cadet commander in charge of the formation. The cadet knew I was having a dressing change and would have the entire formation move forward to avoid the ambulance. For some reason, the LTC became enraged at this suggestion and demanded that the formation do a right face and march straight out through the area occupied by the ambulance. He shouted that the ambulance needed to move. The driver started the engine.

The medic shouted to the driver, "You can't move the ambulance; we have a patient."

The driver responded, "The Colonel says to move the ambulance."

As the medic protested again, I could hear the LTC screaming in the distance. "Move that damn ambulance!"

The driver said, "I'm sorry. He's a colonel, and you're not," and he pulled away.

I had to stop leaning on the ambulance and grab my rifle as it pulled away. As the ambulance moved, the cadet said, "Right face."

The entire formation turned to face me. I stood there with my pants around my ankles and the medic squatting behind me. The formation broke into laughter, and the LTC almost had a stroke. The medic and I were able to move a few feet to clear the path, and the formation marched away. It was a very humbling experience, but not the last encounter I was to have with our LTC.

Our combat veteran sergeant could not stand the LTC. He thought he was an arrogant SOB, an LTC who would never be a COL. Even with my limited exposure to the military at the time, I agreed. We prepared to take our physical fitness test as we neared the end of our six weeks. At that time, the PT test consisted of seven events: sit-ups, push-ups, pull-ups, a horizontal ladder, a grenade toss, a shuttle run, and a one-mile run in combat boots. Several days before the event, the LTC said, "There will be no slackers; no physical profiles will be honored." That was OK with me. I could manage, but the sergeant would have none of it.

"Carr, you got a profile for no running, and you will not do the run."

"But Sergeant, I can do it, and let's not push the LTC," I protested.

"You leave that to me," was the Sergeant's response with a hint of a smile. Oh no, I thought, what has he got planned?

We were out in the field two days later to range fire and familiarize ourselves with the M-60 machine gun. We were eating at lunchtime when I saw the sergeant go over to the LTC, who was having lunch under a tree. There was a brief conversation, and then the sergeant turned on his heel and headed directly over to me. Oh no, this must be it, I thought.

"Carr, come with me," snapped the Sergeant.

I dutifully followed him over to the LTC. When we got there, the sergeant immediately began his argument.

"Sir, this soldier has an injury and a profile for no running and should not do the run on the PT test."

"Sergeant, I have told you that no profiles will be honored for this test," came the response.

"Sir, I don't think you understand the extent of this soldier's injury. Carr, show the Colonel your wound."

Oh no, this is not happening…

My wound had been improving, and I was leaving it open to the air at night and only covered with a 4 by 4 gauze in the daytime.

I mildly protested, but the sergeant was having none of it. "The Colonel needs to see the injury to make the best decision. Make sure you remove the bandage."

I turned around, unbuckled my pants, and mooned the LTC over his lunch.

The LTC said, "That will be enough, Sergeant; he does not have to run."

I pulled up my pants and walked with the sergeant back to my lunch. As we walked, the sergeant grinned and whispered, "That was the best. I love you, Carr!"

ROMANS 5:3-4 Not only so, but we also glory in our sufferings, because we know that suffering produces perseverance; perseverance, character; and character hope.

JAMES 1:2-4 Consider it pure joy, my brothers and sisters, whenever you face trials of many kinds, because you know that the testing of your faith produces perseverance. Let perseverance finish its work so that you may be mature and complete, not lacking anything.

2 CORINTHIANS 13-5 Praise be to the God and Father of our Lord Jesus Christ, the Father of compassion and the God of all comfort, who comforts us in all our troubles, so that we can comfort

those in any trouble with the comfort we ourselves receive. For just as we share abundantly in the sufferings of Christ, so also our comfort abounds through Christ.

Army Teaching Techniques
(*Getting folks to do what ordinary people will not...*)

My first proper exposure to what I would learn was a classic teaching technique of the Army occurred early during my summer camp experience at Fort Bragg, North Carolina. Early one Saturday morning in June of 1970, my father drove me down, dropped me off in a dirt parking lot, and drove away. I signed in and was assigned to a platoon and company. I found myself in a wooden open-bay barracks from World War II. You could almost hear the echoes of soldiers who had occupied those walls as they prepared to take Europe back from Hitler's elite forces.

Summer camp lasted a little more than six weeks and had a very Southeast Asia feel, as we were still heavily involved in the Vietnam War. The silhouettes we would stab during bayonet trials had oriental faces. The targets of our day or night helicopter assaults were apparent copies of small Vietnamese villages. The hot landing zones, which would explode with fire from all sides as we rolled out of our Hueys, were typically tall grass to mimic similar Southeast Asian areas. There was no question about what we were being prepared for. They pretty much had my attention at all times.

The first week of my training involved going to what had been an airborne training center at Fort Bragg. Even by that time, airborne training had shifted south to Fort Benning, but the facilities remained at Bragg, and the trainers at ROTC summer camp put them to good use. We climbed out of our trucks and filed into the bleachers.

These bleachers were in direct sunlight, and it gets hot at Ft Bragg early in the day. We sat virtually shoulder to shoulder as the instructor droned on before us. The instructors were called black caps because they all wore black baseball caps. Behind the instructor was a series of stations where we would sit in smaller bleachers and be called up in small groups to learn how to jump and land correctly. First, from low platforms (several feet high) with no harness, and then gradually

313

to much higher platforms where you would be placed in a harness similar to that of a parachute. Then, you would jump off to experience the sensation of a parachute opening. Then, you would glide/slide down a wire to the ground. Hopefully, you will have learned enough at the previous stations not to break your ankle when you reach the bottom.

So, the instructor spoke, and everyone in the bleachers was either dozing off from the heat and monotone voice or becoming increasingly afraid of going off that high tower. Folks with a fear of heights were probably worried about having to climb the stairs to the top. Most of us were distracted to some degree.

Suddenly, in the middle of a sentence, the instructor said, "Attention" in that monotone voice. If you were not immediately on your feet, you were pulled out of the bleacher and did twenty pushups. You were yelled at for being "stupid" and not following orders, and told to return to your seat. Once everyone was back in place, the instructor resumed his presentation. A few minutes later, another "attention" was mixed into the dialogue. You were doing push-ups if you weren't immediately on your feet this time. If this was your first mistake, you did twenty; if you had the mark of shame from having to do pushups previously, you did forty pushups. When we returned to the bleachers, we were informed that pushups would be doubled with each infraction. Let's see...I just did forty...that means eighty next time...

The infractions would change as we moved from the large bleachers to the smaller ones. If they asked for the next three, and you did not immediately stand up, you were doing pushups. If they asked for the next four and you were number five and stood up (because you had counted wrong or were too anxious), you were told how "stupid" you were, and you had to do push-ups. Soon your arms were burning, and all you could think about was not screwing up again and having to do one hundred and sixty pushups...You did not think about jumping off the low platform or climbing the stairs, or jumping off the high tower and falling through the air; you simply did not want to screw up and have to do more pushups…They had your attention, they had you distracted, and everyone went off that tower.

We were taken to the John F. Kennedy Special Forces Center a week later for several days of training and weapons qualification. We rode out to the site on huge diesel trucks. We called them cattle cars because they were long truck beds with no top. They had a bench down each side and a double bench in the middle. We were all packed shoulder to shoulder, with the folks on the side benches facing inward and two rows in the middle sitting back-to-back, facing outward. You had your weapon and duffel bag between your knees. There was barely room to breathe, but at least you were not walking.

It was about an hour's ride from our billets to the JFK Center. When we arrived, we jumped off the back of the truck, stacked our duffel bags and rifles, and were herded into bleachers. As soon as we were all seated, a sergeant marched out from the right side of the bleachers and proceeded to the midpoint directly in front of us. At that point, he halted, made a sharp right face to look directly at us, and stated: "Gentleman, a brief demonstration." At this point, he did a sharp about-face and looked up at a sixty-foot repelling tower behind him.

On top of the tower were two young soldiers holding M16 rifles in their right hands and a rappelling rope in their left hands. From our perspective, they stood right on the right-hand edge of the top of the tower. Upon a signal from the Sergeant, they went over the edge and walked face-first down the tower's side. All the while, they blazed away with their M16s. When they reached the bottom, the sergeant did an about-face and said: "That gentleman is called the assault rappel. These trainees have been here for the last three hours.

Suddenly, my (and I would imagine most everyone's) pucker factor went to nine. If you are unfamiliar with the pucker factor, it is on a scale of one to ten and deals with how tight your anal sphincter

315

closes when you are under stress. Ten is as high (or tight) as it gets. I had picked this terminology up from my Platoon sergeant, who had done several tours in Vietnam and was well-versed in using the scale.

Oh my God. They expect me to be able to do (or at least attempt) that in three hours! Well, they had my undivided attention. I was alert and "on my game" as they reviewed the knots used in repelling. Before we knew what was happening, we were going off the lower (thirty-foot side of the tower). Luckily, we went over the edge the usual way with our butts toward the ground. Once that was done, we went down the sixty-foot side. We then climbed the stairs a third time to go off what represented the landing pod of a helicopter. This time, we did the helicopter rappel. You go over the side and slide to the ground. There is no wall. If they had told me 24 hours before that I would go over the side and slide down a rope to the ground, I would not have believed them. Yet, here I was (along with everyone else), rappelling down walls and off into thin air. We were all done within hours and off to the next event.

This time, it was the slide for life…a cable angled downward into a ravine with a body of water at the bottom. Now came the familiar, "Gentleman, a brief demonstration." This was followed by a young soldier grasping a small bar attached to the cable via a pulley wheel. With both hands holding the bar and extended arms, he launched himself from a small platform and whizzed down the cable toward the bottom. Before he reached the bottom, he let go of the bar and landed in the water.

More instructions – "Gentleman, three things: first, there is a white line on the cable. When you reach that point, let go of the bar and keep your feet together as you enter the water; second – don't let go too soon, or you might miss the water; third – don't hold on too long, or you might hit the cable mount at the bottom."

OK, I got it – hold on until you reach the white line, and then let go…

We all lined up, and before you knew it, we all stepped off into the air and somehow landed in the water. Amazing.

On the second day at the JFK Special Forces Center, we continued having "fun" by falling into the water. This time, we had to climb a twenty-foot telephone pole and crawl onto a large cable. The cable was stretched between two telephone poles in a pool of water. You would climb out on the cable on your belly, carefully drag yourself out to the middle of the cable, and then swing your legs down so you could hang by your arms over the water. At this point, you were to ask the sergeant in charge for permission to drop. Permission was not immediately granted. You might have been worried about the drop into the water when you first got out there, but by the time the sergeant granted your request to be allowed to drop, your arms were on fire from the strain of holding on. You were disinclined to drop before permission was granted because that would mean you had to climb up again, crawl out, hang, and ask permission again...

The pattern had become apparent, and distraction from the actual event was a major component. You could distract them by preoccupying the group with the fear of punishment (through ever-increasing numbers of push-ups). You could distract them by fear of having to do something even more frightening than what was planned (assault rappel versus routine rappel – rappelling butt first down a 60-foot wall suddenly seemed like cake compared to going face first!). You could distract them with pain (my arms are aching, just let me fall).

The second step was to make the instructions as simple as possible: jump off the platform and roll, jump off the platform and keep your feet together, let go of the handle at the white line, let go of the cable, and fall. The combination of distraction and simple instructions proved to be remarkably effective.

This relatively simple teaching technique was repeated throughout my military career. A touch of distraction can be highly effective when an element of danger is present. A second effective method was to place you in increasingly complex settings, each building on the last, until you found yourself operating at a high level in situations that most people might find uncomfortable.

In Desert Storm, I served in the burn and neurosurgery intensive care units at Landstuhl Army Medical Center in Germany. I wanted to be in the desert, but that did not happen. Instead, I spent my time in intensive care units. It was my first exposure to severely wounded soldiers, and I was forever changed. While we were busy, the initial care had been rendered in the desert before they arrived in Germany. A decade and several promotions later, I became Deputy Commander for Clinical Services at Camp Bondsteel in Kosovo. This time, I was responsible for all clinical aspects of the hospital. It was a hectic and rewarding job, and we were the first physicians to care for wounded service members. In my last tour of active duty, I was near Mosul, Iraq, at Forward Operating Base Diamondback with the 28th Combat Support Hospital out of Fort Bragg (I guess I had come full circle). Now, we were right in the middle of the fight, and we got patients within minutes of their wounding. It was a very explosive atmosphere, and we typically got multiple patients, many of whom were severely wounded – numerous gunshot wounds, feet, legs, hands, and arms blown off...and you just did your job. You stopped bleeding; you got patients into surgery, and you treated whatever was going to kill your patient quickly. You did this twenty-four hours a day, seven days a week. You also weathered mortar attacks several times per week, and a really poor sniper who sometimes took shots at folks as they tried to get to the gym. Only later, when I was removed from the events, did I have time to truly comprehend the inhumanity in which I had existed. It was a privilege to work with the most dedicated bunch of medical folks I had ever met. It was an honor to care for real heroes. The kind of heroes who get up every day and do complex jobs in dangerous places. The kind that literally risks everything and sometimes comes back in pieces. I was glad that the Army had me ready. Going to medical school was not nearly enough preparation.

PROVERBS 4:7 The beginning of wisdom is this: Get wisdom. Though it cost all you have, get understanding.

PROVERBS 16:16 How much better to get wisdom than gold, to get insight rather than silver!

JAMES 1:5 If any of you lacks wisdom, you should ask God, who gives generously to all without finding fault, and it will be given to you.

Making a Good First Impression
(*A "broken" scale and reading instructions…that guy is a genius!*)

In the summer of 1975, after being allowed to delay my entry onto active duty to go to graduate school, I was scheduled to report for active duty for six months of training (basic officer course) and OJT (on-the-job training). I had been commissioned in the Signal Corps, but while my record sat in the "control group" in St. Louis, I had several branch transfers and one promotion! As I neared the end of my PhD program in Biomedical Engineering and Mathematics (BMME) at UNC-Chapel Hill, I was notified that I had once again been branch transferred – this time to the Medical Service Corp.

I had no idea what they did, so I called to ask. I was told that they were guys who kept the hospital units running, much like hospital administrators in the civilian world. Well, that sounded more down my line than infantry.

I asked where they did their basic officer training, and I was told it was at the Health Sciences Academy at Fort Sam Houston in San Antonio. Well, now we are talking. Sign me up!

A month later, I was in Durham having a new in-processing physical examination, and by September of 1975, I was in wonderful San Antonio. My living conditions were good. I had a private room in the high-rise junior officer BOQ (Bachelor Officers' Quarters), and it was a quick walk up the hill to the academy. That was good because I had no car and I walked everywhere. I got several sets of the new permanent-press khaki uniforms. They were easy to wash and looked good and sharp without being pressed! I did a little cooking at the BOQ, but I took most of my meals at the mess hall, where the food was excellent and free. Classes were held five days a week, and if we were not in the field at Camp Bullis (located north of San Antonio in the foothill country), we had the weekends off. I made some good friends (the best one being Sam B), and before I knew what was happening, ten weeks flew by, and I was an "Honor" graduate of the Health Services Academy.

Well, now what do I do? I was scheduled to be at Fort Sam for six months, so the remainder of my stay was spent doing on-the-job training (OJT). Since my career to this point had been primarily that of a lab rat, the powers that be thought that's where I should be. I was to report and serve as an expert consultant to a laboratory doing specialized blood testing.

"So, what is my job?" I inquired.

"Oh…you just go there and help them out with any problems they might be having," came the response.

Well, that seemed global and vague enough for me to live with.

After a weekend to bask in the glory of my recent "graduation" from AHS, I reported to work in the laboratory on Monday morning. My boss was too busy to show me around (apparently, he was also a new graduate, and this was his first job in the Army), so I found an empty desk in a side office and set up shop. I then walked around, introduced myself, and asked if there was anything I could help with.

The responses were always, "No, Sir, we are doing fine – no problems."

"Well, if you need me or if I can be of any assistance, I will be right in that office."

At that point, I decided to go to the local eatery and have a hot breakfast of eggs, biscuits, and gravy. It was excellent. I returned to the lab, walked around a little, read a little, and finally made it through to the end of the day. After one day, I knew I had to find something to do, or I would go crazy.

The next day, I went in, asked if there were problems, and was told there were none. I'm off to another excellent breakfast and then back to sit in the office. This time, I didn't ask questions; I walked around the lab, looking at things. I saw what appeared to be a new top-loading Mettler balance with a sticker attached, indicating that it was broken.

It looked new. I asked the fellow at the adjoining bench what was wrong with the balance. He said that he did not know, but it had never worked. When they unpacked it and turned it on, the window where the weight should have been displayed lit up, but the rotating scale on which the numbers should have been displayed never appeared. They had sent the device to maintenance, but it did not work when it returned. They planned to return it to the manufacturer, but it had been over six months, and it was still sitting on the bench.

"Do you mind if I take a look at it?" I asked.

"Sure, go ahead; I don't think you could hurt it."

I smiled at that ringing endorsement, picked up the device, and took it to my desk. I could not find the manual, but I had the power cord, so I plugged it in and turned it on. When I turned it on, I saw a light shining underneath the cover. As I had been told, the scale did not appear in the window where one would look for the measured weight. I unplugged the unit and decided to look under the cover by removing the outer housing. I found what I thought must be the screws that secured the housing and borrowed a Philips head screwdriver from the tool drawer in the lab. I removed three screws and was in the process of trying to lift the cover off the scale when I heard what sounded like a spring moving, followed by a brief, high-pitched buzz. It was as if something had been pinned against the housing, and when I tried to move the cover, whatever was jammed was freed. Could it have been the scale mechanism? I gently put the cover back in place, plugged the unit into the receptacle, and flipped the switch. The light came on, the scale swung into view, and the reading went to a weight of zero. I entered the lab, picked up a set of standard weights, and checked to see if the scale was reading the weights accurately. It was dead on. I carefully replaced the screws and made sure the unit was still working.

I carried the unit back into the lab, carefully placed it on the bench, and stated that it was fixed and seemed to function appropriately. I provided no further explanation for what I had done. I had been in the office for about five minutes.

Several folks got up to come over and check out this minor miracle. All were impressed that it was working and pleased to have a new balance. They were also pleased that they did not have to deal with the paperwork of returning it. I had made an impression. It was also clear that when this unit was sent to the maintenance shop, no one had touched it. I was sure they would have "fixed it" as quickly as I had if they had.

I rode the wave of awe associated with that event for a few days, but I could not simply sit in the office. By Thursday, I was out looking for something to do. I found a lab tech who said she had trouble getting a fibrinogen assay to work. Hey, I studied fibrinogen for my dissertation, and I knew I could help!

"What seems to be the problem?" I asked.

"I'm not sure. I've been trying to get this to work for two weeks. I have followed the protocol and done the complete assay at least five times, and I cannot get consistent results," was the bewildered response.

"Do you mind if I review the protocol?"

"Sure, go ahead, but I have followed it exactly…"

I took the protocol to my office and recognized it as a modified "Claus" assay named after the scientist who had developed it. The protocol was relatively standard, so I had trouble figuring out where things went wrong. I returned to the lab to review the setup and noted that the assay had been performed using plastic test tubes. I had always used glass test tubes, and the protocol specifically called for glass tubes.

I found the technician and asked if she had glass test tubes. She said they had shifted primarily to plastic but still had a supply of glass tubes. I then suggested that she repeat the assay, but this time use glass test tubes instead of plastic. She gave me a flat (you've got to be kidding me) look and said she would.

About an hour and a half later, she appeared at my door with a huge smile and announced that the assay had "worked beautifully!" I congratulated her on her success, and she thanked me for my assistance.

I later heard her telling others in the lab how I had solved the problem "within minutes." My reputation was made! That new guy is a genius!

From then on, people were more than willing to have me assist when things didn't appear to be working. It was great. They always started with, "I don't want to bother you, but could you take a look at this for me?" I was sure they did not want to bother the "genius" with the mundane, but at least I had something to do.

I've often thought that it is not difficult to be a genius. You need to know how to turn a screw and read instructions. Oh, and you also need to turn the screw and read the instructions…

COLOSSIANS 3:23 Whatever you do, work at it with all your heart, as working for the Lord, not for human masters.

PROVERBS 12:24 Diligent hands will rule, but laziness ends in forced labor.

ECCLESIASTES 9:10 Whatever your hand finds to do, do it with all your might , for in the realm of the dead, where you are going, there is neither working nor planning nor knowledge nor wisdom.

Surviving Two Gasoline Explosions
(*Having lived through one...how dumb can one guy be...*)

My Momma always told me that God cares for young children and fools. Well, there have been a few times in my life when I was nowhere near the age of a young child, but God took care of me when I did some foolish (OK...stupid...) things. Some of the most dramatic involved gasoline.

As my father neared 65 years of age, when all the children had left the house, and most of the first wave of grandchildren were already in school, my parents sold their three-bedroom house within Greensboro city limits and moved to the southeastern part of Guilford County, North Carolina. The house was slightly smaller, but they had more land. That was good because my father always had a large garden.

A shallow creek ran behind my father's yard and then through a culvert under the road they lived on. My father's property line ran with the creek down to the culvert. All was well until the county upgraded the culvert with a large pipe. Unfortunately, instead of putting the pipe where the original culvert was, they placed it parallel to and slightly uphill of the previous culvert. The result was a dam when they removed the original culvert and filled the area with dirt. The creek still wanted to run where it had before, but now that the culvert was gone, the water would back up until it was high enough to flow through the new pipe. There was a swamp on part of my father's property, which served as an excellent breeding ground for mosquitoes. What genius came up with this feat of engineering...?

Since the county would do nothing to correct their error, my father decided to re-channel the creek so that it would flow through the new pipe. It was no small task; he was over 70 years old, and his tools were an axe, a mattock, and a shovel. When I asked Momma what Daddy was doing, she said he was down in the creek up to his calves in water, drying to cut out tree roots with an axe. I decided it was time to help Dad for a few days.

I was in my late twenties and reasonably shape, but the three days I worked with my father were no picnic. We dug the channel deeper by cutting roots and removing rocks, which we stacked along his side of the creek to reinforce the bank. It was hard, hot, sweaty work, but the flow rate increased each time you made the channel flow a little better.

A month or so after the new creek bed was in place, the swamp was dry, and the wedge of land had greened up nicely. Now, my father got the idea that we should clean out all the underbrush and reclaim that portion of his property as part of his yard. We would leave the "good trees" but remove all the "weed trees."

This would take more than my Dad and me, so brothers-in-law and older grandsons were brought in for support. We wanted to complete this quickly, so we employed better tools, including chainsaws. With the crew we had, the work progressed rather quickly. We had decided that the cut material would be stacked and burned on the spot. This is a fairly standard technique for clearing land, as it eliminates the need to load trucks to haul away materials or pay landfill fees.

The accelerant typically used for this type of work is kerosene, and we had a five-gallon can. Kerosene is used because it is less volatile than gasoline. When burning green wood and brush, you need an accelerant to get things started and keep them going. You light the fire, let it burn down, put on more fuel and accelerant, let it burn down, and repeat the cycle.

After several hours, we were running low on kerosene. So, we sent someone (I can't remember who, but I think it was someone no longer in the family) to get more kerosene. They went away and returned with a whole can. The fire was pretty much out, so we had been putting more cuttings on the pile. When our young hero returned, he said something like, "I'll get this thing going!"

As he started to pour the liquid in the can onto the pile, the pile exploded. The percussion knocked the fellow with the can to the ground, and the rest of us felt it. Immediately, flames soared twenty to thirty feet into the air, and a wave of heat pushed us back further. I looked up to see the leaves in adjacent trees begin to curl from the heat, but thankfully, they did not catch fire.

Luckily, the large can landed on its bottom and sat upright. We quickly pulled it away from the fire and asked, "What in the name of God is in that can?"

"Well, I could not find kerosene, so I got gasoline..." came the response.

I knew that gasoline was explosive – we had all heard of Molotov cocktails, but I had never seen it in action. It was a real bomb! Luckily, none of us were hurt, and we did not cause a forest fire...Hopefully, we have all learned a lesson.

Well, maybe, and maybe not...

Fast forward twenty years, move to Virginia, and buy an older house with a large stump in the front yard. It had been cut off about a foot above the ground, and this, given the appearance of the stump and the ivy that had grown up around it, must have occurred at least ten years prior. I had been planning to have the stump taken out. This course of action was accelerated when I began to be buzzed by bumble bees whenever I mowed near the stump. Several minutes of sitting in a lawn chair and watching the stump confirmed that the bees were coming to and going out of the stump.

I would need to handle the bee problem to get the stump ground out. I had previously handled several large nests of yellowjackets (sometimes known as ground bees). This was accomplished by identifying the nest opening (by careful observation) in the daylight, waiting for the bees to return to the nest at night, pouring in gasoline, moving several paces back, and throwing a match. You could watch the whole nest explode underground with the percussion blast and a moment of exposed flame that followed as it emerged from the underground tunnels. It is all pretty nifty and definitely fun. I thought: I got this.

The first step was to remove the ivy. I managed this without too much difficulty and without getting stung. Now that the stump was nicely exposed, the next step was to identify the entrance point for the bumblebees. Once again, a few minutes in the lawn chair was all that was required. Now, all I need to do is pour gasoline into that hole, step back, and throw a match to dispatch the bees. All appeared to go well.

After about twenty minutes, I noticed bees buzzing around the stump. At this point, I thought I should do a second round of "extermination." I had a distant memory of gasoline being poured on what was once a fire, so I carefully walked over and laid my hand on the stump to see if it was hot. It did not feel hot, so I thought all was a go.

I retrieved my red plastic fuel can with the yellow plastic nozzle, walked up to the stump, and began pouring fuel down into the nest opening.

The next thing I know, I am flying through the air and landing flat on my back about eight feet from the stump. When I look up, I see a flame fifteen to twenty feet up in the air, and the leaves in a nearby oak are beginning to curl back. My ears were ringing, and there was something surreal yet familiar about the scene. As I lay there, I turned my head to one side to see the red plastic fuel container neatly sitting upright on its bottom.

Well, that was good. What was not good was the fact that the end of the yellow nozzle was on fire. Oh God. Now I have a real Molotov cocktail, containing about a half-gallon of gasoline, sitting several feet from my head.

What should I do...? I crawled over and blew the flame out...Then, I crawled over to the base of a nearby tree and sat. I watched the fire burn down. I considered the question of how stupid I had to be... I wondered why that bomb in my hand did not go off. How and why had the plastic container landed on its bottom without slouching gasoline up that spout? There should have been a second explosion... Mostly, I just sat and thanked God that I was still alive and not hurt.

As I sat, my mother's words came to me, and I once again knew what category of human God was taking care of that day...and it was not the young child variety...

PSALMS 107:17 Some became fools through their rebellious ways and suffered affliction because of their iniquities.

PSALMS 107:19 Then they cried to the Lord in their trouble, and he saved them from their distress.

PROVERBS 1:32 For the waywardness of the simple will kill them, and the complacency of fools will destroy them;

EPHESIANS 5:15 Be very careful, then, how you live – not as unwise but as wise

Memorial Day
(*Talking about things that are too close to the bone...*)

In April of 2011, I was approached by two fellows from a group called the "Guardians of the National Cemetery" and asked if I would be willing to deliver a few remarks about what Memorial Day meant to me as part of their annual Memorial Day program. I immediately agreed to participate when I found that the Guardians was a volunteer organization formed to present honors (including 21-gun salutes) at veteran funerals. These guys were all veterans, and most were well above 65 years of age; yet they showed up in all kinds of weather to do their jobs for free. I was told that it was not infrequent for the Guardians to be the only people present during the internment. I could not have said no.

So, I dutifully put together a short speech, partially based on entries from a journal I kept while serving as a physician with the 28th Combat Support Hospital in Iraq. I had no idea how difficult it would be to make that presentation. Tears ran down my face, and I almost lost my voice.

Someone told me later that the two-star General sitting behind me also cried. I guess there are some things you never get over.

Memorial Day Remarks
Washington Crossing National Cemetery
Marcus E. Carr, Jr, COL USAR (ret.)
30 May 2011

We are here today to honor those who have fallen in service to our country. I have been asked to share a few words about what Memorial Day means to me, and in doing so, I offer a perspective that is undoubtedly held by many in this audience.

You might ask why they asked "this guy" to speak. My response is, "Good question." I asked it myself. So, let me introduce myself by addressing a few additional questions that I would ask if I were you.

You're a hematologist – what did you do for the Army?

The short answer is – I did whatever they told me to do.

OK. Then what is the most important thing you did for the Army?

This answer is simple – I always tried to stop the bleeding.

Soldiers are typically healthy and in excellent physical condition. Therefore, when wounded, they have a better-than-average chance of surviving. Most mortal combat wounds are lethal from the moment of impact – gunshot wounds to the head or heart, devastating explosions, etc. Nothing a medic, nurse, or doctor can do in these cases will make a difference. Most soldiers who die of a potentially survivable injury do so from bleeding. Therefore, stopping bleeding has the highest potential for saving lives in combat trauma. The effort to stop bleeding begins with the first hands on the scene. These may be the hands of the wounded soldier. Therefore, the new combat tourniquet is designed to be used by someone with only one hand. The hands may belong to a fellow soldier who applies pressure. They may be the hands of a medic applying a bandage made of materials designed to promote blood clotting. As the soldier passes from hand to hand, each receiving caregiver will continue and increase the efforts to stop the blood flow. In the first medical facility with nurses and doctors, this effort will include administering blood products and blood clotting proteins, as well as considering surgery to close large vessels.

A famous pathologist once told me, "All bleeding stops. Your job is to stop it while the patient is still alive." So, that is one of the main things I did for the army. It was undoubtedly the most important thing I tried to do.

So, what does "Memorial Day" mean to an old Army Doc?

I think the best way to answer this question is to give a "real", un-edited insight into my most recent tour in Iraq in the spring of 2007, just ahead of the surge. I served with one of the finest medical teams I have ever seen – the 28th Combat Support Hospital based out of Fort Bragg. First formed during World War II and known to the Army as the "China Dragons," the 28th CSH is one of the most deployed units in the military, having served in every major conflict (and many minor ones) since its formation. Although you may not be familiar with the name "China Dragons," you may have heard them referred to as "Baghdad ER," a series that aired documenting some of their work in Iraq. During early 2007, the area around Mosul was very active, requiring more direct medical support for the Army and Marine personnel operating in the heart of Saddam's childhood home. The 28th CSH was split into two components, with approximately one-third of the unit deployed to Forward Operating Base Diamondback, located just north of Mosul. The ability to conduct split operations in two areas of active combat and the high level of medical care delivered earned the 28th CSH a Meritorious Unit Citation for 2007.

I can offer you two statistics to give you a sense of the quality of care. First, during the time I was in Mosul, the average time required to get a patient from the helicopter to the operating room (if they were deemed to require immediate surgery) was 13 minutes. You will not find a result comparable to this in the best trauma centers in the United States. Second, if you arrived at our door with a pulse, you survived.

This was the case despite the fact that most of the patients were severely injured and the fact that the facility routinely received multiple simultaneous casualties. Additionally, mass casualty situations (with more than five simultaneous patients) occurred virtually every week. Of course, there was also the slight inconvenience of being mortared about three times per week.

I would like to read a short entry from a journal I kept while in Iraq.

Many (too many) years ago, I was told by a very wise old soldier that if I truly wanted to remember things as they actually happened, I would have to write them down. Otherwise, the mind suppresses the parts that are "too close to the bone." I first took this to heart during Desert Shield/Desert Storm when I worked in the burn center and neurosurgery intensive care unit at Landstuhl Army Medical Center. I carefully cataloged each day. When I got home, I put that journal in a box and did not touch it for three years. Then, someone convinced me to give a medical lecture, titled "Medical Grand Rounds," to the medical staff on Memorial Day, sharing my experience during the Gulf War. When I opened the journal, I finally understood why I had packed it away. Since then, I have "journaled" through Paraguay, Kosovo, the Dominican Republic, Guyana, and Iraq.

This is a partial entry from 25 May 2007 and captures (as closely as I can come to it anyway) what Memorial Day means to me.

"...In the afternoon, at 1800, we had an appreciation ceremony and party for the interpreters. Then, we experienced the most touching moment of the day. We had a bad IDE incident last night. HUMVEE hit and rolled. Three were badly hurt, and one was killed on the spot – all were American, all from our FOB (Forward Operating Base). The Angel flight picked the flag-draped coffin up at the flight line in 1910. Big C-17 with just one passenger – that flag-draped coffin. His unit marched out to the aircraft and formed an honor guard that extended from the plane to where the ambulance stopped. Everyone

334

came to attention and saluted as the casket was carried aboard. Then, the formation broke and moved to the foot of the ramp at the tail of the plane. They knelt for a prayer, then fell back into formation and marched off the tarmac. Hospital personnel formed a single line along the wall on our side of the field in front of the hospital, stood at attention, and saluted. I think their unit photographer was surprised by our being there because he turned and took photos of our salute. It was all so dignified, quiet, honorable, and profoundly moving. I could not help but think that this is Memorial Day weekend, and while most will be at parties, car races, and cookouts, an Angel Flight will take one soldier home, and some families will never view Memorial Day the same way again. Some son, brother, husband, or father will never take his former place in his family. Hard for me to think about – it is difficult to comprehend such a sacrifice...."

So Memorial Day is a time of fun, family, warm sunshine, and good food. It is also a time to take a moment to say a prayer for those who have fallen and to remember their sacrifice, as well as that of their family and friends. Only those who hold these heroes in their hearts (close to the bone) can ever truly know the price paid when soldiers go to war. That is why the last toast is always to absent comrades.

As I turn the program over to the next speaker, I would just like to pause for a minute to pay tribute to the Army Medic. Medics do incredible things under unimaginable conditions. As a group, they have been awarded more Congressional Medals of Honor than any other group in the US military. They are the heart and soul of the medical team. When you are handed a patient kept alive by a combat medic, you will do whatever it takes to make sure that patient remains alive.

These are truly exceptional people, and to my mind, they represent the best citizens our country is capable of producing. Though it is not perfect, the United States of America is exceptional. Now, let us reflect on what we mean by exceptional.

Addendum:

Memorial Day is a day to remember those who have died while defending our country. I have seen the remains of such heroes, felt their loss, and thought about what their ultimate sacrifice means to their family and others who loved them. We should never diminish what their service and dedication mean. Service members are part of units, and when they are involved in armed conflict, those units become like family. These bands of brothers fight for their country, but they will die for their friends.

JOHN 15:13 Greater love has no one than this: to lay down one's life for one's friends.

Made in the USA
Columbia, SC
12 December 2025

75787963R00186